AMERICA'S JACK THE RIPPER: THE DEFINITIVE ACCOUNT OF THE ZODIAC KILLER

www.korsgaardpublishing.com
ISBN 978-87-93987-06-7

PUBLISHING HISTORY
First edition: 2017
Second Edition: 2020

ACKNOWLEDGMENTS

My sincere gratitude goes to the following list of friends and associates who have assisted me with this book. Kayode Olawuyi, CEO of Pneuma Communications, www.pneumacommunications.com, spent hours editing the book and pointing out aspects that needed improvement. Caroline Cheruiyot read the book and made many recommendations and was always fast to answer my questions. I also acknowledge Tyler Hedalen for his insights pertaining to tire track calculations and for reading the book and pointing out two dozens aspects that needed improvement. Dave Toschi (1931-2018) answered my questions about the Zodiac case. Bill Crow provided a detailed account of his encounter with the Zodiac. Mark McClish, a former Supervisory Deputy United States Marshal, reviewed a draft of Chapter 14. Nancy Slover (1942-2012), who spoke to the Zodiac in 1969, answered my questions one night in 2010. Mark Hewitt, my good friend and zodiologist, provided valuable insights and analyses. My gratitude also extends to Beatrice Meseno Meshuko and Lady Jane Emefa Addy. My friend and mentor, John Remington Graham, is a great inspiration to me.

PREFACE

This book was originally published in 2017 under the title, “America’s Jack the Ripper: The Crimes and Psychology of the Zodiac Killer.” Since then, more chapters have been added and the book has overall been updated and revised.

LE LIVRE EST DÉDICACÉ À ÈMERAUDE, AVEC TOUT MON AMOUR, SØREN.

TABLE OF CONTENTS

INTRODUCTION

In the late 1960s, a maniac murdered his way into the media spotlight. He was not aiming for 15 minutes of fame, but for years of nationwide publicity. He named himself, "the Zodiac," in his bloodstained communications. He demanded publication of his bizarre musings, and habitually indulged in extortion and terrorism. He shrewdly manipulated readers by providing cryptic clues to his identity, yet swore that the police would never catch him. He used a gun, he used a knife, and he varied his actions to such a high degree that nobody could predict where his demons would guide him next. His killings and decision to go public entailed a high risk of apprehension, but it was worth it to him. His obsession with notoriety and control even led him to threaten to kill schoolchildren, a move that paralyzed California with fear. It has been observed that his actions carry an uncanny resemblance to those of Jack the Ripper, perhaps the most famous serial killer in world history, and many researchers have called the Zodiac, "America's Jack the Ripper."

The Zodiac committed his first official killings in 1968, though his first murder may have taken place in 1966, or possibly even in 1962. Very little in this case is straightforward, and as the reader soon will discover, the solution to one problem usually entails a series of complications for other related matters; it is a huge puzzle, and only the Zodiac knows how to put together all the pieces. When the case was at its height, an untold amount of funds and investigators were devoted to bringing the Zodiac to justice. Scores of suspects were investigated and cleared, and hundreds of clues were pursued. Today, it is difficult to justify why resources should be spent on a decades-old case that can, at best, be characterized as stone cold, especially considering that new cases appear every single day. It is therefore now up to the so-called armchair investigators and readers to finally lift the veil of the Zodiac's identity.

Unlike other unsolved crime cases, the Zodiac left an abundance of evidence, both intentionally and inadvertently, for us to pursue. However, it was evidence that bizarrely only led to dead ends. Victims survived, witnesses saw him, composite drawings were made, fingerprints were lifted, tire tracks and shoe prints were examined, and millions of people looked closely at his

unique and disturbed handwriting that was shown on the front page of major newspapers. Hundreds and thousands of people have dedicated time and patience to unveil the Zodiac's identity by gingerly analyzing his cryptic letters and ciphers.
The Zodiac is more fascinating than any other crime case, his ciphers and letters continue to haunt and attract the attention of the public, and the fascination is growing every year. This book is the product of years of research and writing, and provides the definitive account of the Zodiac's crimes, letters, and psychology. Although this book contains more than 650 references, not a single one is related to the alleged "suspects" of the case. The Zodiac left behind a catalogue of evidence, and not a single speck of this evidence has ever been matched to anyone. This means that the Zodiac is still out there, either alive or six feet under.

Søren Roest Korsgaard
Germany, May 2020.
editor@crimeandpower.com
www.crimeandpower.com
www.korsgaardpublishing.com

CHAPTER 1

THE LOVERS' LANE KILLINGS

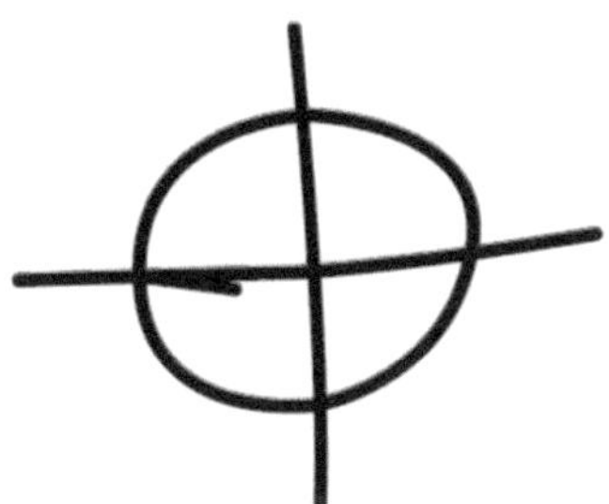

America in the 1960s was characterized by a potpourri of historically significant events and transitions. This tumultuous decade is primarily remembered for the defiant counterculture that challenged the conventional social norms of the 1950s. The counterculture was fueled by the battle for peace in Vietnam, as youth gathered in protests around the nation. Another feature of the decade includes a long list of hotly debated assassinations that shaped the culture and politics of the 1960s. Most people remember where they were on November 22, 1963, when the unforgettable images of John F. Kennedy's demise were broadcast live. Just five years later, his brother, Robert F. Kennedy was also hit by an assassin's bullets. The world was equally cast into shock and horror by the killings of religious and civil rights leaders. This horrific practice climaxed in 1968 when

Martin Luther King Jr. was shot dead. Martin Luther King Jr. continues in our memories today as a prominent activist and eloquent and empowering speaker.

True crime aficionados will also remember that the 1960s gave birth to the Manson Family. This quasi-commune arose in Northern California in the late 1960s. Additionally, the most perplexing and intriguing serial killer since Jack the Ripper entered the scene in 1968. He called himself *the Zodiac.* For those who lived in the San Francisco Bay Area, the memory of the Zodiac killer's reign of terror undoubtedly still stands strong. The Bay Area covers a huge geographical area that extends far beyond San Francisco, encompassing nine counties and just over 100 cities. Vallejo, a Bay Area city, is now the largest city in Solano County. It is located some 25 miles from San Francisco on the northeastern shore of San Pablo Bay. In the late sixties, the city was considered a relatively safe place to live with a desirable "very, very low"[1] crime rate. This was about to change.

Seventeen-year-old David Arthur Faraday, a former San Rafael resident, and his 16-year-old girlfriend, Betty Lou Jensen, a native of Colorado, had never experienced any trouble with the law. By all accounts, they lived a life similar to other teenagers at that time. David, a distinguished Eagle Scout in his spare time, studied at Vallejo Senior High School, while Betty was an honor student at Hogan High School. Despite only being briefly acquainted, they had rapidly grown fond of each other. As they came to know each other better, the attraction intensified to the point where David began to cut classes to see Betty. Then, in late December of 1968, they scheduled their first official date.

Friday, December 20, 1968

It was a brutally cold evening with a temperature of 22 degrees Fahrenheit. At 8 p.m., David, who probably felt the typical teenage anxiety about his upcoming date, reached Betty's home in his mother's 1961, 4-door Rambler station wagon. The two teenagers left with the consent of her parents to attend an event at Hogan High School and a party to be held afterwards. However, they had other plans for the evening.[2] After a short stop to visit Betty's girlfriend, Sharon, David and Betty drove off at roughly 9 p.m. They were not seen again until Helen, an 18-year-old resident of Vallejo, and her boyfriend drove past the couple two times between 10:15 and 10:30 p.m.[3] It was evident that David and Betty had parked at a so-called lovers' lane, an isolated spot that appealed to the younger generation. The location, on the eastern outskirts of Vallejo along Lake Herman Road at the entrance to the Benicia pumping station, ensured a higher degree of privacy than in the city. Homer Your, an employee of the Frederickson Pipe Company, had some duties to attend near the lovers' lane. His wife had nothing better to do and joined him that evening. When he was finished, he turned right at the entrance to Marshall Ranch to reverse their car. Down the road, they saw a red pick-up truck and two men. The Yours turned around and proceeded toward Benicia where they lived. They later reported that David sat in the driver's seat while Betty leaned her head against his shoulder.[4] The men seen by the Yours were Robert Connely and Frank Gasser, two raccoon hunters, and at around 11:05 p.m. they also left the area. When they left, they also noticed the Rambler.[5*] The young couple was enjoying a precious, romantic moment in a place where they did not expect to be disturbed except by passing cars. They wanted all the privacy they could get and the lovers' lane seemed to be a perfect place for them to express their feelings. This should have been the beginning of their lives with many challenges and joys in their paths. Instead, *the Zodiac*, as he would later call himself, destroyed everything.

James Owen, a retired Air Force man, was on his way home after work when he noticed the Rambler, facing east, and a car parked to the right of it. He had no reason to pay attention to the two cars, and he did not see anybody there. He later told the police that he could "not give a description"[6] of the other car, except that it was dark, not particularly large or compact, and lacking in chrome.[7] After he had proceeded roughly a quarter of a mile, he

[*] Detective Pierre Bidou and his colleague may also have passed the scene around the time the hunters left it (David Fincher, Director, Zodiac 2-Disc Director's Cut, 2008).

heard the sound of a gunshot.[8] It would be calculated that he had probably passed the scene at 11:14 p.m.
Stella Borges, a resident of Vallejo, was en route to Benicia. At around 11:20 p.m., she was rapidly approaching the lovers' lane. Suddenly, the bodies of two teenagers came into view. She immediately stepped on the gas and sped to Benicia where she flagged down a police car at 11:25 p.m. It did not take long for police officers to arrive at the scene. Once there, they encountered the gruesome sight: Betty, on her stomach, in a pool of blood, and David lying on the ground with blood emanating from his skull.[9] Betty was dead at the scene, but David was still breathing. An ambulance rushed David to Vallejo General Hospital. Detective Sergeant (Det. Sgt.) Leslie Lundblad told Patrolman Russell T. Butterbach and Officer Wayne Waterman to go to the hospital and get a statement from him, but when they arrived, Barbara Lowe, a nurse at the hospital, told them that Dr. Siebert had pronounced him dead on arrival, at 12:05 a.m.[10]

Lake Herman Activity

Most murders are perpetrated by people who are related in one way or another, such as when an angry husband kills his wife. Investigators knew this and conducted many interviews with friends and family members of the deceased. They scrutinized all sorts of theories and tried to determine who had motive to kill David and Betty. They got nowhere. The detectives probably remembered that Arthur Conan Doyle, via his character Sherlock Holmes, once said, "When you have eliminated the impossible, whatever remains, however improbable, must be the truth."[11] A brutal double murder without a tangible motive or connection to the victims therefore seemed to be the only option left; a deranged thrill killer was on the loose. Even today, random murders are extremely difficult to solve without a copious amount of evidence or witnesses stepping forward. The technical analysis of the bullets and casings yielded a few leads. In retrospect, the investigators should have put more focus on a car seen by several individuals, and on a young couple in a sports car who were chased by another driver.
In the evening hours of December 20, William "Bill" Crow and his girlfriend drove along Lake Herman Road to the lovers' lane.

While he parked there, another vehicle approached the location. The driver began to chase the couple. Bill was able to shake him off by brilliantly navigating the sports car he was driving. After the double murder, Bill was interviewed by two sheriff's deputies who took notes. Many questions have been raised about the report and this author decided to locate Bill and ask him questions about the incident. Bill stated unequivocally that the deputies had misreported his testimony, and that the report contained numerous errors and omissions. He then set the record straight. The following is a summary of his statement (see Appendix for the full statement).

On December 20, 1968, Bill's girlfriend (who was never interviewed by the police) visited him. They decided to test her new, dark colored sports car, and they proceeded to Lake Herman Road. The road was not illuminated by streetlights, and the only artificial light came from a handful of nearby ranches. The couple pulled onto the lovers' lane. Bill turned off the lights and as he started to determine how the various controls of the car worked, a car from the direction of Benicia passed in front of them, continued a little further, and then stopped. Behind the wheel sat a male Caucasian with short hair and glasses. It appears that he had not seen them initially since the sports car was dark-colored and probably blended into the darkness. The aggressive driver put the backup lights on. Bill quickly sensed that something was not right. He needed to get out of there. He put the car in gear and sped toward Benicia while the driver chased them down the deserted road. The aggressive driver gained on Bill and flashed the headlights several times to try to get him to pull over. Bill just drove faster. Seeing a fork in the road ahead, he yanked the wheel hard at the very last moment, and the small and responsive sports car skidded onto the right leg of the fork. The heavier vehicle continued and then stopped. From a 50 yards distance, Bill and his girlfriend watched the other car for a few minutes, until the driver slowly turned around and headed back toward the crime scene. Later, while reading the local newspaper, Bill's attention was drawn to an article about the murder of David and Betty.

It struck him that it had happened at the exact same spot that he had parked the sports car. He took the article, loaded his shotgun, and drove down Lake Herman Road. He determined that the couple had indeed been killed at that spot. He proceeded home and notified the authorities. He felt that the aggressive driver was the man who had killed David and Betty:

> I am reasonably sure that the person who chased me that evening was the Zodiac as I cannot come up with any other reasonable explanation of the events given the time, place and circumstances of what happened that same night sometime later. I believe that what happened is that after the incident with me he went back and parked his car and laid in wait for the next folks to park in that spot. Unfortunately when the young couple did they became his targets.[12]

The remote location of the crime scene suggests that the assailant might have been familiar with the area. Bill would later comment on this aspect: "In 1968 Lake Herman Road was known to the local teens as a park and make out place and the exact spot where the first murders happened was one of the prime spots. That being said, using that road could also have been random."[13]
To the police, the hunters would later explain that at around 9 p.m., they had seen a white, 4-door hardtop 1959 or 1960 Chevrolet Impala parked at the crime scene near the entrance to the Pumping Station.[14] The police also interviewed a local shepherd, Mr. Bingo Wesner, who told them he had seen a white Chevrolet Impala at the entrance at around 10 p.m.[15] Without a doubt, it was the same car seen by the witnesses. An hour and a few minutes later, the murders took place. The chase took place in close proximity to the sightings of the Chevrolet, although the exact time is unclear. The Chevrolet was an important clue that was overlooked by the police. Could it have been the assailant's car? Owen was interviewed twice and repeated that he could not describe the car parked next to the Rambler in any detail. His inattention is understandable as he had no reason to focus on anything else besides getting home from work, and, hence, his general description of the color as dark should not be considered definite. If the assailant did prowl the area in the hours before the crime, he was taking a considerable risk by possibly exposing his car, license plates, and himself to people who could have been observing him by chance. He was also working within a very narrow time-frame with limited escape route possibilities. Lundblad requested in the media that all drivers on Lake Herman Road between 9 to 11:30 p.m. should contact him

"immediately."[16] The driver of the Chevrolet never contacted him, nor did the driver that terrified Bill and his girlfriend (in all probability the same individual).

The Technical Evidence

In 1968, forensic science was in its infancy and investigators had no assistance in solving the crime from an advanced science such as DNA fingerprinting. The evidence would have been subjected to a multitude of analyses had the crime occurred years later. In the following pages, we will detail the physical evidence and reconstruct the sequence of events.

From a Department of Justice report, we learn that Betty was lying on her stomach almost 30 feet from the Rambler toward the road, while David was lying on his back next to the right, front passenger's door.[17] The couple exited the car through this door. David had suffered severe head trauma and blood loss from a single gunshot wound to his head.[18] At the crime scene, Solano County Coroner Daniel Horan observed a dark area around the entrance hole indicating he was shot point-blank.[19] Betty sustained massive injuries to her vital organs as she was shot five times in her back. The bullets struck her in the heart, liver, right kidney, and both lungs. The injuries caused instant unconsciousness, rapid internal exsanguination and death. In addition, the assailant fired his weapon twice at the right side of the Rambler, once through the rear right window and once just above the top door panel into the metal. Two additional shots were unaccounted for.

Bullets, shell casings, and Betty's dress were submitted to Criminalist David Q. Burd for examination. The criminalist's efforts indicated that the bullets

> correspond only with tests fired in J.C. Higgins, Model 80, .22 automatic pistol. It should not be assumed that the exhibits must have been fired in such a weapon but this is the only type presently in our files which corresponds, therefore, it appears somewhat probable that the responsible weapon was of this type.[20]

The J.C. Higgins is an excellent rapid-fire weapon due to its low recoil, and it has a magazine-capacity of 10-rounds. Moreover, the criminalist assessed that a conclusive identification of the weapon would be "extremely difficult, if not impossible,"[21] due to a lack of sufficient unique structures on the bullets. The ammunition was identified as Winchester Western Super X copper-coated .22 long rifle. A single grain of gunpowder was found on Betty's dress indicating that she was shot at a distance of several feet. Only one of the bullets may have been fired at a somewhat closer range.[22] It would appear he first shot David; Betty attempted to escape yet only made it a short distance into the night.

Scattered around were nine empty shell casings, all but one lying close to the car. One was also found on the right floorboard.[23] The bullet that struck the window continued downward forming a sharp angle and lodged itself just above the floor mat. The angle shows that it was fired at a close range and that it was not aimed at the couple who was seated in the front. It can be extrapolated that the shooter forced the teenagers out of the car. He had the opportunity to kill them while they were sitting inside, but this was not his intention. The two shots that did not hit anything may have missed Betty's back as she ran, or were warning shots, fired into the air. Furthermore, when David was found, he held his class ring by the tips of his third and fourth fingers indicating that the killer had used robbery as a ruse to get them out, or simply that David believed it was a robbery.[24] Detectives working on the case reached a similar conclusion.[25]

Thrill killings were almost unheard of back then and it received considerable media coverage. A few selected headlines: "2 Teen-Agers Are Murdered,"[26] "Teen-Agers on 1st Date Fatally Shot,"[27] "Couple Found Shot To Death,"[28] "Police Probe Double Teen Murder,"[29] "Youths on Date Shot to Death,"[30] and "Friends Quizzed in Slaying Of Teen Pair Near Vallejo."[31]

The public and victims' families thirsted for justice; the killer thirsted for blood, but he had just begun his savage hobby. A few months later, he decided that it was time to strike again, this time in another lovers' lane, just minutes away from the Lake Herman Road crime scene.

Friday, July 4, 1969

Twenty-two-year-old Darlene Ferrin, a native of Oakland, worked as a server at Terry's restaurant in Vallejo. She was married to, and lived with, Dean Ferrin. Together they had a daughter, Deena. Michael Renault Mageau, a 19-year-old laborer, had been friends with Darlene for some time, and they confided in each other.[32] Both Darlene and Michael resided in Vallejo. Michael got a call from his friend, Darlene, at approximately 4 p.m. It was Friday and a good day to have some fun, so they made plans to go to the movies in San Francisco. She was to arrive at his place at 7:30 p.m. However, she felt obliged to take her younger sister, Christine, to the local Fourth of July celebrations and she postponed their date. A sparkling smile surfaced on Michael's lips when his popular friend arrived at about 11:35 p.m. They quickly left because they were both hungry. While driving on Springs Road, Darlene said that she wanted to speak with him about something. Michael suggested that they could go to *Blue Rock Springs*. She turned the car around and proceeded there even though they were almost at Mr. Ed's, a local restaurant. From the lovers' lane on Lake Herman Road, if you travel northwest for about 3.2 miles until you reach the crossroad, turn right and proceed 4/5 of a mile, and turn right again, you will have arrived at the parking lot of Blue Rock Springs Park. At night, one might perceive a car or two with misted windows, and hear laughter and voices in the distance. The seclusion of the park made it an attractive lovers' lane for teenagers to make out or seek privacy. Darlene and friends often spent time there at night.[33]

A car driving northeast from the Springs Road direction drew Michael's attention when it proceeded to enter the parking lot. The driver switched off the lights, and the car came to a stop roughly seven feet behind and to the left of Darlene's car. When Michael asked his friend about the driver, she replied, "Oh, never mind."[34] It was unclear to him what she meant.[35] He was not concerned about the intruder, and he did not see the car "too clearly,"[36] though the shape of it resembled Darlene's 1963 Brown Chevrolet Corvair. The darkness concealed the color of the vehicle, but he was able to see that it was a man behind the wheel. About a minute passed and then he raced off at a "fairly fast rate of speed"[37] advancing in the direction from which he came. He returned just moments later. The driver parked roughly ten feet behind and to the right side of the Corvair. He exited his car, kept the lights on, and approached Michael's side, the right passenger's door. He held a large, high-powered flashlight in his hand. His manner of approach led the couple to believe that he was a police officer who wanted to check their IDs. When he reached the door, he blinded them with the flashlight and began shooting through the open window.

In an act of desperation, Michael hurled his body into the backseat. He kept shooting. Believing they were dead, he turned around and walked back toward his car. However, they were not dead, and as the sound of agony reached his ears, he promptly returned to complete his sinister mission. He raised his arm and pulled the trigger, hitting Michael's back and left leg, he then aimed at Darlene and shot her two more times. The killer walked casually to his car.

In a state of pure shock and profound pain, Michael opened the door and fell to the outside; he noticed the man backing up in a turning movement and taking off at "a very high rate of speed."[38] The car had a California license plate; regrettably, the identifying numbers and letters escaped Michael's eyes. It was the same model as Darlene's or very similar. The color was also very similar, but perhaps "a little bit lighter brown."[39] Soon after, another car entered the area. One of the passengers, Jerry, approached Michael and a brief conversation ensued. "Are you all right?"[40] Jerry asked. "I'm shot and the girl's shot, get a doc,"[41] cried Michael. "All right we'll get one,[42]" assured Jerry. "Hurry,"[43] urged Michael. On their way to Jerry's residence, the people in the car spotted the tail lights of a car at the Lake Herman Road turnoff. At 12:10 a.m. one of them phoned the police. Switchboard Operator Nancy L. Slover took the call.[44] From this point, it was only a matter of minutes before the authorities would arrive to assist the victims.

Sergeant Roy Conway, a first-responder, found Michael on the ground in excruciating pain. He felt that it was necessary to question him about the incident. Michael said that it was a young, fat man who had started shooting without saying a word. He drove a brown car.[45] Conway continued to question Michael until the ambulance had arrived. He then passed on the description to other officers at the scene and broadcast it to all police units. Sergeant Douglas Clark found Darlene slumped over the steering wheel. She had a weak pulse and was trying to say something that sounded like "I" or "my."[46] Soon after, she lost consciousness, never to regain it. A doctor pronounced her dead when she arrived at Kaiser Hospital at approximately 12:38 a.m.[47] Her autopsy showed that she had five entry wounds mainly on her posterior thoracic cage resulting in damage to her heart, liver, spleen, and both lungs. Both of her arms had been shot twice. While treated for his wounds by Dr. Jantzen, Michael told Sergeant Richard Hoffman that the shooter was older than himself.[48] Michael was fortunate and survived.

It was decided that Sergeants Ed Rust and John Lynch would be the primary investigative officers in the case.[49]

The Phone Call

Slover picked up the phone again at 12:40 a.m. It was a one-way-conversation. "I want to report a double murder," the caller began. "If you go one mile east on Columbus Parkway to the public park you will find the kids in a brown car. They were shot with a 9 mm Luger. I also killed those kids last year. Goodbye."[50] The killer had left a taunting and horrifying message for the police.

The call was traced to a pay phone at the corner of Tuolumne and Springs Road. From here, if you go 0.1 mile east, then turn west for 0.3 mile, turn south and continue 0.3 mile, and on your right side, you find the Vallejo Police Department. The pay phone was located some 10 minutes from the crime scene though the killer spent an additional 30 minutes before placing the call. He may have switched his car, changed his clothes, discarded the weapon, and so forth, and after this he headed to the pay phone. Just as he took considerable risks before and during the killing of David and Betty, in this instance, he similarly took risks by calling the police and driving around in the area of the crime scene. He must have realized that there was a possibility he could have been pulled over by a police officer or that his call was recorded (it was not since they did not have the equipment at that time).

Slover filled out a report about the call and gave a comprehensive description of the killer's voice. She typed that she could not discern an accent, and he "seemed to be reading or had rehearsed what he was saying." His voice was even, consistent, mature, and she added in parentheses, "rather soft but forceful." He raised his voice when she tried to interrupt with questions. When he ended the call by saying "goodbye," his voice "deepened and became taunting."[51]

Although her report was detailed, she did not assign a number to her presumed intuitive estimate of his age. In June 2010, we contacted Slover who reported that the caller had horrified her, and even more so when she learned that it indeed had been the killer on the other end. The conversation was still fresh in her mind despite the 41 years that had passed. She stated, "I estimated him anywhere between late '20s - mid '30s."

She was also asked if she got the impression that it was a local man. "I really don't know," his specific wording "led me to believe he was not that familiar with Vallejo, but that could have just been him playing with me too, because he referred to the park as the 'public park,' and it was never referred to as 'the public park,' it was Blue Rock Springs,"[52] she said.

The Technical Analysis

No significant leads emerged after a criminalist had analyzed the slugs and shell casings, and it was not even possible to pinpoint the specific pistol that the killer had used to kill Ferrin and injure Michael. It only appeared to have been one of the following brands: Browning, Smith & Wesson, Star, Astra, Llama, Neuhausen, Zbrojovka, Husqvarna, or Esperanza.[53] The pistol had been loaded with 9 mm Winchester Western ammunition, the type commonly called 9 mm Luger. The killer had chosen not to use the J.C. Higgins from the December crime. He probably knew that the .22 bullets were potential fingerprints that could tie his weapon to the crime via a forensic firearm examination. He probably destroyed or sold the J.C. Higgins shortly after December 20, 1968.

Interviews

No witnesses stepped forward who had seen the actual shooting or phone call. However, George Bryant showed up at the police station and said that he lived approximately 800 feet away from the crime scene, and at "approximately midnight,"[54] while lying in his bed, he distinctly heard two gunshots that were followed by rapid gunfire, and subsequently a car took off at "super speed."[55] He said that it "burned rubber and was squealing its tires as it sped along the road."[56] He thought that it was someone celebrating and was not greatly concerned.

On July 7, while Michael was in the intensive care unit, Sergeant Rust paid him a visit and asked him a number of questions. Even though Michael was medicated and in a critical condition, he was able to give a detailed and coherent account of the shooting and describe the killer's appearance. Michael said that the killer "appeared to be short, possibly 5'8", was real heavy set, beefy build." However, he was "not blubbery fat, but real beefy, possibly 195 to 200 [lb.], or maybe even larger." He had "short, curly hair, light brown, almost blonde." He had on a bluish short-sleeved shirt. He noticed that his face appeared to be large, and that he was not bearded or wearing glasses. He was about 26-30 years old. He mostly got a profile view of him. Michael added that he did not believe anyone had a reason to kill him or Darlene. If someone had wanted to kill her, he was sure she would have told him.[57]

Overview

The killer, or the Zodiac as he would later call himself, had committed two crimes with a very similar *modus operandi*. His anger seemed directed at couples, and he definitely had a propensity to taunt the police. Clearly, the killer's self-confidence had been amplified since December and he was already becoming more brazen. But at the same time, he was taking more precautions. When he entered the parking lot the first time, he was most likely checking if the couple was compatible with his desires. Upon seeing that Michael and Darlene did, he then left to check if anybody was nearby. He then returned to pull the trigger.

He had been disturbed and frightened by Owen's presence in December.

In both crimes, it appears that he had used a ruse to facilitate the killings or get the victims to act in accordance with his presumed fantasies of the crimes. In December, he pretended to be a robber, and in July he gave the impression that he was a police officer checking out on the couple. His flashlight, bluish shirt, and manner of approach point in that direction.

The investigative officers had little to work on apart from checking out leads the public had sent the Vallejo Police Department.

In retrospect, if the necessary records existed, investigators could have identified all those living in Vallejo and adjacent cities having one or both of the cars suspected to be in the possession of the killer. The pool of possible suspects could then be reduced to males matching the physical characteristics outlined by Bill Crow and Michael Mageau. Although this strategy would have been highly tedious and extremely time consuming, with no guarantees provided, it could have led the police in the right direction.

APPENDIX A

Figure 1
The 1961, 4-door Rambler station wagon.
Figure 2
Another view of the Rambler station wagon from a distance.
Figure 3
In focus is one of the bullet holes in the Rambler station wagon.
Figure 4
Aerial overview of the Lake Herman Road crime scene.
Figure 5
Betty Lou Jensen and David Faraday.
Figure 6
Darlene Ferrin and Michael Mageau.
Figure 7
Email to Søren Korsgaard. Bill Crow.
Figure 8
Email to Søren Korsgaard. Bill Crow.

Figure 1

Figure 2

Figure 3

Figure 4

Figure 5

Figure 6

Figure 7

"What you sent are some of the comments from the police report that I saw for the first time a few years back when a researcher sent me a copy. I knew the Sheriff who wrote the report and never reviewed it nor was there ever any follow up. What I find somewhat strange is that at no time did anyone to my knowledge ever interview the girl I was with on the night that this happened. I will be happy to provide you with a copy of the police report. The below is not accurate in the details and reflect what the officer wrote in response to questions that I was asked. For example, I never said the car I saw was possibility a Valiant. What I said was that I noticed the back up lights come on after the car passed my location. I was then asked to describe the lights and I said they were round. At [that] time Valiant was not part of my vocabulary and the only thing I can think of was that the officer was familiar with the Valiant automobile and its tail lights. I also never said how many were in the car. I said I saw that the driver was Caucasian. I was then asked if there could have been more than one person in the car. I responded that there could have been, I could not see the passenger side as it was nighttime and there are no lights in the area. The Sheriff decided to include a they into the report. I have a memory of what occurred and live within a few miles of the scene. From time to time I still drive out Lake Herman Road. I will send a complete account in a few days."

Figure 8

"It is important from my point of view to keep two things in mind. First, on December 20, 1968 the Zodiac Killer did not yet exist. Secondly, the first time I ever saw a copy the police report relating to my incident was October 6, 2003 when a copy was faxed to me by a person investigating the Zodiac. I never reviewed or knew what the investigators wrote of my interview with them until that time.

On December 20, 1968 I was living with my parents in Vallejo where I was born, raised and still live. My girlfriend had moved from her parent's home in Napa, California to San Francisco. She contacted me and was coming for the weekend to visit her parents and wanted to come by that day and show me her new sports car. It was a small dark colored car with two seats and a standard transmission. We decided to take it for a drive and she suggested that I drive and try it out. Lake Herman Road is basically a desolate two lane winding county type road that runs between east Vallejo and Benicia. There are few lights and some scattered ranch type homes. It has changed very little over the years and today my home is located a few minutes' drive away. Back then Lake Herman Road was known to the local youth as a place that had a few well known places to park and make out. The spot where the two youths were killed is one of those places. On this evening I chose Lake Herman Road because I thought it would be a good place to test out the sports car.

We drove down Lake Herman Road from Vallejo towards Benicia. I pulled into the entrance to the Benicia Water Pumping Station. There is [located a] gate back off the main road and thus room to park. I pulled in and turned around with the car on the far right fringe of the entrance driveway with the lights off and the car still running. It was a cold night and I had the heater on. The car had toggle switches on the dashboard as controls which were new to me. I was in the process of determining how they worked when I noticed a car coming from the direction of Benicia. As it passed in front of me I did not recognize the car (back in that day your car was part of your identity) and could only see that the driver was a white male with short hair and glasses. Again, at that time there was no Zodiac. The car passed where I was parked and I noticed that it started to stop. I do not think the driver initially saw the car we were in as I was parked at the extreme north side of the driveway facing the road and our car was a small dark sports car that would have blended into the night.

I noticed the back up lights of the other car come on and I remember they were round in shape. My senses told me that this was not a good thing and I turned on the lights, put the car in gear and took off towards Benicia. The other car pulled into the driveway of the pump station, turned around and came in my direction of travel. I sped up and so did he. The next thing that happened was that he started to flash his headlights, high beam, low beam, high beam, etc. in an attempt to get me to pull over. I did not stop but sped up and so did he. Contrary to what the police report indicates he was gaining on me as we sped down the road. There is a fork in the road with one leg going on towards Benicia and the other heading back towards Vallejo. I waited to the last possible second and turned the sports car towards the right fork. The larger car could not make the maneuver. I went down about fifty yards and stopped. I looked back and the other car had stopped. At that point my youthful testosterone kicked in and I started yelling that I was going to go back and kick his [ass]. My girlfriend was upset, concerned and started to cry. I watched the other car as it sat stopped in roadway. After a few minutes the other car slowly turned around and went back in the direction we had come from, back towards the pumping station. I decided that good judgment out weighed valor and decided to continue on home [and] we did. I was aware of the time because before I left my father reminded me that we were going hunting the next day and I needed to get some sleep as we were getting up early.

There was an article in the local newspaper about the killings of David Faraday and Betty Jensen. The description of the place of the killings seemed to be the same exact spot where I had been parked earlier that same night. I took the article and my shotgun (as if the person was still going to be there in the daylight) and drove down Lake Herman Road. I determined that the killings had taken place in the exact same place where I had been. When I came back home I shared with my mother what had happened to me and asked her what I should do. She suggested that I inform the police and I called the Vallejo Police Department. They indicated that it was the Sheriff's jurisdiction and I called them. They sent out two Sheriff's Deputies and I knew Deputy Lundblad because I played organized baseball with his son. They asked some questions, wrote some notes and left. That was the one and only contact I had with the authorities.

In 2003 I was contacted by a man from New Jersey who was researching the Zodiac. During our telephone [conversation] I asked him how he found his way to me and he indicated that my name appeared in a police report that he had. I asked and he agreed to fax me a copy.

It was not long after my incident that the Zodiac Killer emerged. That caused me to relive that evening many times over the years. When I reviewed the police report I noted the following discrepancies. When I stopped I was not adjusting the motor as the report states. To adjust the motor would have required me to be outside the car with the hood up. I never got out of the car and was experimenting with the toggle switches that evening. The toggle switches have nothing to do with adjusting the motor. I did not indicate the car was blue or that it was a [Valiant]. Back then I did not know [what] a [Valiant] looked like. I responded to the question I was asked about the shape of the back up lights. I indicated that the backup lights were round and the officer suggested and evidently wrote down that the other car was a [Valiant]. The report further states that the other car did not attempt to gain on me. What I think he meant to write is that it did. The entry before that states that the car followed me at a high rate of speed. In addition, I absolutely never stated that I could see more than one person in the other car. I was asked if there could have been more than one person in the other car and I indicated that it was dark, I could not see into the passenger seat, but there could have been. I did indicate that the driver of the other car was Caucasian as stated in the report and that suggests and confirms that I did get a brief look at him. You can tell from the report that the interview was brief."

ENDNOTES A

[1] David Fincher, Director, Zodiac 2-Disc Director's Cut, 2008.
[2] Solano County Sheriff's Office Report, Vallejo, Case Number V25564, 3.
[3] Ibid, 47.
[4] Ibid, 37.
[5] Ibid, 56.
[6] Ibid, 20.
[7] Ibid, 4.
[8] Ibid, 22.
[9] Ibid, 8.
[10] Ibid, 14.
[11] "Sherlock Holmes," https://en.wikiquote.org/wiki/Sherlock_Holmes (retrieved April 2020).
[12] Crow, William. Email to Søren Roest Korsgaard. September 24, 2010.
[13] Ibid.
[14] Solano County Sheriff's Office Report, Vallejo, Case Number V25564, 40.
[15] Ibid, 19.
[16] "Appeal Is Made For Help," December 26, 1968.
[17] Department of Justice, Bureau of Criminal Investigation and Investigation Report, Case Number 1-15-311-F9-5861, 23.
[18] Death Certificate for David Arthur Faraday, County of Solano, File No. 101653.
[19] Solano County Sheriff's Office Report, Vallejo, Case Number V25564, 17.
[20] Department of Justice, Bureau of Criminal Identification and Investigation, Case Number 37-F-2795, report by David Q. Burd, 2.
[21] Ibid.
[22] Ibid, 2-3.
[23] Solano County Sheriff's Office Report, Vallejo, Case Number V25564, 8.
[24] Ibid, 15.
[25] Ibid, 5.
[26] "2 Teen-Agers Are Murdered," Fresno Bee Republican, December 21, 1968, 6.
[27] "Teen-Agers on 1st Date Fatally Shot," Independent Press-Telegram, December 22, 1968, 17.
[28] "Couple Found Shot To Death," Abilene Reporter News, December 22, 1968, 11.
[29] "Police Probe Double Teen Murder," Press-Courier, December 22 1968, 35.
[30] "Youths on Date Shot to Death," Albuquerque Journal, December 22, 1968, 19.
[31] "Friends Quizzed in Slaying Of Teen Pair Near Vallejo." San Francisco Chronicle, December 22, 1968, 10.

[32] Crime Report, Vallejo Police Department, Case Number 243 146, 23.
[33] Ibid, 28.
[34] Ibid, 21.
[35] Ibid.
[36] Ibid.
[37] Ibid, 22.
[38] Ibid.
[39] Ibid.
[40] Ibid, 30.
[41] Ibid.
[42] Ibid.
[43] Ibid.
[44] Ibid, 10.
[45] Ibid, 13.
[46] Ibid, 14.
[47] Ibid, 12.
[48] Ibid.
[49] Ibid, 13.
[50] Ibid, 10.
[51] Ibid.
[52] Nancy Slover. Telephone interview. June 7, 2010.
[53] California Department of Justice/Division of Law Enforcement/Bureau of Investigation, Zodiac Homicides, for Law Enforcement Use Only, 4.
[54] Crime Report, Vallejo Police Department, Case Number 243 146, 18.
[55] Ibid.
[56] Ibid.
[57] Crime Report, Vallejo Police Department, Case Number 243 146, 23.

CHAPTER 2

PLEASE RUSH TO EDITOR

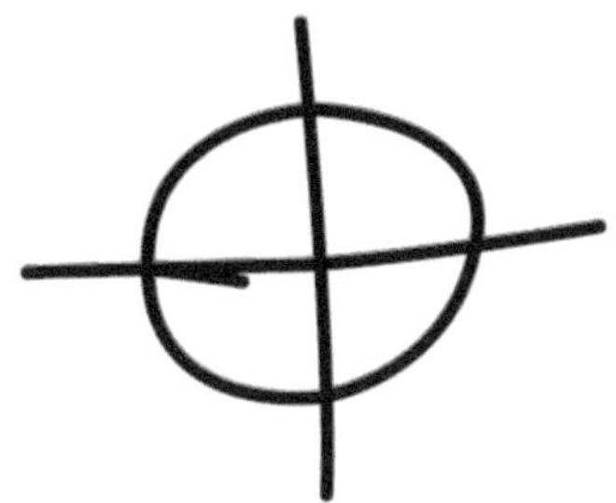

Thursday, July 31, 1969

Almost a month elapsed, and the behavioral pattern established by the assailant changed again, this time radically. In longhand, the killer penned three letters and constructed a complex cryptogram. The editors at the San Francisco Chronicle, the San Francisco Examiner, and the Vallejo Times-Herald each received a letter with one third of the cryptogram on August 1. The envelopes were postmarked on July 31 in San Francisco. They contained excess postage, almost as if he was impatient and wanted them delivered in a hurry or compulsively wanted to make sure the letters would arrive. On the front and back of the envelopes, the assailant had written, "Please Rush to Editor!" In the letters, he communicated detailed information about the killings and promised that his identity would be uncovered if the arcane cipher was solved. He concluded each letter with a threat that he would go on a killing rampage if they did not give him front-page coverage. On August 2, 1969, the Chronicle published its part of the cryptogram on page four underneath the headline, "Coded Clue in Murders."[1] Police Chief of Vallejo Police Department, Jack E. Stiltz, commented, "We're not satisfied that the letter was written by the murderer, but it could have been," and he urged the writer to send a second letter "with more facts to prove it."[2] The cops obviously welcomed the communications and hoped for more correspondence. With luck on their side, it would lead to his arrest.

The three messages when placed side-by-side read as follows:

The San Francisco Chronicle	**The San Francisco Examiner**	**The Vallejo Times-Herald**
Dear Editor	Dear Editor	Dear Editor
This is the murderer of the 2 teenagers last Christmass at Lake Herman + the girl on the 4th of July near the golf course in Vallejo	I am the killer of the 2 teenagers last christmass at Lake Herman + the girl last 4th of July.	I am the killer of the 2 teenagers last Christmass at Lake Herman and the Girl last 4th of July.
To prove I killed them I shall state some facts which only I + the police know.	To prove this I shall state some facts which only I + the police know.	To Prove this I shall state some facts which only I + the police know
Christmass	Christmass	Christmass
1 Brand name of ammo Super X	1 brandname of ammo - Super X	1 Brand name of ammo Super X
2 10 shots were fired	2 10 shots fired	2 10 shots fired
3 the boy was on his back with his feet to the car	3 Boy was on his back with feet to car	3 Boy was on back feet to car
4 the girl was on her right side feet to the west	4 Girl was lyeing on right side feet to west	4 Girl was lyeing on right side

4 th July	4th of July	4th of July
1 girl was wearing paterned slacks	1 girl was wearing patterned pants	1 Girl was wearing patterned Pants
2 The boy was also shot in the knee.	2 boy was also shot in knee	2 Boy was also shot in knee
3 Brand name of ammo was western	3 ammo was made by Western	3 Brand name of ammo was Western
Over	Here is a ciPher or that is part of one. The other 2 parTs are being mailed to the Vallejo Times + S.F. Chronicle	Here is a cyipher or that is part of one. the other 2 parts have been mailed to the S.F. Examiner + the S.F. Chronicle
Here is part of a cipher the other 2 parts of this cipher are being mailed to the editors of the Vallejo times + SF Examiner	I want you to print this cipher on the frunt page by Fry afternoon Aug 1-69.	I want you to print this cipher on your frunt page by Fry Afternoon Aug 1-69, If you do not do this I will go on a Kill rampage Fry night that will last the whole week end.
I want you to print this cipher on the frunt page of your paper.	If you do not print this cipher, I will go on a Kill rampage Fry night.	I will cruse around and pick of all stray people or coupples that are alone then move on to kill some more untill I have killed over a dozen people. ⊕

In this cipher is my idenity.	This will last the whole weekend, I will cruse around killing people who are alone at night untill Sun Night or untill I kill a dozen people. ⌖	
If you do not print this cipher by the afternoon of Fry. 1st of Aug 69, I will go on a Kill ramPage Fry. night.		
I will cruse around all weekend killing lone people in the night then move on to kill again, untill I end up with a dozen people over the weekend. ⌖		

Analysis

In retrospect, we know that the writer of the letters did not embark on a killing-streak even though the editors did not publish his cipher exactly as demanded. Therefore, the "killer" or "murderer," as he called himself, demonstrated through his deceptive display of aggression that he was a bluffer and was aiming for widespread horror and attention.
From the factual points he listed in the letters, we get the impression that it was easy for him to navigate. For example, he demonstrated visual-spatial abilities by accurately recalling the position of Betty's feet using a cardinal direction. He similarly described Blue Rock Springs in this manner to Slover, except this time he was a bit unclear, as he did not pick a point of reference when he stated, "If you go one mile east on Columbus Parkway to the public park you will find the kids in a brown car." The statement is inaccurate or very imprecise if he was trying to direct the authorities from the pay phone or police station to the crime scene. We should note, however, that he knew Columbus Parkway, indicating that he was well acquainted with the area. He must also have had a good recall of the crimes, given that he provided details that he had a limited time to memorize, according to our established timeline.
Moreover, it has been observed that his estimate of the victims' maturity signifies that he was significantly older than they were. For example, he referred to Darlene and Michael as "kids" even though they were 22 and 19 years old respectively.

Monday, August 4

The killer could not stand the challenge issued by Stiltz and sent a reply in the form of a San Francisco postmarked envelope containing a three-page letter to the Examiner. It was received on August 4. The content eliminated any doubt that the actual killer was the mysterious pen pal. By this point, the police had already contacted the FBI for assistance. Many of the correspondences between them have been made public in the ensuing years. One document affirms the opinion of the police vis-á-vis the culpability of the writer: "Police officials are of [the] opinion that the letters were written by [the] person responsible for the murder

of the three and the wounding of the fourth victim. They have no idea as to the significance of the ciphers."[3†]
The killer's decision to enter the public stage was not without risk, because he might accidentally have revealed clues to his identity or location. Perhaps someone would recognize his handwriting, tone of communication or abilities, and phone the cops to tell them about their suspect. The actual paper and envelopes yielded clues to pursue after the FBI had conducted their forensic analyses. They determined that the paper contained the watermark of the F. W. Woolworth Company, "FIFTH AVENUE."[4] Latent prints were lifted from page two and three.[5] Elimination prints were taken from the personnel at the Chronicle who had handled the material, and they were all excluded as the source of the latents.

The August letter.

Page 1 read:

Dear Editor

This is the Zodiac speaking.
In answer to your asking for
more details about the good
times I have had in Vallejo,
I shall be very happy to
supply even more material.
By the way, are the police
haveing a good time with the
code? If not, tell them to cheer
up; when they do crack it
they will have me.

[†] The Zodiac crimes did not fall under federal jurisdiction, so the FBI never actively investigated the crimes.

On the 4th of July:
I did not open the car door, The window was rolled down all ready. The boy was origionaly sitting in the frunt seat when I began fireing. When I fired the first shot at his head, he leaped backwords at the same time thus spoiling my aim. He ended up on the back seat then the floor in back thashing out very violently with his legs; thats how I shot him in the

Page 2 read:

knee. I did not leave the cene of the killing with squealling tires + raceing engine as described in the Vallejo paper. I drove away quite slowly so as not to draw attention to my car.
The man who told the police that my car was brown was a negro about 40-45 rather shabbly dressed. I was at this phone booth haveing some fun with the Vallejo cops when he was walking by. When I hung the phone up the dam x@ thing beganto ring + that drew his attention to me + my car.
Last Christmass
In that epasode the police were wondering as to how I could shoot + hit my victoms in the dark. They did not openly state this, but implied this by say ing it was a well lit night + I could see the silowets on the horizon.

Bullshit that area is srounded

Page 3 read:

by high hills + trees. What I did
was tape a small pencel flash
light to the barrel of my gun.
If you notice, in the center
of the beam of lighT if you aim
it at a wall or celling you will
see a black or darck spot in
the center of the cirCle of
light aprox 3 to 6 in. acrosS.
When taped to a gun barrel,
the bullet will strike exactly
in the center of the black
dot in the light. All I had to do
was spray them as if it was
a water hose; there was no
need to use the gun sights.
I was not happy to see that I
did not get frunt page cover -
age.
⌖
NO ADDRESS

Analysis

Instead of "the murderer" and "the killer" which he had initially called himself, the serial killer finally settled on the now-infamous pseudonym, "the Zodiac." It has become quite clear over the years that the noun, "Zodiac," appears in a myriad of places from boats to astrology. We will now detail some of the most significant findings that have been made. The most compelling origin appears to be Zodiac watches. This Swiss manufactured brand uses the name Zodiac and the crosshair symbol, which the Zodiac signed his letter with, on the face of their watches. Based on ads from the 1960s, they were relatively expensive timepieces. Although manufactured in Europe, they were sold across the globe, and prior to the Zodiac crimes in the late 1960s there were ads for Zodiac watches in the San Francisco Chronicle and the San Francisco Examiner.[6] Much more assessable than these watches was the concept of Zodiac as it pertained to astrology, which, unlike today's skeptical age, experienced increased popularity around the time the letter was sent. Astrology.com.au defines Zodiac:

> The word Zodiac literally means animals and refers to the patterns or configurations of creatures as seen in the twinkling stars at night. The Zodiac belt is the great circle around which our luminescent Sun apparently moves month by month throughout the year, transceiving the energy of those different constellational signs and thereby transmitting the celestial radiations to our Earth. As the planets revolve around the Sun in their respective cycles we can observe the influences associated with those celestial movements. Broadly speaking, the 12 signs of the Zodiac can be divided into both masculine and feminine, positive and negative, or, active and passive. The masculine signs are Aries, Gemini, Leo, Libra, Sagittarius and Aquarius, whereas the feminine signs are Taurus, Cancer, Virgo, Scorpio, Capricorn and Pisces.[7]

Zodiac is also a reoccurring theme in the 1939 short-film, *Treasure Island.*[8] The Chinese-American Detective Charlie Chan investigates a mysterious psychic, Dr. Zodiac, and his complicity in several suicides that turnout to be murders. A telegram received by a victim of Dr. Zodiac is of interest,

> "SIGN OF SCORPIO INDICATES
> DISASTER IF ZODIAC
> OBLIGATIONS IGNORED
> UNSIGNED."

In his first three letters, the Zodiac also threatened disaster if his demands went unmet, coincidentally. It is briefly mentioned that a character in the movie is a reporter for the San Francisco Chronicle. The climax is Chan's characterization of Dr. Zodiac: He is a "man of great ego, enjoys using power to dominate lives of others. Advise caution. To destroy false prophet must first unmask him before eyes of believers." After consulting *History of Psychiatry*, he elaborates on his criminal profile of Dr. Zodiac:

> But Dr. Zodiac not ordinary criminal, he is man of great ego with disease known to science as pseudologia fantastica. Listen: Pathological liars and swindlers suffer from exaggerated fantasy, unleashed vanity, and great ambition, which robs them of caution known to saner men. [...] Criminal egotist finds pleasure in laughing at police.

The similarities continue to accumulate as Dr. Zodiac responds to a paranormal challenge by writing this message in his distinctive handwriting: "I accept your challenge to a demonstration of my powers. I shall appear on your stage to-night. Dr. Zodiac." As the keen readers already have noticed, the portrayal by Chan could easily have been applied to the Zodiac killer! The desire for communicating in handwriting as well as his use of the modal verb, "shall," instead of, "will," which is more commonly used in American English, are also Zodiac characteristics. Was the Zodiac a movie aficionado?

Let us move further back in time to November 1931 when *Popular Science* published "Hidden Crime CLUES," an article that contains conspicuous parallels to the Zodiac case. The article details the efforts of Detective Luke S. May to solve a "weird 'Zodiac Murder.'"[9] Dr. Fred Covell had been wrongfully accused of killing his wife, Ebba Covell, on September 3, 1923, in Bandon, Oregon. Ebba had been found by Dr. Covell's disabled brother, Arthur, who "spent his days in a wheelchair poring over charts, zodiacs, and horoscopes, absorbed in the 'black art' of astrology."[10] Luke S. May was not impressed by the evidence that had been presented against Dr. Covell. He therefore entered the case and discovered that a miscarriage of justice was about to take place.

The detective aimed his attention at the crippled brother in order to gain further insights. He found that he was a "man of unusually keen intellect and tremendous will power,"[11] and he had "an almost hypnotic effect upon those around him."[12] The detective noticed that among the brother's belongings were "curious messages in code, using signs of the zodiac as key symbols."[13] While the detective was a "cryptographer of note," he was mostly unfamiliar with astrology, so he began a thorough study of it. He then "reexamined the notes, grouped the symbols, found the key to the baffling code, and uncovered one of the most fantastic and diabolical murder plots of criminal history."[14] The crippled brother had a kill list of 17 people that ended with his 16-year-old nephew, Alton Covell, who under his spell had carried out the actual murder of Dr. Covell's wife. When Arthur had cast "the horoscopes of his victims, the astrological assassin had set the time of their deaths for the hours when the stars boded most evil for them,"[15] the article reads. From other sources, we learn that Alton was sentenced to life in prison, but pardoned in October 1934. He died in Texas in 2002.[16] Arthur was less fortunate: A group of prison guards carried him to the gallows and hanged him on May 28, 1925.[17]

With the above synchronism in mind, it is easy to picture that the Zodiac could have picked up the major aspects of his criminal persona in quite a few places. In fact, an entire volume could be penned detailing hundreds if not thousands of possible Zodiac influences. We shall not plague the readers to such a degree, but continue our analysis of his letter.

The Zodiac indirectly discounted the observation of Bryant and Mageau when he asserted that he drove away *slowly* from the crime scene. He was lying, obviously. The objective of the August letter was ostensibly to convince everyone of his guilt; nevertheless, he must have been reasonably sure all along that the police were satisfied with the information he had provided. Why else would he insert deception into his letter and possibly undermine his efforts? We might conjecture that he felt portrayed as a coward, and it was paramount for him to repair the scratches of his perceived public image.

No evidence has emerged that backs his claim that a man reported the color of his car at the phone booth. It must have been clear to the Zodiac that Michael said it was brown because this was stated in the Vallejo Times-Herald, which he had evidently read.[18] In addition, Zodiac stated in the beginning of the letter that Michael was the one who had opened the car door of Darlene's Corvair. When Michael fell outside, he saw the color of the Zodiac's car. There is no doubt that Zodiac was aware that Michael was the one who had reported the color. So we must question why Zodiac confirmed that his car was brown. Why comment on this aspect at all? First, Mageau could have been mistaken about the color, and, therefore, the Zodiac was eager to play along. Second, Zodiac could have included the elaborate story to get the police to look for a witness who did not exist. Third, he specified that he was at the phone booth when his car was seen. In other words, he did not change his car to one with a different color after the shooting. His manipulation may indicate that he did make a switch. Having access to more than one car is also backed up by physical evidence, as we shall see. It is indicated that Zodiac lived close to the crime scene. If we recall, Zodiac spent 40 minutes before making the phone call, even though it was a 10 minute drive from the crime scene.

The Zodiac's flashlight-gun-sight is similar to modern laser sights, which first became available to the public several years later. It seems like a clever piece of creativity. However, the notion of mounting a flashlight to a weapon goes at least as far back as 1922, when Popular Mechanics gave a description of such a devise.[19] Furthermore, on February 4, 2011, author James Wm. Lewis confirmed that the method was prevalent among hunters in Missouri in the 1950s and '60s and probably long before that. During daytime, raccoons and rabbits could easily escape the hunter. However, at night, the use of a flashlight made the eyes of the animals glow—making them easy targets.
It has been observed that the Zodiac's description of his flashlight-sight is almost identical to one characterized in Museum Piece, an episode of Alfred Hitchcock Presents.[20]
In the episode, Hollister owns a small museum, and one evening after a guided tour, he recounts to an interested guest how a determined district attorney had been responsible for the innocent conviction of his son, Ben. In jail, the son lost interest in life and died. Recounting the incident that led to the conviction, the son is shown with a rifle that has a flashlight mounted to the barrel. At this point, Hollister says, "He'd invented a foolproof gadget for night shooting, a spotlight mounted on his .22 in such a way that his shot would strike the exact center of the circle of light." Evidently, Hollister sought revenge and killed the district attorney, and started to exhibit his skeleton in his museum. While looking at the skeleton, he says to the guest, "you know it took almost a year to put him there. I remember the excitement of the manhunt, the most dangerous game." As will be shown in this chapter, the Zodiac's affection for Museum Piece is further established when he communicated that man is *the most dangerous* animal. Hollister's narrative also bears a strong resemblance to the words used by the Zodiac when he stated, "the bullet will strike exactly in the center of the black dot in the light," while Hollister said, "his shot would strike the exact center of the circle of light."

Friday, August 8

At 6:35 p.m., the Vallejo Police Department (VPD) got a call from George Murphy, an employee of the San Francisco

Chronicle.[21] He advised the officer that Donald Gene Harden had sent him a letter that stated that he had broken the cipher. Experts later authenticated the solution. The Chronicle published it the next day in the article called, "A 'Murder Code' Broken."[22] The front-page of the Vallejo-Times-Herald read, "Cryptogram Deciphered By Teacher." Their article stated, "Det. Sgt. John Lynch, who with Det. Sgt. Ed Rust is in charge of the murder cryptogram case, said: 'There is no doubt in my mind that this is a true translation of the cipher and that the murderer wrote it. You can almost check the cipher against itself.'"[23] Around the same time, the FBI in Washington had independently broken the cipher.[24] It was never disclosed how the FBI agents had deciphered it. Harden was a high-school teacher and amateur cryptographer, and naturally the arcane cipher intrigued him when he saw it in the newspaper. He and his wife, Bettye June Harden, had begun decrypting the cipher by looking for four-letter patterns such as in the word "kill."[25] Relatively soon after launching their attack on the cipher, they had broken it. The deciphered message read as follows:

> I like killing people because it is so much fun it is more fun than killing wild game in the forrest because man is the moat dangeroue anamal of all to kill something gives me the moat thrilling experence it is even better than getting your rocks off with a girl the best part of it ia thae when I die I will be reborn in paradice snd all the I have killed will become my slaves I wil not give you my name because you will try to sloi down or stop my collecting of slaves for my afterlife ebeorietemethhpiti

Apart from completing the symmetry of the cipher, the last eighteen symbols do not yield a meaningful message.

Analysis of the Zodiac's cipher

The cipher is 408 characters long of which 54 are unique; they include ordinary and reversed letters and symbols, some of which are used in astrology. Visually, the symbols and methodical arrangement of the cipher appear sophisticated, but the cipher system is very basic. The primary encryption scheme involves substituting the alphabet with symbols, reversed letters, etc. Some letters are substituted by a single character, others by multiple ones. If he had used numbers instead, the letters A, B, C could analogously be represented like this:
A= 1,2,3,4,
B = 5
C = 6
To encrypt ABC, we can write 156, 256, 356, or 456. B and C always remain the same. A, on the other hand, varies between four different numbers. In technical terms the cipher is a combination between a homophonic substitution cipher and a simple substitution cipher, or, as an FBI expert wrote, it is a unilateral, "substitution cryptosystem with variants."[26]
The creator of the code allocated the highest number of characters to the specific letters that are most frequently used in the English language, namely: E, T, A, O, I, and N. Frequency analysis is a powerful tool and obscuring letters this way makes it more difficult to decrypt the cipher. Furthermore, Harden said that Zodiac had used a reversed Q multiple times trying to lure the analyst into believing that it was the letter E.[27]
The cipher message is riddled with misspellings, and these have been observed to be the result of sloppiness, such as when he encoded "AND" and picked the wrong symbols and it became "SND" instead. The two symbols he confused were very similar. He displayed the same confusion of symbols when he misspelled several of the other words. However, some do not fall in this category, such as the misspelling of *forest*.
The Zodiac demonstrated knowledge of cryptography equivalent of what a student would learn through a swift study of an introductory book. However, he may have had knowledge and experience beyond this. He could have made the cipher easy so he could enjoy the additional front-page coverage when it was decrypted. While this may be true, he was nevertheless not a

perfectionist, since he made numerous errors as Harden mentioned. On the other hand, D. C. B. Marsh, a mathematician and head of the American Cryptogram Association, said, shortly after the cipher had been solved, that it was "complicated" and deemed it the work of someone who "knows his business."[28]

The Zodiac may have read the 1968 book "SECRET CODES and CIPHERS,"[29] and followed the instructions outlined on the pages. The author, Bernice Kohn, presents ciphers in equal length sentences and he writes that if the message is too short to complete the symmetry one should add on "any letters."[30] At the end of the 408 cipher, the Zodiac added extra letters to complete the overall symmetry. Kohn also introduces suppression of frequencies: "This type uses more than one symbol for the very common letters, or for all of the letters."[31]

Observations

The Zodiac compared killing people with the pursuit of animals, indicating a disturbed mind and an outrageous fantasy life. In addition, he chose to attack defenseless teenagers giving them no chance, and hardly creating any sport.

As previously mentioned, Museum Piece most likely inspired the Zodiac's selection of words in the cipher. Furthermore, the iconic phrase, *the most dangerous game*, is also the title of a 1924 short story that was adapted into a film in 1932.[32] The short story and movie center around the skilled hunter Zaroff who has lost his passion for hunting animals and, as a substitute, hunts humans on his island. He says in the film, "Here on my island, I hunt the most dangerous game." The phrase is worded slightly differently in the short story: "'Here in my preserve on this island,' he said in the same slow tone, 'I hunt more dangerous game.'"

In 1967, Daniel P. Mannix authored the book, *A Sporting Chance, Unusual Methods of Hunting*. Mannix, an expert of hunting, elucidates various atypical methods of hunting, such as with a boomerang and bow and arrow. The final chapter, *The Most Dangerous Game*, may have been of interest to the Zodiac: Mannix recounts various scenarios in which man has been the target of the hunt.[33]

The Zodiac's cryptic clues and letters had awakened the public, and many individuals from a variety of settings flooded the cops with their insights and analyses, though most were useless. A notable exception was Donald Harden who offered some valid points to the media when he was asked about his impression of the Zodiac. "He is bright enough, but not necessarily of high intellect," Harden said, and, "he may be in or near middle age," because he uses the term *getting your rocks off* that has dropped out of general slang use.[34] Years later, in 2007, Harden gave an interview just before his death. He revealed the sad story of his life and admitted that he wished he had never solved the cipher. "It cost me my family,"[35] he said.

The Zodiac's disturbed concept of victims becoming slaves in the afterlife caught the attention of Professor Fred from the Stanford Research Center. He contacted VPD by mail and stated that the concept originates in South East Asia and particularly at Mindanao in the Southern Philippines. He felt that the Zodiac either was of South East Asian extraction or had knowledge of the area.[36] Another possibility is that the Zodiac attained his inspiration for the slave concept by plagiarizing ancient Egyptian mythology. In that culture, slaves were murdered so they could accompany the Pharaoh into the afterlife.

A psychiatrist who was employed by the California Medical Facility in Vacaville had analyzed the Zodiac's letters and crimes and concluded that it was "the work of someone you would expect to be brooding and isolated."[37] He continued, "He probably is a guy who broods about cutoff feelings, about being cut off from his fellow man … comparing the thrill of killing to the satisfaction of sex is usually an expression of inadequacy. He probably feels his fellow man looks down on him for some reason."[38] The news outlet, which cited the criminal profile, states at this point:

> The belief that his victims would be his slaves in an afterlife reflects a feeling of omnipotence, the unnamed psychiatrist added, indicating a paranoid delusion of grandeur — expressed through a belief common among primitive peoples throughout history. And the taunting notes and phone calls may be a plea to be found out, exposed, perhaps cornered — in which event, the psychiatrist said, a grandiose paranoid quite likely might take his own life, as a grand gesture, to punish the world for its neglect of him in life.

And could it still be a hoax? The psychiatrist was asked. ‘If this is a put-on, then it’s the product of a very, very disturbed person. If this is not a put-on, the man probably will kill again.’”[39]

APPENDIX B

Figure 1
Zodiac letter. Mailed July 31, 1969.
The San Francisco Chronicle.
Figure 2
Zodiac letter. Mailed July 31, 1969.
The San Francisco Examiner.
Figure 3
Zodiac letter. Mailed July 31, 1969.
The Vallejo Times Herald.
Figure 4
The envelopes belonging to the July letters.
Figure 5
The three cipher parts.
Figure 6
Zodiac letter. Received August 4, 1969.
The San Francisco Examiner.

Figure 1

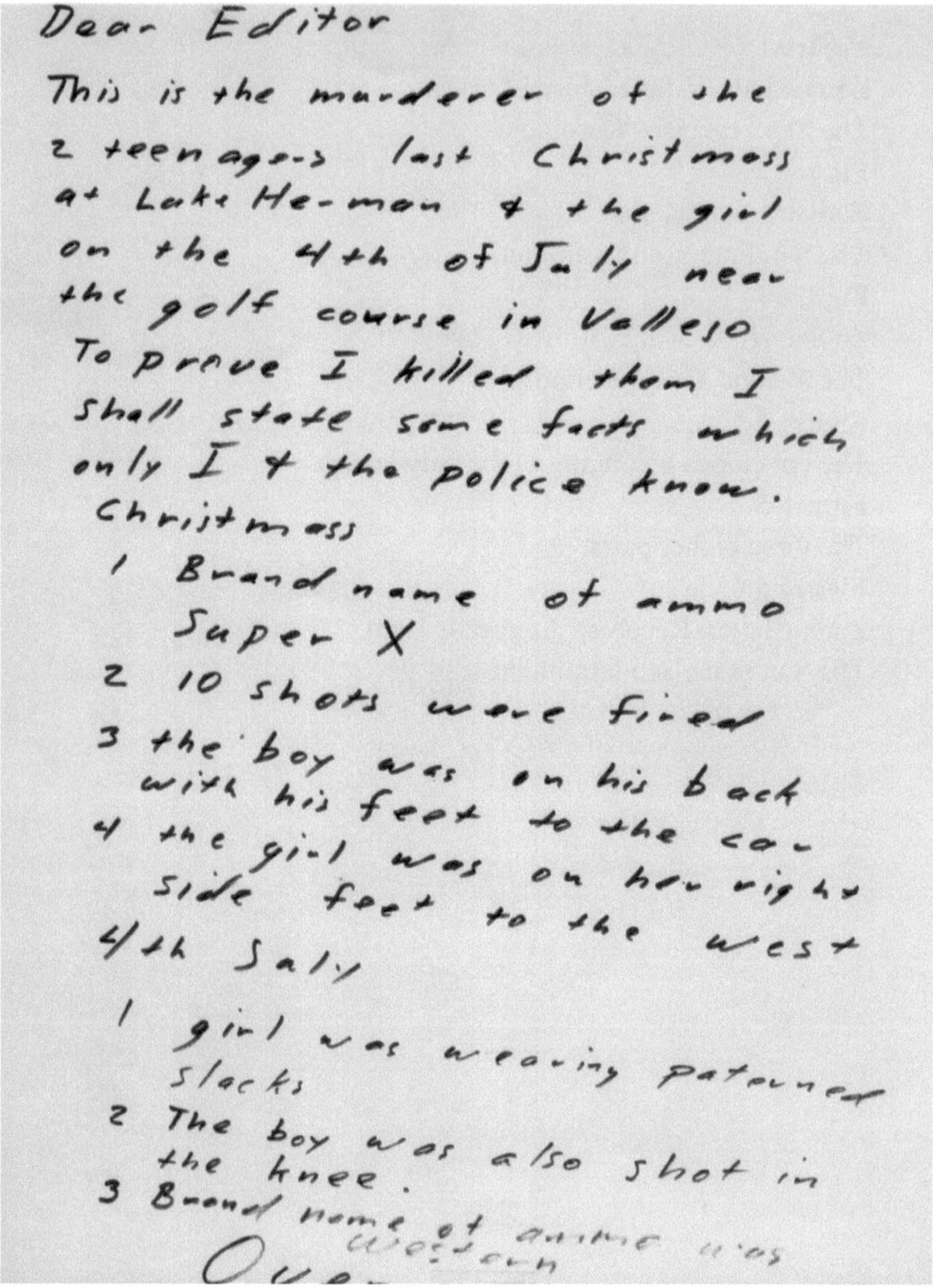

Dear Editor

This is the murderer of the 2 teenagers last Christmass at Lake Herman & the girl on the 4th of July near the golf course in Vallejo To prove I killed them I shall state some facts which only I & the police know.

Christmass

1 Brand name of ammo Super X

2 10 shots were fired

3 the boy was on his back with his feet to the car

4 the girl was on her right side feet to the west

4th July

1 girl was wearing patterned slacks

2 The boy was also shot in the knee.

3 Brand name of ammo was Western

Over

Here is part of a cipher the
other 2 parts of this cipher are
being mailed to the editors of
the Vallejo times + SF Exam
iner.

I want you to print this cipher
on the front page of your
paper. In this cipher is my
idenity.

If you do not print this cipher
by the afternoon of Fry. 1st of
Aug 69, I will go on a kill ram-
Page Fry. night. I will crase
around all weekend killing lone
People in the night then move
on to kill again, untill I end
up with a dozen people over
the weekend.

Figure 2

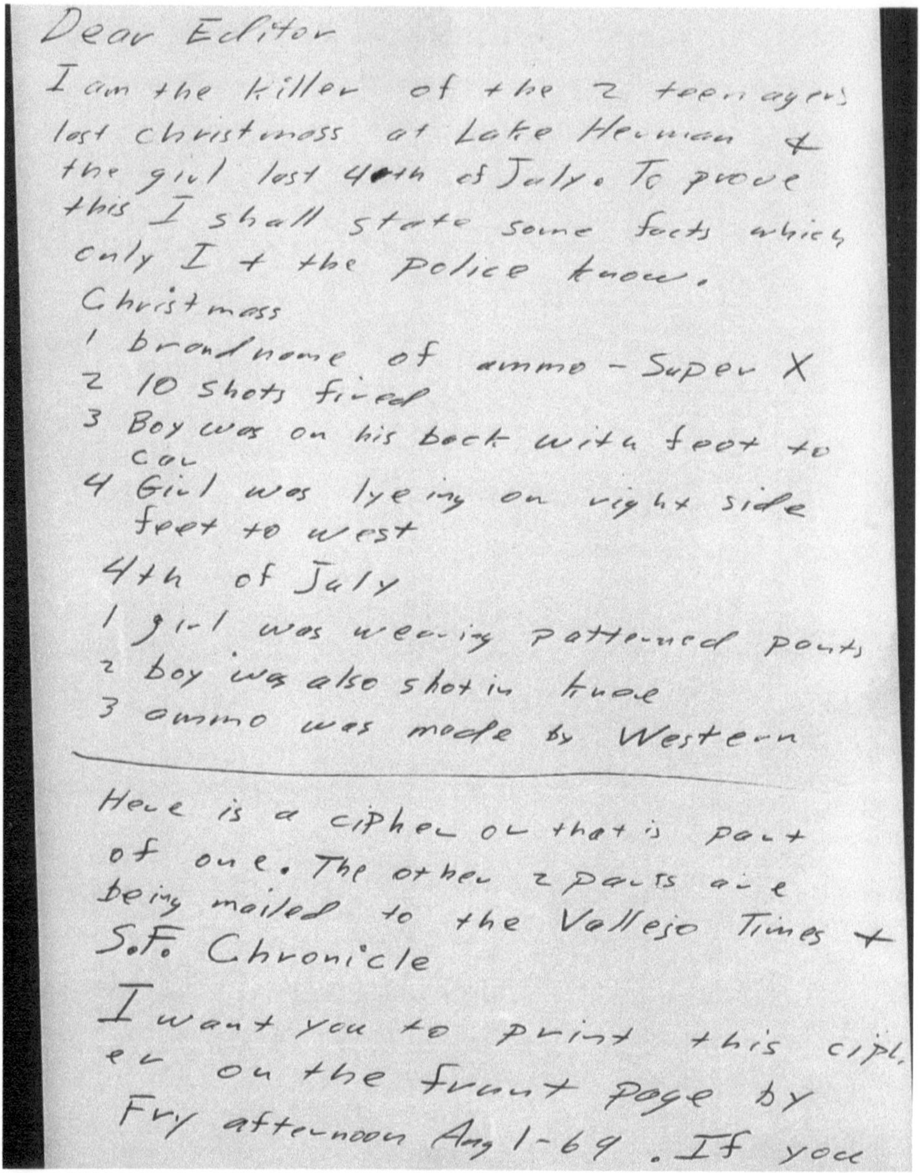

Dear Editor

I am the killer of the 2 teenagers last christmass at Lake Herman & the girl last 4th of July. To prove this I shall state some facts which only I + the police know.

Christmass

1 brand name of ammo - Super X

2 10 shots fired

3 Boy was on his back with feet to car

4 Girl was lyeing on right side feet to west

4th of July

1 girl was wearing patterned pants

2 boy was also shot in knee

3 ammo was made by Western

Here is a cipher or that is part of one. The other 2 parts are being mailed to the Vallejo Times + S.F. Chronicle

I want you to print this cipher on the front page by Fry afternoon Aug 1-69. If you

do not print this cipher, I
will go on a kill rampage
Fry night. This will last the
whole weekend, I will cruse
around killing people who are
alone at night untill Sun Night
or untill I kill a dozen
people.

Figure 3

I am the killer of the 2 teen
agers last Christmass at Lake Herman
and the Girl last 4th of July. To
Prove this I shall state some facts
which only I + the police know
Christmass
1 Brand name of ammo Super X
2 10 Shots fired
3 Boy was on back feet to car
4 Girl was lyeing on right side
feet to west
4th of July
1 Girl was wearing patterned
Pants
2 Boy was also shot in knee
3 Brand name of ammo was
Western

Here is a cyipher or that is
part of one. the other 2 parts
have been mailed to the S.F.
Examiner + the S.F. Chronicle.
I want you to print it.

cipher on your front page by
Fry Afternoon Aug 1-69, If you
do not do this I will go on a
kill rampage Fry night that
will last the whole week end.
I will crase around and pick
of all stray people or coupples
that are alone then move on to
kill some more untill I have
killed over a dozen people.

Figure 4

Mailed July 31, 1969.

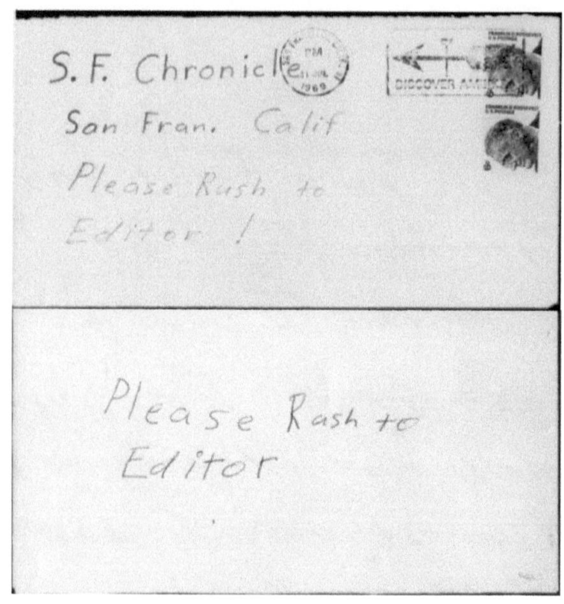

Mailed July 31, 1969.

Mailed July 31, 1969.

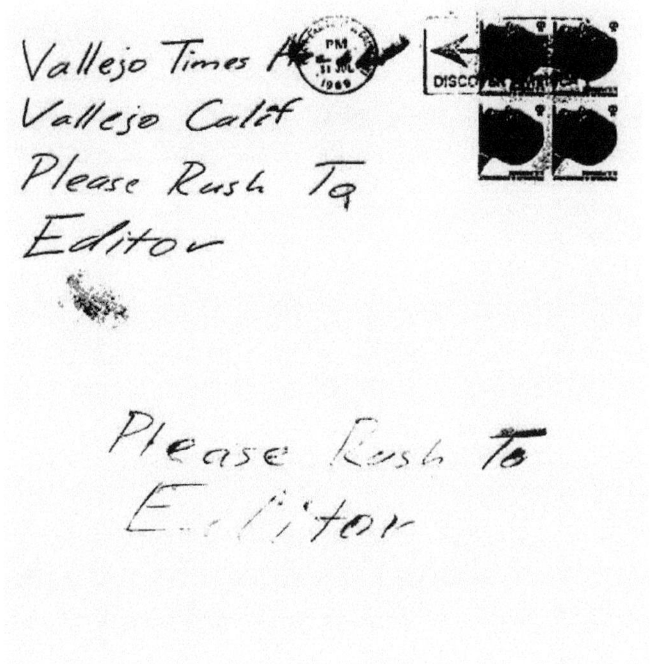

Figure 5

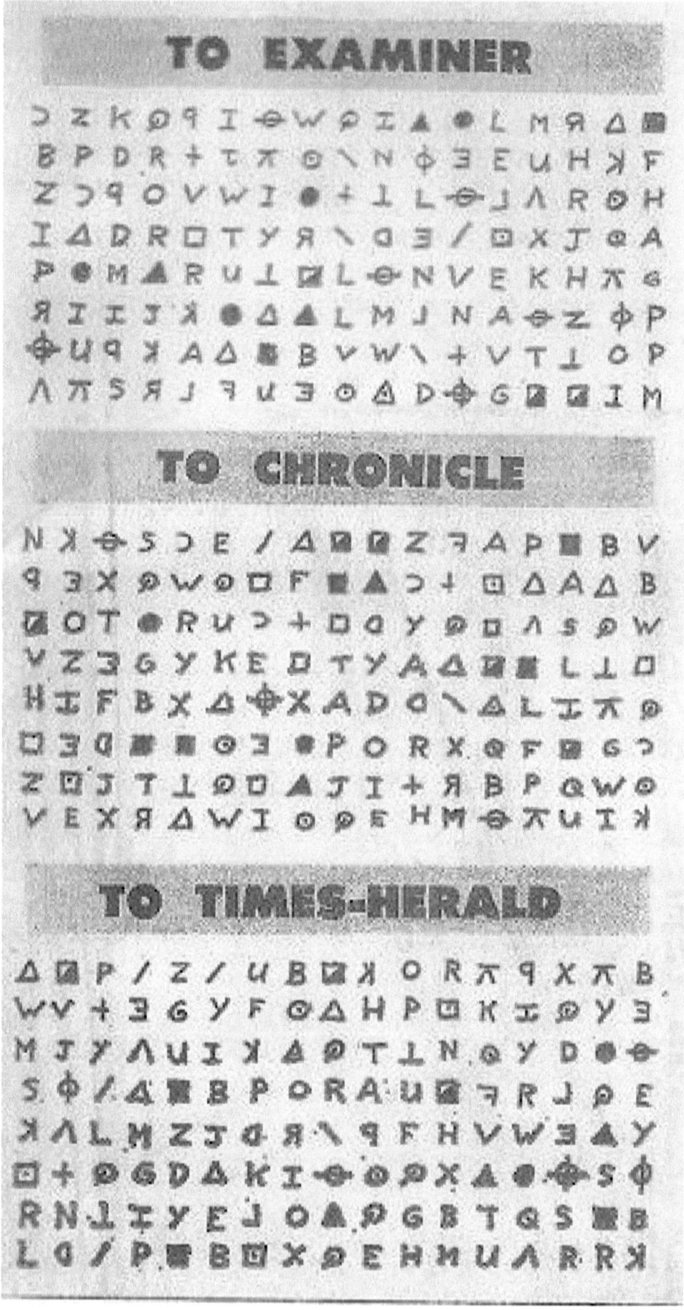

TO EXAMINER

TO CHRONICLE

TO TIMES-HERALD

Figure 6

Q1 D-6?0808059 LL
FBI
LABORATORY

Dear Editor
This is the Zodiac speaking.
In answer to your asking for
more details about the good
times I have had in Vallejo,
I shall be very happy to
supply even more material.
By the way, are the police
haveing a good time with the
code? If not, tell them to cheer
up; when they do crack it
they will have me.
On the 4th of July:
I did not open the car door, The
window was rolled down all ready.
The boy was origionaly sitting in
the front seat when I began
fireing. When I fired the first
shot at his head, he leaped
backwards at the same time
thus spoiling my aim. He end
ed up on the back seat then
the floor in back thrashing out
very violently with his legs;
thats how I shot him in the

Q2 D-600808059 LL
FBI
LABORATORY
L.C. A-15042

knee. I didn't leave the cene of the killing with squealling tires & raceing engine as described in the Vallejo paper. I drove away quite slowly so as not to draw attention to my car.
The man who told the police that my car was brown was a negro about 40-45 rather shabbly dressed. I was at this phone booth haveing some fun with the Vallejo cops when he was walking by. When I hung the phone up the dam X@ thing began to ring & that drew his attention to me & my car.
Last Christmass
In that epasode the police were wondering as to how I could shoot & hit my victoms in the dark. They did not openly state this, but implied this by saying it was a well lit night & I could see the silowets on the horizon. Bull Shit that area is srounded

by high hills & trees. What I did
was tape a small pencel flash
light to the barrel of my gun.
If you notice, in the center
of the beam of light if you aim
it at a wall or ceilling you will
see a black or darck spot in
the center of the circle of
light about 3 to 6 in. across.
When taped to a gun barrel,
the bullet will strike exactly
in the center of the black
dot in the light. All I had to do
was spray them as if it was
a water hose; there was no
need to use the gun sights.
I was not happy to see that I
did not get front page coverage.

NO ADDRESS

ENDNOTES B

[1] "Coded Clue in Murders," San Francisco Chronicle, August 2, 1969, 4.
[2] Ibid.
[3] Freedom of Information and Privacy Acts, Subject: Zodiac Killer, File Number: 9-HQ-49911, Section 1, Federal Bureau of Investigation, 4.
[4] Ibid, 9.
[5] Ibid, 27.
[6] "The Zodiac Watch Ads," www.mk-zodiac.com/ZodiacWatchAds.html (retrieval date April 2016).
[7] "The Twelve Signs of the Zodiac," http://astrology.com.au/astrology/zodiac-signs (retrieved June 2016).
[8] Norman Foster, Director, Charlie Chan at Treasure Island, 1939.
[9] "Hidden Crime CLUES," Popular Science, November 1931, 22.
[10] Ibid.
[11] Ibid.
[12] Ibid.
[13] Ibid.
[14] Ibid.
[15] Ibid.
[16] "Arthur Covell," https://www.findagrave.com/memorial/68407525/arthur-covell (retrieved April 2020).
[17] "Under a Bad Sign," https://malefactorsregister.com/wp/the-fault-is-in-ourselves (retrieved April 2020).
[18] "Police Still Hunt For Shooting Clues," Vallejo Times-Herald, July 8, 1969, 2.
[19] "AUTOMATIC PISTOL COMBINED WITH HAND FLASHLIGHT," Popular Science, August 1922, 244.
[20] Paul Henreid, Director, Museum Piece, Season 6, Episode 25, 1961.
[21] Crime Report, Vallejo Police Department, Case Number 243 146, 43.
[22] "A 'Murder Code' Broken," San Francisco Chronicle, August 9, 1969, 2.
[23] "Cryptogram Deciphered By Teacher," Vallejo-Times-Herald, August 9, 1969, 1.
[24] Napa County Sheriff's Department Report, Case Number 105907, 12.
[25] "A 'Murder Code' Broken," San Francisco Chronicle, August 9, 1969, 2.
[26] Ibid, 23.
[27] "Salinas Teacher Breaks Code on Vallejo Murders," San Francisco Sunday Examiner and Chronicle, August 10, 1969, A26.
[28] Ibid.
[29] Bernice Kohn, SECRET CODES and CIPHERS (Prentice-Hall, 1968).
[30] Ibid, 22.
[31] Ibid, 32.

[32] Richard Connell, Collier's Weekly, 1924. The movie adaptation (1932) was directed by Irving Pichel and Ernest B. Schoedsack.
[33] Daniel P. Mannix, A Sporting Chance, Unusual Methods of Hunting (Dutton 1967).
[34] "Zodiac, A Quiet, Bright Man - - Who Likes To Kill," St. Petersburg Times, October 18, 1969, 13.
[35] "Ich töte gerne Menschen," http://archive.is/py9Bz#selection-428.0-428.1 (retrieved August 2015).
[36] Crime Report, Vallejo Police Department, Case Number 243 146, 44.
[37] "ZODIAC THE KILLER," The Tuscaloosa News, October 17, 1969, 2.
[38] Ibid.
[39] Ibid.

CHAPTER 3

BY KNIFE

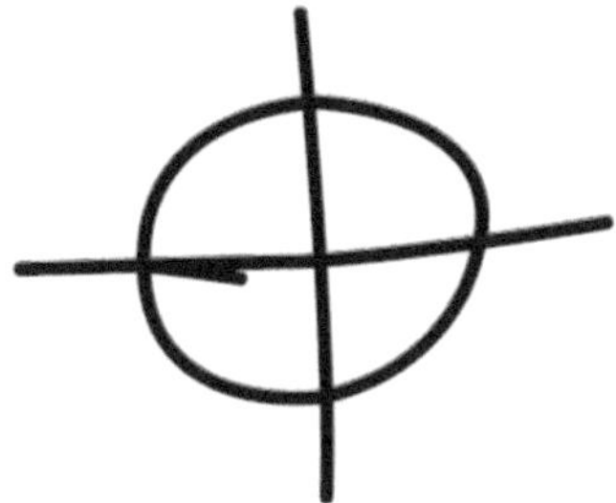

Saturday, September 27, 1969

Twenty-year-old Bryan Calvin Hartnell studied at Pacific Union College at Angwin, Napa County, California. At the college, he bumped into his twenty-two-year-old friend, Cecelia Ann Shepard, who attended the University of California in Riverside. He asked her if she wanted to spend some time together, and suggested going to San Francisco. She readily accepted the invitation. As the day progressed and it started getting late, they changed their minds about going to San Francisco. Instead they decided on impulse to go to Lake Berryessa, one of the largest lakes in Napa County, located at least 44 miles from the Lake Herman crime scene. In Bryan's 1956 Karmann Ghia they cruised past two acquaintances about one mile south of Lake Berryessa Marina at 5:15 p.m. As they drove by, Bryan waved out of the window and said, "Hi, John,"[1] to his friend. Bryan parked his car on Knoxville road about 500 yards from Twin Oak Ridge, a small peninsula that jutted into Lake Berryessa. They walked to the water on foot. At the location, Bryan and Cecelia reminisced about old times and enjoyed the outing. It was getting romantic between them. Suddenly, Bryan's attention was directed to the noise of rustling leaves. The ensuing is the conversation that took place (C: Cecelia, B: Bryan):

B: "You have your specs on. Why don't you see what the deal is over there"?
C: "Oh, it's some man."
B: "Is he alone?"
C: "Yeah."
C: "Well, he just stepped behind the tree."
B: "What's the idea of that? To take a leak?"
B: "Well, keep looking and tell me what happens."
Cecelia squeezed his arm and said, "Oh my God, he's got a gun!"[2]

A man, dressed in a ceremonial type costume, briskly walked toward them. He began a conversation with Bryan (reproduced later). He claimed that he was a fugitive who had escaped from the Deer Lodge prison in Montana, and had killed a couple of guards during the escape.[3] He was en route to Mexico and was in need of a car and money. The couple did not have much to offer him. Soon after, at gunpoint, he ordered Cecelia to tie Bryan's wrists with precut lengths of plastic clothesline, which he had brought to the scene in his back pocket. She complied and "tied a couple of loose knots."[4] In a state of intrepidness, Bryan whispered to Cecelia that he thought he could wrestle the gun out of the stranger's hand, and asked her if she would mind. Cecelia became fearful about his plan, and Bryan did not proceed. Instead, the man tied Cecelia "terribly tight,"[5] and retied Bryan's loose bindings. Bryan noticed that the stranger became very nervous while tying her.[6] The man continued to assert control when he told them, "Now I want you both to lay face down so I can tie up your feet."[7] A defiant Bryan started to argue with him and said it could get cold at night. In turn, the man pointed his gun directly at him and told him, "GET DOWN! RIGHT NOW!"[8] Bryan finally complied and the couple was hogtied. At some point, Bryan asked the stranger to show him whether his pistol was loaded or not. Bryan, an avid reader, had read in a magazine that criminals usually do not use a loaded weapon. After he had tied the couple, the stranger showed Bryan a bullet from the magazine and returned the gun in its holster. Bryan turned toward Cecelia to say something, and during that instance, he caught a glimpse of the man pulling out a large knife. The man proceeded to stab Bryan in the back repeatedly. Cecelia became "hysterical."[9] After several brutal thrusts, the man believed that Bryan was dead—but he was not. He was playing dead. With murder still in his mind, the man commenced his attack on Cecelia. She was injured to a much greater extent than Bryan, presumably because her reflexes made her twist and turn. Leaving them for dead, the man walked to Bryan's car and scrawled a message on its passenger door with a black, felt tip pen. The man had taken neither the keys nor any other items that the couple had brought to the scene. Handwriting analysis would later confirm that the Zodiac had penned the message. It read:

⌖
Vallejo
12-20-68
7-4-69
Sept 27-69-6:30
By knife

By printing these words and dates, the Zodiac proudly referred to his two previous crimes and his most recent one. He wanted everyone to know that he had struck again. It is not clear whether 6:30 designates the time of the attack, or when he wrote the message. What it does signify, however, is that he was wearing a watch. Upon leaving the crime scene, the Zodiac felt compelled to continue his communicative pattern that he had begun in July, and he located a pay phone. At 7:40 p.m. he called the Napa Police Department (NPD). Officer David Slaight picked up the phone and said, "Napa Police [Department], Officer Slaight." "I want to report a murder, no, a double murder. They are two miles North of Park Headquarters. They were in a white Volkswagen [Karmann]-Ghia," Zodiac told the officer. The dumbfounded officer replied, “Where are you now?” Zodiac chillingly replied, “I’m the one that did it.”[10‡]

The telephone line was left open, and Slaight could hear traffic passing and possibly female voices. He got the impression that the Zodiac had a male voice, young sounding, possibly early twenties. Earlier, we argued the case that Zodiac concocted the story about being spotted in the phone booth in Vallejo. Since he did not hang up the phone in Napa, it may be true that it rang in Vallejo, but there was nobody nearby. So he had been mixing truth with deception in his August letter.

The Napa police did not know where the phone booth was located, and “virtually any official with a radio was asked to help.”[11] Luck enabled them to locate it fast at 1231 Main Street in Napa, just a few blocks away from the Napa Police Department. Zodiac was provoking the police just as he did in July. Lake Berryessa was actually within the jurisdiction of the Napa Sheriff’s Department, but he may have decided to call the NPD due to its proximity to the phone booth he used. If the Zodiac took off after writing the message on the car door at around 6.30 p.m., he spent an hour and 10 minutes to get to the phone booth. Had he traveled the shortest path, it would not have taken him more than an hour to get there. It is indicated that he carefully got rid of his costume and other equipment before he placed the call. Considering the organized nature of the crime, it is likely that he parked close by and walked to the phone booth. He would certainly have anticipated that the cops would track down the phone booth and question people in the vicinity.

Back at the crime scene, Bryan and Cecelia struggled to stay alive and to free themselves from the bindings. Unfortunately, it took a long time before they got the necessary medical attention. They arrived at Queen of the Valley Hospital at 8:50 p.m. Doctors desperately tried to save their lives, but two days later Cecelia passed away while Bryan was fortunate to recover. The

‡ The victims were actually located 0.7 mile north of Park Headquarters and not two miles as he stated during the call).

next day, two pathologists Drs. Wilmer A. De Petris and Dwight G. Straub examined Cecelia's body and prepared a postmortem. Dr. Petris estimated that the weapon would be "from nine to eleven inches in length, one inch in width and possibly sharpened on both sides on the top of the blade similar to a bayonet type weapon. In addition, the wounds indicated it would be a heavy or sturdy type blade."[12]

On Thursday, October 2, Cecelia was buried in St. Helene. During the funeral services at the Pacific Union College Chapel, Det. Sgts. Kenneth Narlow and Richard Lonergan positioned themselves inside the chapel, and Criminalist Harold Snook, Sergeant Thomas Butler, and Detective Ronald Montgomery on the outside of the chapel. The Zodiac's risk-taking nature led them to conjecture that he might attend the funeral. Inside the church, they observed the attendants. On the outside, they photographed people entering and leaving.[13]

Close Contact with the Zodiac

Unlike the two previous crimes, the Zodiac inadvertently left promising evidence, and he had failed to kill Bryan. Bryan later gave a detailed description of what had happened, and of the Zodiac's physical characteristics. According to a Napa police report, Bryan estimated that the Zodiac had spent 15 minutes with them in total.[14] It is an open question why the Zodiac would expose himself to this risk, knowing fully well that other people could have seen him. He could have committed the crime faster and in other ways – such as with his pistol. It would appear that the way the act was carried out had a meaning to the killer psychologically. We may also see this crime fulfilling a fantasy or a psychological need in his use of the grotesque and ludicrous costume. Most likely, he had fantasized about the crime for a long time as evidenced by his creation of the equipment including the modified knife and case, which must have taken hours if not days to make. It would appear that his fantasy life centered on him being an executioner-type killer and punisher.

During that quarter-of-an-hour, Bryan and the Zodiac had had a rather long and unusual conversation. He worked with investigators to produce a transcript of it to the best of his ability.

The conversation went as follows (C: Cecelia, B: Bryan, A: Zodiac):

C: "What do you want?"
A: "Now take it easy - all I want's your money. There is nothing to worry about - all I want is your money."
B: "O.K. – whatever you say, I want you to know now that I will cooperate so you don't have to worry – whatever you say we'll do. Do you want us to come up with our hands up or down?"
A: "Just don't make any fast moves – come up slowly."
B: "But we don't have any money – all I have is 75¢."
A: "That doesn't matter – every little bit helps (pause) – I'm on my way to Mexico – I escaped from Deer Lodge Prison in Montana, Deer Lodge. I need some money to get there."
B: "You're welcome to the money I have, but isn't there something else I can do for you? Give you a check or get some more?"
A: "No."
B: "I can give you my phone number and you can call me."
A: "(No reply)."
B: "I want to get in contact with you. I am a sociology major and maybe I can even offer you more help than you think you need."
A: "No."
B: "Well, is there any other thing you need?"
A: "Yes. One more thing – I want your car keys. My car is hot."
B: "(Reaching into pockets, then patting first front then back pockets) I guess in all the excitement I don't remember where I put them. Let's see. Are they in my shirt, in the ignition, on the blanket.... Say! would you answer a question for me? I've always wondered. On T.V. movies and in an article in the Readers Digest they say that thieves really keep their guns loaded. Is yours?"
A: "(excited slightly) Yes, it is! (then calm and matter-of-fact) I killed a couple of men before."
B: "What? I didn't hear you."
A: "I killed a couple of guards getting out of prison. And I'm not afraid to kill again."
C: "Bryan – do what he says!"
A: "Now I want the girl to tie you up."
C: "(reaches for rope that he pulls from back pocket)."

B: "This is really strange. I wonder why someone hasn't thought of this before. I'll bet there's good money in it."
A: "(no reply)."
B: "What was the name of that prison?"
A: "(no reply)."
B: "No really, what did you say the name of it was? I'm just curious."
A: "(begrudgingly) Deer Lodge in Montana."
"(There must have been some dialogue at this point but I can't remember any until we are both tied up)."
A: "Now I want you both to lay face down so I can tie up your feet."
B: "Come on – we could be out here for a long time and it could get cold at night."
A: "Come on – get down!"
B: "Listen, I didn't complain when you tied our hands, but this is ridiculous!"
A: "I told you."
B: "We aren't going anywhere – anyway, I don't think that it's necessary (or – Aw, come on – we don't want to.)."
A: "(Pointing gun directly at me at point blank range) I told you to get down!"
"(He ties me, then her)."
B: "Your hands are shaking. Are you nervous?"
A: "Yes, I guess so. (Laughed in a very relaxed manner)."
B: "Well, I suppose that I'd be nervous too."
"(Then after we were tied and hog-tired)."
B: "Now that everything is all said and done, could you show me that your gun is loaded? (Or, and probably this: "Now that all is said and done, was that gun really loaded?")."
A: "Yes, it was! (or) Sure, I'll show you."
"(He then opened cartridge or whatever)."[15]

Despite being armed with a pistol and knife, the Zodiac was paranoid about the possibility of Bryan fighting back. He even felt the need to concoct a story to make sure that they would not resist him. Was the Zodiac generally paranoid and anxious or was this the result of a previous bad experience?

It was easily determined that Zodiac had invented the prison escape to trick the victims. Montana State Prison at Deer Lodge was located over 1000 miles from the crime scene. The latest prison escape from that institution was in 1968. Numerous California prisons could have served as the basis for the ruse, such as the notorious San Quentin State Prison, located just north of San Francisco in Marin County.

When detectives visited the hospital to ask Bryan questions, the Zodiac's voice was still vivid in his mind. Bryan described the Zodiac's voice as medium pitched, and that he had a unique way of talking. He did not sound educated or illiterate. Intriguingly Bryan said, "His voice… I can remember … almost like I'd heard it before. You know there's some drawls that a lot of people have similar. And… almost as if I'd heard it before… couldn't think where."[16] In 2007, Bryan further elaborated on the voice, saying, "he had a very precise cadence to his voice. Not an accent but slow and measured. 'All I want's your money' had a real distinctive tone about it, where - which - I told the police then that if I ever heard it again, I would be able to recognize it. I haven't heard it again. But it did have a unique sound."[17]

Bryan judged that the Zodiac was 20-30 years of age.[18] He had concealed his facial characteristics by what appeared to be an "ingeniously devised"[19] costume that had four corners at the top - similar to the top of a paper sack. Clip-on sunglasses were affixed to the hood covering the eyes. Bryan did not believe he wore glasses underneath.[20] The costume came down almost to his waist. Near the solar plexus the Zodiac had his crossed-circle signature measuring approximately three inches in diameter. It "looked like it was made with a machine, or with some degree of care. It wasn't just scrawled on with white paint. It was proportional,"[21] Bryan later said.

Bryan also said that he did not have any compliments for the Zodiac's clothes. He was sloppily dressed and looked unprofessional. He wore a pair of pleated pants, described as old suit pants that were black or dark blue. He had used gloves.[22]

Bryan estimated that his height may have been somewhere between 5'8" and 6'. Apart from his sloppy appearance, he also appeared to be a heavy individual, weighing somewhere between 225 and 250 pounds. He had greasy, brownish hair, and it looked combed. The knife was in a case, possibly made of wood, attached to his belt. The handle was of hardwood and held in place by two brass rivets. Cotton surgical tape approximately 1" wide was wrapped around the handle. The blade was 12" long and ¾" wide. It may have been a modified bread knife.[23] He kept his pistol in a smooth, black leather case.

Later in the hospital, Bryan was shown many different types of pistols and bullets. He was relatively certain that he had seen a .45 bullet in Zodiac's hand.[24] He could not identify the pistol.

Cecelia was unable to give any statements at the hospital before expiring of sustained wounds. However, in a 2007 interview, Deputy Dave Collins, one of the first people to arrive at the scene of the attack, revealed that he had taken a statement from Cecelia at the crime scene. He said the following:

> When we arrived at the scene, Cecelia Shepard was in a fetal position on the ground, at the base of an oak tree. [...]. She said, 'Bryan and I were here on the blanket. We're down by the water and we're just enjoying the afternoon, we're having a nice time talking, and I saw this guy. He was coming down the hillside, and he seemed to stop and watch us. He's looking at us." And I said, 'what distance? How far away was he?' And she pointed to an area, and I said, 'that's about - looks like 200 to 300 yards away.' She said, 'that's where I first saw him. And then as we continued enjoying the afternoon and watching the water and reading, I would glance and I'd notice he'd get closer, and he was closer, and then pretty soon, he was within 75 to 100 feet away. And I told Bryan, 'that guy has come down here.'' And then she looked again and, she said, 'he was gone.' And I said, 'well, where did he go?' She said, 'he stepped behind a tree and the tree was 50 to 75 feet away. And when he stepped out he was pulling a hood over his head.' And I said, 'a hood?' [...]. And I asked her if she saw him clearly before he put the hood on and she said, 'yes, I did.' I said, 'what did he look like,' and she said, 'well, he had...' I said, 'what color was his hair?' She said, 'well, it

was brown.' And, 'what race was he?' 'He was white.' And I said, 'well, how about his eyes? Could you see the color of his eyes?' And she said, 'no, he had dark glasses on underneath the hood.' But she said his hair hung down across his forehead and was showing through the eyeholes. I said, 'well, how tall? Let me stand where he was when he came up to you, and look at me I'm 5'10" tell me how he matches my height.' Because she was lying on the ground. She said, 'well, he's just a little bit taller than you, probably an inch or two taller than you.' I said, 'okay, how much did he weigh?' She said, 'he was overweight he was bulky-looking. His clothing was all dark, dark pants, dark shirt, dark jacket, and the jacket was bulky.' And I said, 'well, I'm 170, look at me, and judge by my weight, and see what you can tell.' She said, 'well, he'd have to be at least 20 or 30 pounds heavier.'[25]

Physical Evidence

Physical evidence was collected as the investigators sifted through the site. The Zodiac had left a lot of "excellent" clues for investigators and they were in turn "working around the clock to put"[26] him off the streets.

First, Sherwood Morrill, head of the Questioned Documents Section of California's Criminal Identification and Investigation Bureau, identified the Zodiac as the author of the message on Bryan's car door.[27]

Second, distinctive shoe prints were "tracked from the road to the scene of the crime and back to the passenger side of the victim's car."[28] Investigators concluded that they were the killer's shoe prints.[29] Butler photographed them and Snook made plaster casts.[30] Without success, numerous shoe stores were searched meticulously in an effort to find a shoe that made a corresponding impression. On September 29, Probation Officer H. B. Schotte, who had seen the plaster casts, introduced Narlow and Lonergan to Mr. Bassel, a retired Master Sergeant in the US Air Force. Bassel had brought along a pair of his Air Force shoes. The two detectives noted that the sole matched the design of those worn by the Zodiac.

Finally, they had identified the shoes as so-called Wing Walkers. It was easily determined that Zodiac's shoe size was 10.5 D.[31] The sergeant went on to describe the shoes as Government Issue and said that "most Air Force personnel and many of the civilian personnel employed at Air Force bases had this type of shoe."[32] Over one million pairs had been produced in 1966. Later, a large quantity was shipped to the Air Force Depot in Ogden, Utah, and from there distributed upon requisition to various military installations on the West Coast. The investigators also determined that Wing Walkers were sold as surplus at the Travis Air Force base near Fairfield, Solano County, California and possibly at other surplus sales locations.[33] The name *Zodiac* also points to the military.

In the 1950s, Zodiac watches of the type *Hermetic Leatherneck Award* were issued in the US Marine Corps to top performers in their Officer Candidate School. If the military was his profession, it explains his knowledge of cryptography, his use of Wing Walker shoes, and other aspects covered in the next chapters.

Footwear and tire impression evidence is very valuable to investigators as it can be used to place a vehicle and/or a suspect at a scene. An organized criminal can minimize or eliminate physical evidence such as DNA, fibers, and fingerprints, but will invariably leave evidence when entering and exiting a crime scene unless they are floating in air.[34] Sometimes a shoe print has been the key evidence that led the police directly to the perpetrator.[35] The Zodiac's shoe prints led the investigators to the tire impressions of his car, located approximately 20 feet to the rear of Bryan's Karmann Ghia.[36] The impressions indicated that he had not left the area at a high rate of speed.

Going into further details in his report, Snook noted that one of the tire impressions was measured to be about 4.5" in width and had a parallel tread design. The other one was slightly larger, 5.5", and had a different pattern. The fact that the patterns and sizes are different may indicate that the Zodiac had put a spare tire on his car as these are almost always slimmer than the original. The distance in-between the two tire impressions was about 52".[37] However, industry track width is "the distance between the centerlines of the left and right tires."[38] We can calculate a track width based on this data. We have to add the average width of the treads to the reported measurement.

However, his car did not leave the factory with a 4.5" left tire and a 5.5" right tire. If it had 5.5" tires, it results in the following industry track width:

$$\frac{5.5" + 5.5"}{2} + 52" = 57.5"$$

This calculation is, at best, an approximation for several reasons. One is that front and rear tires, in almost all cases, have different track widths. Based on the description in the police report, the police did not know what they were measuring. Retired FBI agent, William J. Bodziak, the world's foremost expert on footwear and tire tread impressions, informed us in a private communiqué that "if a vehicle drives perfectly straight, the offset between the front and rear tracks will result in a small additional impression on the inner or outer edge of the rear tracks. This is often not recognized and believed to be a tire track of just one tire and therefore any measurement of it would include the additional width and would be inaccurate."[39] Furthermore, when we inspect the reported tire tread widths, namely, 4.5" and 5.5", they do obviously not correspond to the actual tire width of the Zodiac's car as they are too small. Bodziak also pointed out that "police at the crime scene, even today, are unaware of the proper way to measure 'tire track width' as well as 'tire tread width.' So these measurements are more often than not recovered improperly."[40] Bodziak's book, *Tire Tread and Tire Track Evidence: Recovery and Forensic Examination*, informs us that "The tire industry defines the tread arc width as a measurement across a tire's full tread that coincides with the radially outmost surfaces of the various tread blocks, ribs, or lugs. However, when a tire leaves its impression at a scene, that impression rarely represents the entire tread arc width."[41] In his book, Bodziak then cites an example of a vehicle that "showed 8.22 inches of its tread width recorded in soft soil, 7.32 inches of its tread width recorded in firm soil, and only 6.54 inches of its tread width recorded on a hard concrete surface."[42] This observation explains why the tread widths of the Zodiac's car are very small, and they can therefore not be used to determine the tire widths of his car and, consequently, the calculated track width is imprecise.

Today during a criminal investigation, the track width of a suspect's vehicle would simply be entered into a computer database that would furnish the data of vehicles that have a corresponding track width.[43] The police reports do not specify the types and makes of vehicles that match, so we have searched databases and identified cars that could have left a 57.5" track width despite it being an estimate (discussed later).
In his report, Snook also outlined a collection of 35 latent impressions (finger and palm prints) lifted from the phone booth used by the Zodiac.[44] One of them was a "still-wet palm print."[45] "Captain Donald Townsend of the Napa County Sheriff's Office said, "It was very, very heartily done by our Criminalist Hal Snook and we're very pleased with the results."[46] The phone was most likely not used after the call as it was found shortly afterwards, and it was still off the hook.[47] Eight latent impressions were also lifted from Bryan's Karmann Ghia.[48] Because the Zodiac wore gloves at the time of the stabbing, the prints on the door are questionable whereas he may have felt that wearing gloves in public would attract unnecessary attention. A green bottle was found close to the crime scene on the suspected path walked by the Zodiac. It was also dusted for fingerprints and five latent impressions were lifted from it.[49]

The Voyeur and the Mysterious Man

On September 28, Narlow and Lonergan interviewed Dr. Clifton Rayfield and his son David. At around 6:30 p.m. the previous evening, just less than a mile from Bryan's Ghia, the father and son spotted a male Caucasian. He was about 5'10" and heavily built. He was dressed in a long-sleeved dark shirt with some red features. His pants were dark.[50] As soon as he noticed David, he departed by changing direction. The two investigators opined that it was unlikely to have been the Zodiac due to the timing and geography of the area.[51] It is interesting that the man did not report his presence to the Napa Sheriff's Department since he had been near a murder scene at just the right time. Considering the direction of the Zodiac's shoe prints and the 15 minutes that he spent with Bryan and Cecelia, the killer could not have approached Clifton and David before the stabbing, only after it.

Although the individual was heavy and wore dark clothes – like the Zodiac - it is unlikely to have been him.

A few hours prior to the crime, the erratic behavior of a man agitated three girls, Joanne, Linda, and Linda Lee. They told their story to Lonergan, Snook, and Townsend on September 28.[52] They believed that their experience could be related to the stabbing of Bryan and Cecelia. Two days later a sketch of the man was published in the Napa Register. Robert McKenzie, a Register staff member, had made it using an "Identi-Kit." The article, "Officials Sifting Clues In Hunt For Murderer,"[53] stated that he had not been "connected with the crime. However, they would like to question him or talk to anyone else who might have seen him."[54] Although McKenzie was not a professional artist, investigators showed the sketch to potential witnesses.[55] It is apparent then that the girls felt the sketch was reasonably accurate.

The investigators took notes while interviewing them. When we compare the notes, there is variation as expected. However, taken as a whole, the notes suggest that between 2:55 p.m. and 3:30 p.m., the girls parked at Lake Berryessa on Knoxville Road, approximately two miles north of the A&W Root Beer stand. They soon noticed a 1966 or 1967, sky or silver blue, 2-door Chevrolet Sedan with long rather than round tail lights. The driver, a white male adult, parked noticeably close to their car to the point that the rear bumpers were nearly touching. Roughly 30 minutes after the initial sighting, the driver of the car reappeared while the girls were sunbathing in their bikinis. He stared at them from the edge of some trees. He would look away when they looked back at him. He stayed close to the girls for about 30-45 minutes. His car was gone when they departed at about 4:30 p.m. Is the voyeur the Zodiac?

The first step in examining that question is to compare the physical characteristics of the two, and then determine if the specific type of car they observed has a track width of about 57.5". The girls said that the voyeur was 6' to 6'2", 200 to 225 lb., muscular, well or stocky built. His dark or black hair was without curls and combed/styled. Zodiac's height was estimated to be anywhere between 5'8" and 6'.

His age was ostensibly difficult to judge for witnesses and listeners who reported it as low as 25 to as high as 45.[§] His weight was anywhere between 180 to 250 lb. and his body type was characterized as heavy, beefy, stout, overweight, and bulky looking. Zodiac's hair was long enough for Bryan to see it was combed, greasy, and dark brown. Bryan also said the Zodiac wore black or dark blue suit pants and a super-thin cotton coat. The voyeur wore a dark, short-sleeved shirt and dark or dark blue slacks. From the data on the two individuals, it is a distinct possibility that they are one and the same. At least, it is not possible to eliminate the man as being the Zodiac based on the variation: It jibes with what would be expected from a collection of witnesses who made their observation during various circumstances. For example, the girls could easily have mistaken black or dark hair for darkish brown hair.

As for the car driven by the voyeur, a database search shows that a 1966 and a 1967 Chevrolet Chevelle Sedan has an industry track width of 58", which is indistinguishable from the calculation as it is an estimate. It also has long tail lights from the factory. The girls characterized the car as a 1966 or 1967, 2-door Chevrolet Sedan with long tail lights. With this in mind and the other similarities, it is very likely that the voyeur was the Zodiac scouting the area for potential victims.

Michael Mageau thought that the Zodiac might have been driving a 1963 Chevrolet Corvair. This particular model may not have been used by the Zodiac in September as the industry track width is probably too far off, unless Michael actually saw a newer model from 1965-1969 where the General Motors Company produced a Corvair with a rear track width of 57.2" (see Appendix).

The industry track width of a 1959 or 1960 4-door Hardtop Chevrolet Impala, which was associated with the killing of

[§] See next chapter.

Faraday and Jensen, is far off from the measured track width.[56] Just as the Zodiac varied his weapons, he may also have changed cars between the crimes, possibly using as many as three different ones.

On September 30, Captain Townsend told the media that they had suppressed a portion of the message on Bryan's car door, but added that it "vaguely"[57] mentioned the Vallejo killings. He dared the killer to write or call them again to prove that he was indeed the man who "loves to kill."[58] A few days later, Townsend declared, "Unless we capture this man, he will kill again."[59]

The evidence left by the Zodiac enabled investigators to gather more knowledge about him and establish facts. For example, when the Zodiac penned the dates and numbers on the car door, he would not have had time to elaborately disguise his handwriting. The foremost experts on his handwriting have also reached the conclusion that his handwriting appeared not to be disguised.[60] He probably had a secure income given his access to at least two cars, multiple weapons, etc. He appeared to be a heavy-set, clumsily dressed individual who was nervous around women. He had an unmistakable habit of risk-taking. He had also displayed craftsmanship such as sewing, knowledge of cryptography, and was possibly associated with the military. Unfortunately, he was extremely lucky as none of the evidence had led to his capture.

The stabbing received massive publicity. The following are some of the headlines: "Hooded Assailant Ties, Stabs Pair,"[61] "'Good clues' in 'hood murder',"[62] "Berryessa Killer Termed a Deviate,"[63] "Slaying Suspect 'May Strike Again',"[64] and "Seek Madman After Attack At Berryessa."[65]

APPENDIX C

Figure 1

Sketches made by the police of how the Zodiac appeared in his costume.

Figure 2

The plastic clothesline used to tie the victims.

Figure 3

An investigator examining the tire impressions.

Figure 4

An impression in the sand of the Zodiac's shoe.

Figure 5

A pair of Wing Walker shoes.

Figure 6

The Zodiac's message on Bryan's car door.

Figure 7

The composite drawing of the man who intimidated the three girls.

Figure 8

The industry track width of cars associated with the Zodiac case.

Figure 1

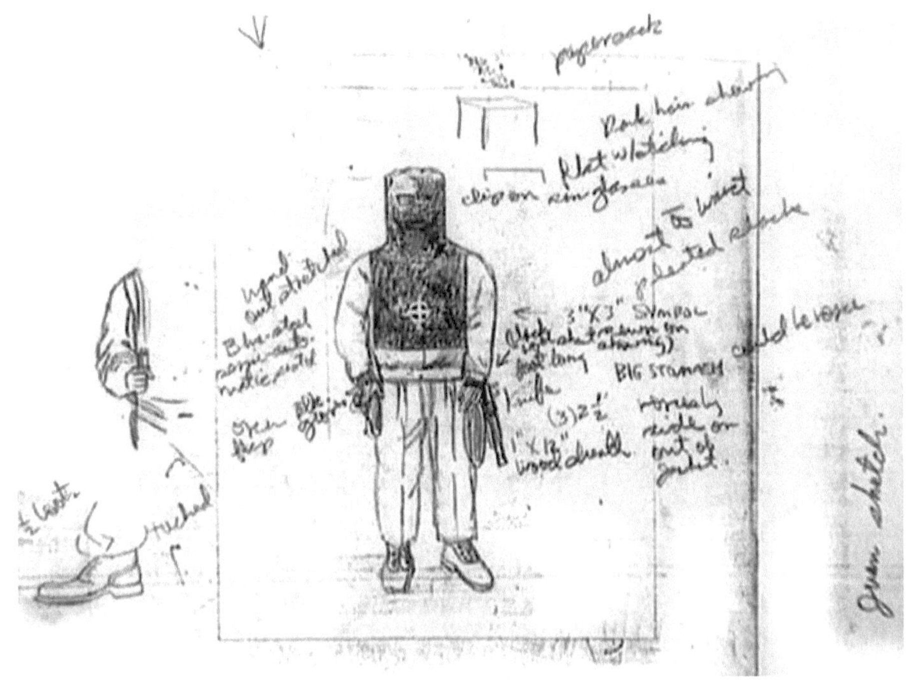

Figure 2

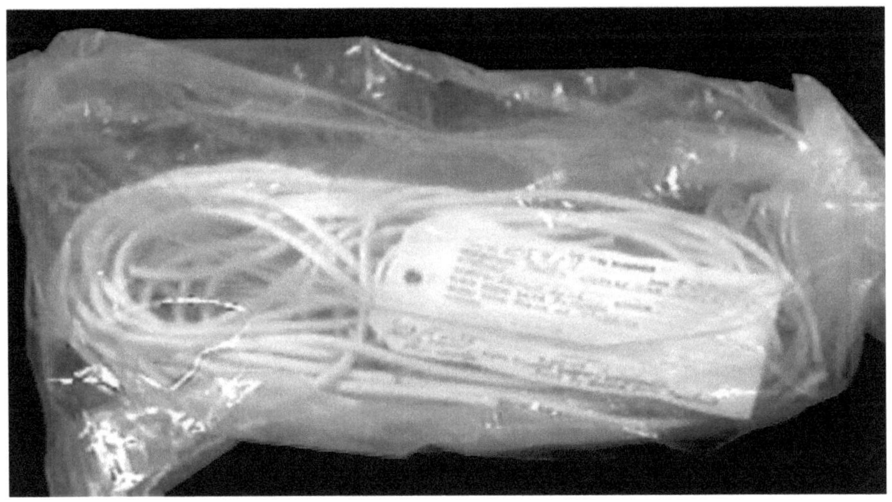

Figure 3

Figure 4

Figure 5

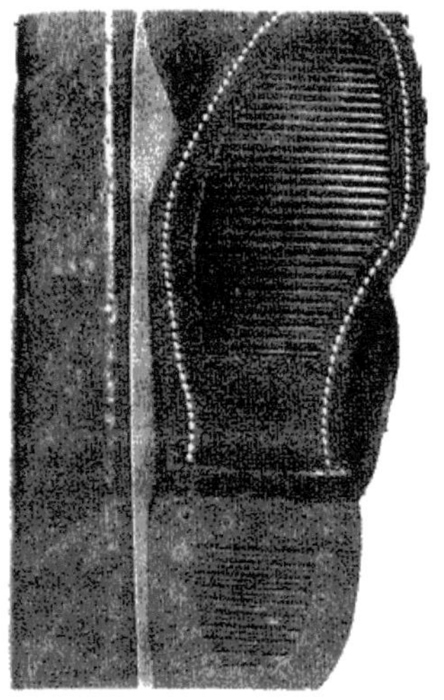

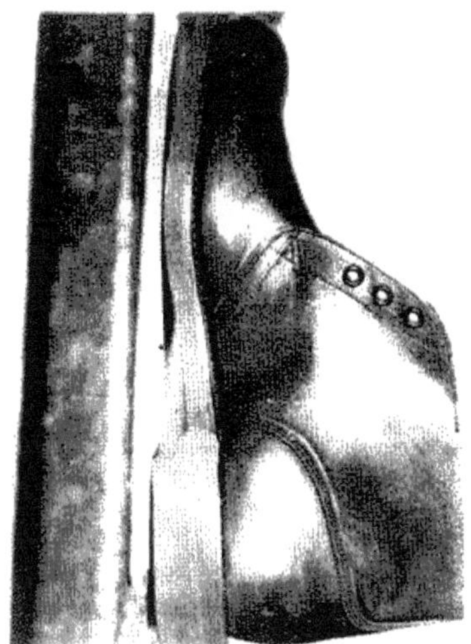

Figure 6

Figure 7

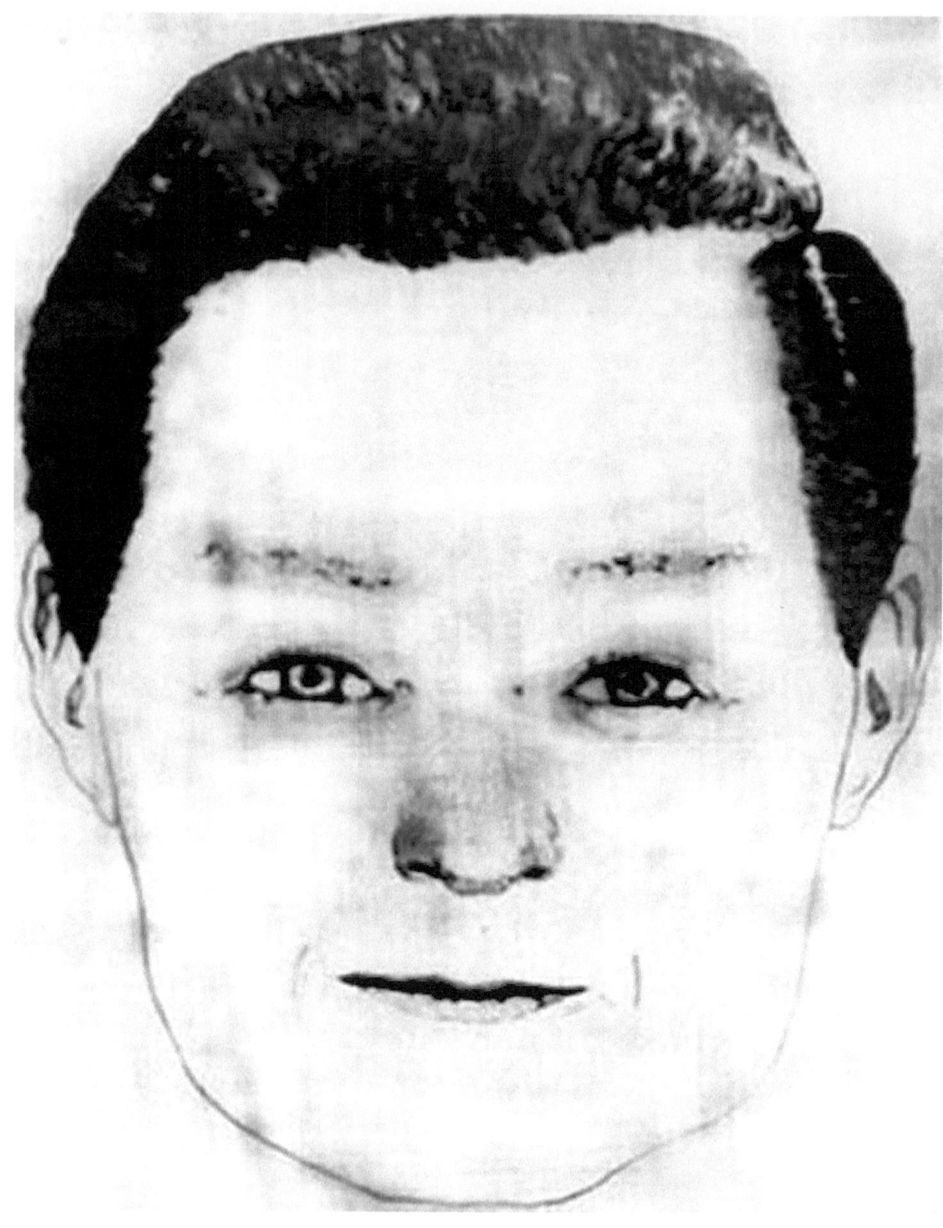

Figure 8

Lake Herman Road

Front Track 60.3"
Rear Track: 59.3"
1959 Chevrolet Impala
Body types: 4-door Sedan, Convertible, Hardtop Coupe, and Hardtop Sedan.

Front Track 60.3"
Rear Track: 59.3"
1960 Chevrolet Impala
Body types: 4-door Sedan, Convertible, Hardtop Coupe, and Hardtop Sedan.

July 4

Front Track 54.5"
Rear Track: 54.5"
1963 Chevrolet Corvair Series 1
Body types: 4-door Sedan, Club Coupe, and Convertible.

A front track of 55" and a rear track of 57.2" are valid for the following:

1965 Chevrolet Corvair Series 2
Body types: Convertible, Sport Coupe, and Sport Sedan.

1966 Chevrolet Corvair Series 2
Body types: Convertible, Sport Coupe, and Sport Sedan.

1967 Chevrolet Corvair Series 2
Body types: Convertible, Sport Coupe, and Sport Sedan.

1968 Chevrolet Corvair Series 2
Body types: Convertible and Sport Coupe.

1969 Chevrolet Corvair Series 2
Body types: Convertible and Sport Coupe.

Lake Berryessa

Front Track 56.8"
Rear Track: 56.3"
1966 Chevrolet Chevy II
Body types: 100 Sedan, Nova Sedan, Nova Sport Coupe, and Nova Super Sport Coupe.

Front Track 56.8"
Rear Track: 56.3"
1967 Chevrolet Chevy II
Body types: 100 Sedan, Nova Sedan, Nova Sport Coupe, and Nova Super Sport Coupe.

Front Track: 58"
Rear Track: 58"
1966 Chevrolet Chevelle
Body types: 2-door Sedan, Malibu Hardtop Sedan, and Malibu Sedan.

Front Track: 58"
Rear Track: 58"
1967 Chevrolet Chevelle
Body types: 2-door Sedan, Malibu Hardtop Sedan, and Malibu Sedan.

ENDNOTES C

[1] Napa County Sheriff's Department Report, Case Number 105907, 10.
[2] Interview of Bryan Calvin Hartnell by Det./Sgt. John Robertson at Queen of the Valley Hospital, Sunday, September 28, 1969, 2.
[3] Napa Sheriff's Office. Dialogue between an unknown assailant and Bryan Hartnell, 1-2.
[4] Interview of Bryan Calvin Hartnell by Det./Sgt. John Robertson at Queen of the Valley Hospital, Sunday, September 28, 1969, 3.
[5] Ibid.
[6] Napa County Sheriff's Department Report, Case Number 105907, 17.
[7] Napa Sheriff's Office. Dialogue between an unknown assailant and Bryan Hartnell, 2.
[8] Interview of Bryan Calvin Hartnell by Det./Sgt. John Robertson at Queen of the Valley Hospital, Sunday, September 28, 1969, 3.
[9] Ibid, 5.
[10] Napa County Sheriff's Department Supplementary Report, Case Number 105907, David Slaight.
[11] "Zodiac on the line …," http://napavalleyregister.com/news/local/zodiac-on-the-line/article_8eb37c90-9581-544e-87ea-6aa1ba3f6b90.html (retrieved May 2016).
[12] Department of Justice, Bureau of Criminal Investigation and Investigation Report, Case Number 1-15-311-F9-5861, 19.
[13] Napa County Sheriff's Department Report, Case Number 105907, 12-13.
[14] Ibid, 17.
[15] Napa Sheriff's Office. Dialogue between an unknown assailant and Bryan Hartnell, 1-2.
[16] Interview of Bryan Calvin Hartnell by Det./Sgt. John Robertson at Queen of the Valley Hospital, Sunday, September 28, 1969, 4.
[17] David Fincher, Director, Zodiac 2-Disc Director's Cut, 2008.
[18] Napa County Sheriff's Department Report, Case Number 105907, 16.
[19] Interview of Bryan Calvin Hartnell by Det./Sgt. John Robertson at Queen of the Valley Hospital, Sunday, September 28, 1969, 4.
[20] Ibid, 5.
[21] David Fincher, Director, Zodiac 2-Disc Director's Cut, 2008.
[22] Napa County Sheriff's Department Report, Case Number 105907, 7.
[23] Ibid, 27.
[24] Napa County Sheriff's Department Report, Case Number 105907 (Det./Sgt. Robertson contacts Hartnell at the hospital attempting to identify the Zodiac's weapon and ammunition).
[25] David Fincher, Director, Zodiac 2-Disc Director's Cut, 2008.

[26] "Officials Sifting Clues In Hunt For Murderer," Napa Register, October 2, 1969.
[27] Department of Justice, Bureau of Criminal Investigation and Investigation Report, Case Number 1-15-311-F9-5861, 23.
[28] California Department of Justice/Division of Law Enforcement/Bureau of Investigation, Zodiac Homicides, for Law Enforcement Use Only, 6.
[29] Department of Justice, Bureau of Criminal Investigation and Investigation Report, Case Number 1-15-311-F9-5861, 6.
[30] Report by Det./Sgt. Hal Snook, Napa County Sheriff's Department Supplement Crime Report, Case Number 105907, 2-3.
[31] Ibid, 11.
[32] Napa County Sheriff's Department Report, Case Number 105907, 10.
[33] California Department of Justice/Division of Law Enforcement/Bureau of Investigation, Zodiac Homicides, for Law Enforcement Use Only, 10.
[34] "Latent Prints-Footwear and Tires," http://www.maine.gov/dps/msp/criminal_investigation/crimelab/footwear.htm (retrieved April 2011).
[35] "Skosålen afslørede 15-årig morder," http://ekstrabladet.dk/112/article4305743.ece (retrieved April 2016).
[36] Department of Justice, Bureau of Criminal Investigation and Investigation Report, Case Number 1-15-311-F9-5861, 9.
[37] Report by Det./Sgt. Hal Snook, Napa County Sheriff's Department Supplement Crime Report, Case Number 105907, 2.
[38] "Vehicle Dimensions," http://excelmathmike.blogspot.com/2010/09/vehicle-dimensions.html (retrieved September 2011).
[39] Bodziak, William. Email to Søren Roest Korsgaard. April 21, 2020.
[40] Ibid.
[41] Bodziak, William, "Tire Tread and Tire Track Evidence: Recovery and Forensic Examination" (CRC Press 2008), 27.
[42] Ibid, 29.
[43] Stuart H. James et al, Forensic Science: An Introduction to Scientific and Investigative Techniques 2nd ed. (Taylor & Francis, 2005), 383.
[44] Report by Det./Sgt. Hal Snook, Napa County Sheriff's Department Supplement Crime Report, Case Number 105907, 1.
[45] "Zodiac on the line …" http://napavalleyregister.com/news/local/zodiac-on-the-line/article_8eb37c90-9581-544e-87ea-6aa1ba3f6b90.html (retrieved March 2017).
[46] "Track Clues To Berryessa Mad Killer," The Times San Mateo, September 30, 1969, 11.
[47] Report by Det./Sgt. Hal Snook, Napa County Sheriff's Department Supplement Crime Report, Case Number 105907, 1.
[48] Department of Justice, Bureau of Criminal Investigation and Investigation Report, Case Number 1-15-311-F9-5861, 9.

[49] Report by Det./Sgt. Hal Snook, Napa County Sheriff's Department Supplement Crime Report, Case Number 105907, 3.
[50] Napa County Sheriff's Department Report, Case Number 105907, 5.
[51] Ibid.
[52] Ibid, 8-9.
[53] Napa Register, September 30, 1969, 1.
[54] Ibid.
[55] "Officials Sifting Clues In Hunt For Murderer," Napa Register, October 2, 1969.
[56] "Vehicle specifications," http://www.automobile-catalog.com (retrieved September 2011).
[57] "Police Dare Cipher Killer" San Francisco Examiner, September 30, 1969.
[58] Ibid.
[59] "Slaying Suspect 'May Strike Again'" Corpus Christi Times, October 2, 1969, 9A.
[60] Notes by movie producer for the 1989 documentary: Crimes of the Century: The Zodiac Killer, 37. Also see: "He'd 'Recognize' Zodiac," San Francisco Chronicle, May 8 1973.
[61] "Hooded Assailant Ties, Stabs Pair," The Press Courier, September 29, 1969, 3.
[62] "'Good clues' in 'hood murder'," The Daily Review, September 30, 1969, 3.
[63] "Berryessa Killer Termed a Deviate," The Times San Mateo, October 1, 1969, 1.
[64] "Slaying Suspect 'May Strike Again'," Corpus Christi Times, October 2, 1969, 9A.
[65] "Seek Madman After Attack At Berryessa." The Times San Mateo, September 29, 1969, 2.

CHAPTER 4

MURDER IN PRESIDIO HEIGHTS

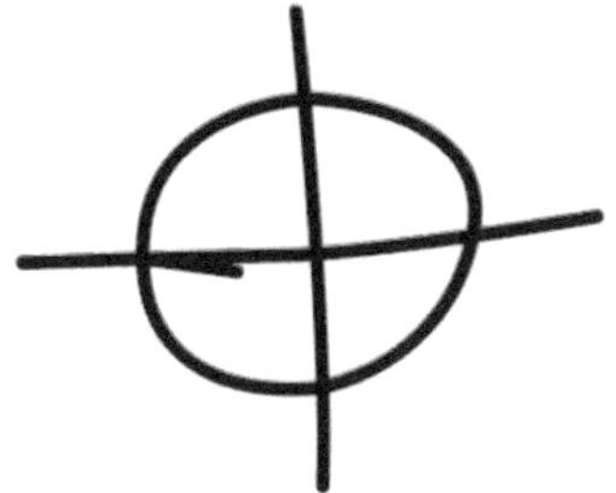

Paul Lee Stine, age 29, and his spouse Claudia S. Stine resided on Fell Street in San Francisco. Paul was ambitious and intelligent. He wanted to become a professor, his brother later said. To pay for his studies, he worked as a cab driver for the Yellow Cab Company.[1]

Saturday, October 11, 1969

Paul Stine reported to work at 8:45 p.m. Shortly after that, he took a passenger from Pier 64 to the San Francisco Air Terminal. At 9:45 p.m., he was dispatched to 500 9th Avenue. En route to the destination, he picked up a fare at Mason and Geary Streets.[2]

Stine and his passenger then proceeded to Presidio Heights – probably at Washington and Maple Streets.** They drove a short distance further to the corner of Washington and Cherry Streets and stopped. Stine probably only caught a glimpse of it before the passenger placed a 9 mm pistol against his head and pulled the trigger. The gunshot caused instant unconsciousness and death followed soon after. Paul Stine had just been killed in Presidio Heights, a small affluent neighborhood with plenty of luxurious million dollar residences and exclusive multi-room mansions. People come from afar to admire the grand living spaces and staggering outdoor acreage, as well as the obligatory rolling lawns, golf courses, and Hollywood heritage.

Obviously, a murder in this area results in media coverage beyond the norm. Houses surround the crime scene and there could be many potential witnesses. And there were witnesses. Three teenagers, Trevor, Rebecca, and Lindsey, saw the killer on the front seat of Stine's cab at around 10 p.m. They were positioned across the street in their house on the second floor about 50 feet from the cab. They had not seen or heard the gun being fired. From their vantage point, they saw that Stine was "slumped partially over his lap."[3] He appeared to be searching Stine's pockets, and later it would be learned that he had stolen his ignition keys, wallet, and cut off a piece of his shirt. He did not take several other keys and a few other items. Subsequently, he wiped the interior of the cab, including the driver's compartment, with a white rag - possibly a handkerchief. He exited the cab by the front passenger's door and wiped it off. He then walked around the cab to the driver's side and wiped the exterior part of the door. They lost track of him when he "nonchalantly"[4] walked north on Cherry Street in the direction of the Presidio. For over two centuries, the Presidio of San Francisco served as an army post until the mid-1990s when it

** There is some confusion as to whether they stopped at Washington and Maple or the Washington and Laurel area.

became a national park. It has many areas with dense vegetation and forestry.

One of the teenagers phoned the police and reported the crime. The dispatcher got the impression that the killer was a Negro Male Adult (NMA) and not a White Male Adult (WMA) and broadcast this erroneous information to all police units. It later turned out that this was a critical error. Officers Armond Pelissetti and Frank Peda arrived shortly after the departure of the killer. Pelissetti would later say that as he approached the cab, he could see fingerprints with traces of blood.[5] They immediately checked the cab and found Stine "slumped over the front seat with his upper torso"[6] in the passenger's side. His head was resting on the floorboard. One of the teenagers outlined to Pelissetti what had happened and said that the perpetrator was a white man. Pelissetti then quickly ran to his police car and made sure that other officers became aware of the initial error.

At 10:10 p.m., Stine was pronounced dead.[7] A few minutes later, after about two hours of sleep, Homicide Inspector Dave Toschi was woken by the noise of his telephone. "I was exhausted,"[8] he would later recall. The voice on the other end said, "You've got a sloppy one near the Presidio. Cab driver shot in the head."[9] The inspector got dressed, entered his vehicle, picked up his partner, William Armstrong, and drove to the crime scene. Around the same time, a meticulous search for the killer was carried out by several police units, dog units, and a fire department spotlight vehicle was utilized but to no avail.

The Physical Evidence

The physical examination of the cab revealed one 9 mm Winchester Western shell casing on the front floor of the passenger's side. An examination revealed that the killer had used a semi-automatic pistol, possibly a new model produced by the Browning Arms Company. A ballistics test established that it was not the same weapon as he had used in July to kill Ferrin and injure Mageau.[10]

A technician dusted the cab with fine powders to bring friction ridges to light. A total of thirty latent fingerprints, three latent palm prints, and one latent impression that came from either a lower joint area or palm print were found.[11] Some of them contained "traces of blood" and were "believed"[12] to be the killer's. They were found on the post between the doors on the driver's side. According to the witnesses, the killer walked to the driver's side and made contact with the cab as he apparently wiped the surface of it. In addition, prints lifted from the right front door handle were also "believed to be"[13] the killer's. The others "may or may not"[14] have been left by him. The prints have been used along with other evidence to eliminate suspects over the years. Unlike the offenses we covered in the first chapters, only a fraction of the police reports have been released regarding the Stine murder. In the publically available material, it is not stated how the integrity of the prints was established and whether or not it is reasonable that someone other than the Zodiac could have left the prints. We contacted the former lead-investigator, Dave Toschi, now 79 years old. Through an intermediary, he was asked if they took elimination prints and excluded those present at the scene as the source. Toschi answered, "Yes." He then went on to describe the meticulousness of the technicians: "The cab was towed from the scene with the crime lab following behind to make sure no one else touched it. The next morning the crime lab took many prints."[15] The fact that they obtained elimination prints changes the low probability that an unrelated individual left the ones in question to approaching zero. If the killer left prints, it is almost expected that some of them were stained with blood to some degree, as per Toschi there was blood everywhere inside the cab. Pelissetti would later categorize it in the same way: "Based on the crime scene, there would have been a lot of blood on that person."[16] The integrity of the prints is further strengthened by the fact that Pelissetti and Peda secured the crime scene within minutes of the killer leaving the cab and the prints with blood were seen at this time. In 2009, Toschi said this about the evidence, "We had witnesses, we had a description, we had fingerprints - we just figured we're gonna get the guy."[17] Unlike in a typical serial offender case, the Zodiac left a lot of evidence that cannot reasonably be questioned. The evidence will undoubtedly identify an individual as the killer if a comparison is made. The fact that none of the evidence, handwriting included, has ever been tied to any individual shows that the Zodiac was never interrogated or even investigated. If he had been, the physical evidence would have implicated him in the crimes.

The Teenagers

Pelissetti and Peda listened carefully to what the teenagers said about the killer's movements, how he looked, and how he was dressed. In the initial police report, they summarized the killer's appearance as a white male adult in his early forties, 5'8" tall, heavily built, reddish-blond "crew-cut" hair. The killer was wearing eyeglasses and had on a pair of dark brown trousers. The teenagers also told them that the killer was wearing a navy blue or black "Parka" jacket as well as dark shoes. Pelissetti and Peda added in their report that the murderer "should have many blood stains on his person and clothing."[18]

The cops later interviewed the teenagers extensively. They had been upstairs in their house and having fun when their attention was drawn to Stine's cab because the interior light was on, which was very bright. One of them remarked that the driver looked "sick, or something."[19] Something nefarious was going on. Stine was lying across the front seat with his head in the passenger's lap. Rebecca perceived blood and the glimpse of a knife. Horrified, she screamed, "He's stabbing that man."[20] In reality, he was busy cutting off a piece of Stine's shirt. Lindsey, the oldest of the teens, age 16, walked downstairs to get a good view of what was happening. He knew that he could not be seen by the passenger because downstairs the lights were off. Upstairs, one of them called the police. He walked real close to the window and observed the man's actions. Rebecca joined Lindsey at the window soon after. "They both watched and observed in silence as [the man] pushed the driver to an upright position behind the steering wheel, exited the car, and walked around the rear of the car and opened the driver's door. Stine had fallen over onto the seat, and [the man] pulled him back up into the seated position and had some difficulty keeping him upright."[21] When he had finished wiping off the cab, he calmly walked away. Lindsey showed great courage when he ran outside to see where the killer was going. “He ran to the corner of Cherry and watched as [the man] continued his casual pace right up to the corner of Jackson & Cherry.”[22] At this moment in time, Pelissetti and Peda arrived, and started to question him about what had happened. Lindsey explained that the killer was still in sight on Cherry Street. When they both looked, the man was out of sight.

Sunday, October 12

All of the articles that were published assumed it was a so-called “routine robbery” gone wrong. Zodiac had not entered the picture, yet. The Chronicle covered the killing under the headline, “Robbery Victim, Cabbie Slain in Presidio Hts.”[23] They reported a description of the killer and mentioned certain aspects of the crime, such that he had been wiping off the cab.

Monday, October 13

Toschi tasked Juan Morales, a talented artist at the SFPD, to work-up a composite drawing of the killer. Morales listened carefully as the teenagers described the facial structures of the man they had seen. On Monday, October 13, it was released to the public. The wanted poster described the killer as 25-30 years old, 5’8” to 5’9,” reddish brown hair, crew cut, heavy-rimmed glasses, and wearing a navy blue or black jacket.

Tuesday, October 14

A letter arrived at the Chronicle. The Zodiac had once again decided to communicate - this time he had enclosed a piece of Stine’s blood soaked shirt as a testimony to his guilt. Zodiac concluded his message to the Chronicle by stating that he would “wipe out a school bus”! The aforementioned article in the Chronicle mentioned that the witnesses were teenagers. Perhaps this motivated the Zodiac to issue this particular threat.
The FBI concluded in their characteristic cautious tone that all of the four letters that had been received at this point had likely been prepared by the same hand.[24] Using excess postage had apparently become one of the Zodiac’s trademarks. The envelope was postmarked in San Francisco.

The new letter read:

This is the Zodiac speaking.
I am the murderer of the
taxi driver over by
Washington St + Maple St last
night, to prove this here is
a blood stained piece of his
shirt. I am the same man
who did in the people in the
north bay area.
The S.F. Police could have caught
me last night if they had
searched the park properly
in stead of holding road races
with their motercicles seeing who
could make the most noise. The
car drivers should have just
parked their cars + sat there
quietly waiting for me to come
out of cover.
School children make nice targets, I think I shall wipe out
a school bus some morning. Just
shoot out the frunt tire + then
pick off the kiddies as they come
bouncing out.

The envelope read:

S.F. Chronicle
San Fran.
Calif.
Please Rush To Editor[††]

[††] Zodiac had drawn his signature symbol at the top left corner of the envelope.

Wednesday, October 15

It was now all over the media that Zodiac had committed another murder. Chronicle gave him a new name: "The Boastful 'Slayer,'"[25] which was their headline. They reproduced the letter except for the school bus menace. The consequences of publishing the threat were considered.

Thursday, October 16

It was reported in the *Napa Register* that police officials were "certain" that the Vallejo, Lake Berryessa, and Presidio Heights crimes had been committed by one person. It was stated that they had made a "preliminary match of fingerprints and handwriting."[26] Undersheriff Tom Johnson told the newspaper that "specialists have not completed, as yet, extensive examinations to verify that identity," but he added, "I'm fairly certain it's the same man."[27] The next day, it was reported in the *Lodi Sentinel* that a "preliminary analysis of partial fingerprints obtained from crime scenes in Napa County, Vallejo and San Francisco indicated they came from the same man. But [Undersheriff Johnson] said the prints were not complete enough for an identification of the killer."[28] On October 21, 1969, Captain Martin Lee of the San Francisco Police Department declared that "handwriting, ballistics and fingerprint experts" had "linked the same man to five slayings in the San Francisco Bay Area."[29] Years later, Inspector Toschi said, "Police have enough fingerprints from the Stine murder scene and from a Napa County telephone booth, where Zodiac once called police, to make a positive identification if he is captured or surrenders."[30]
It is uncertain why Vallejo was mentioned as a source of prints as the Zodiac ostensibly did not leave any prints prior to September 1969. It is, however, more important that a preliminary match between the prints had been made, showing it was the same perpetrator. When Johnson told the journalists that the prints were not enough to identify the killer, he was alluding to the partial nature of the prints. The specific criteria for making a match between two prints (fingers, palms, feet, etc. can all make an impression that can identify a person) varies depending on which expert is consulted. Some experts will declare a match

based on 12 points in common, while others require significantly more. The partial prints in this case were likely not enough to absolutely match them to an individual, but they could be used to rule out suspects, and they have been used for this ever since they were lifted. However, we only have an article describing the preliminary match. The statements from Lee and Toschi, which were made after an exhaustive examination had been conducted, strongly suggest that the prints could identify the Zodiac, and not just rule out suspects. To this day, these prints, which "came from the same man," have, without exception, ruled out all alleged suspects who had their prints compared to them, meaning that the Zodiac is still out there, dead or alive.

Friday, October 17

The Zodiac had exhibited violent, bizarre, and erratic behavior in a pattern that carried little consistency, and it seemed difficult if not impossible to predict which way he would go next. Clearly, it was not an option to discount his threat of wiping out a bus full of children, and on October 17 it was published. The public did not receive it lightly and a virtual epidemic of fear and paranoia spread across the Bay Area. Officers now boarded school buses with loaded shotguns or followed them in police cars. Headlines: "Kids Next, 'Zodiac Killer' Warns,"[31] "Zodiac Killer Wants A Bus,"[32] "Zodiac Killer Wants to Add School Bus 'Kiddies' to List,"[33] and "'Zodiac' To Stalk School Bus?"[34]

Saturday, October 18

Paul Avery was the leading investigative journalist working on the Zodiac case for the Chronicle. On October 18, 1969, the Chronicle published his most recent article, titled, "Zodiac Portrait of a killer,"[35] a fearless piece that manifestly provoked the Zodiac and tore permanent holes in his perceived public image. In the article, Avery went on to characterize the Zodiac as "a clumsy criminal, a liar and possibly a latent homosexual."[36] He also quoted SFPD Captain Lee who had said that the Zodiac had made mistakes, like leaving fingerprints, letting three teenagers see him, and failing to kill two of his victims. "Two young men who may one day pick him out of a lineup,"[37] Lee said. These clumsy errors show that the Zodiac is "not to be the master criminal he apparently considers himself."[38] Lee then said, "His boast of being in the area we were searching while we were searching it is a lie."[39] He then detailed why it remained clear that Zodiac had lied about it.

After the initial wanted poster was released, it was opined that it could be improved if Morales did not incorporate the input from all three teenagers into the drawing. After listening to the kids' observations again, it was determined that Rebecca was the most artistically inclined. The final sketch was made using only her input. When it was finished, the kids agreed that it was very close to what they had seen. On October 18, it was circulated. The revised wanted poster described the Zodiac as 35-45 years old, about 5'8", heavily built, short brown hair, possibly with a reddish shade. After the stabbing at Lake Berryessa, Zodiac clearly had a haircut. He may have gotten that haircut because he felt he resembled the man with moderately long hair on the September composite drawing. We should note that composite drawings have a widespread success rate of 30%-80%.[40] The two drawings are placed here side by side.

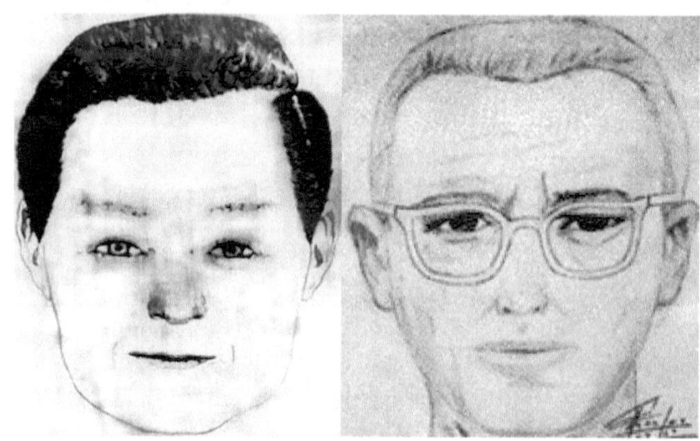

While writing this book, we contacted a leading company that specializes in forensic compositing, age progression, and animation. We tasked them with creating a realistic rendering of the October 18 composite drawing using their sophisticated software, which has made them famous for age progressing well-known actors. The rendering provides the readers with a more realistic view of how the Zodiac may have looked (see

Appendix). We provided Bill Crow with the rendering and the original composite drawing. He responded,

> To be honest with you it has been 42 years ago and what I noticed was general aspects of the person in the other car and a memory that I did not recognize the person as someone I knew... I only had a momentary glimpse as he drove past and at that time I had no reason to pay more attention. I do not think that I should comment on the pictures.[41]

Tuesday, October 21

The Examiner consulted William F. Baker, a well-educated psychologist and handwriting analyst of 35 years. After an exhaustive study of one of the letters, Baker said that the Zodiac "feels suspended between heaven and hell, not sure of himself and feels caught in a trap of merely existing."[42] Baker went on to say, "His vanity and ego know no bounds. He's a 'nobody' to those who know him but he is now a 'somebody' because everybody knows he has killed five persons although they don't know his identity. 'And he is glorifying in his anonymity.' He is a methodical planner and extremely shrewd."[43] While writing the letter, Zodiac "was under a great emotional strain and excitement."[44] The handwriting appeared to be "very contrived,"[45] and Baker judged that "he has a post-high school education, although it could be self-education. He is probably trying to steer people off."[46] Controversially, Baker also said, "The probability is that he is impotent and a watcher rather than a participant in sex."[47] The expert also speculated about the Zodiac's motive: "The strong slant to the left of the lower letters denotes a 'mother hostility' and an unhappy childhood. Carry that trait further and you find the man who is afraid of women and hates them. Carry that to a further extreme and you have a man who is capable of killing women to get even with his mother."[48] Baker concluded the interview by saying that Zodiac is "unquestionably paranoid and schizophrenic."[49]

Wednesday, October 22

Although the Zodiac case was bizarre on a whole new level, it would still take a new, unanticipated twist. At 2 a.m., the dispatcher of the Oakland Police Department picked up the phone. The caller said he was the Zodiac killer and went on to demand that Francis Lee Bailey, a famous attorney involved in many high profile cases, appear on the Jim Dunbar TV show. If this were not possible, he would settle with Melvin Belli, a prominent defense attorney who notably defended Muhammad Ali and Jack Ruby. The request was not dismissed as a crank call, and Belli joined the Dunbar show later that morning. Belli probably saw it as a great opportunity for marketing himself while doing service in the public's interest.

In one of the most dramatic moments in the history of the Dunbar show, a man, "Sam," who purported to be the Zodiac called the show a total of 13 times. He apparently hung up frequently to avoid being traced. His speech was muffled, fragmented, sometimes aggressive, and at other times calm, indicating a mental patient was on the other end.

Belli was able to get Sam to explain that he suffered from recurring headaches and violent impulses to kill. The dramatic morning came to a close when Belli agreed to go to the San Francisco district attorney's office "to see if prosecutors would assure him they would not ask for the death penalty."[50] In another call off camera, Belli and Sam arranged to meet at a secret location after he had talked with the district attorney. Of course, Sam did not show up.

Nancy Slover, Bryan Hartnell, and David Slaight, the three individuals who had heard the Zodiac's voice, were summoned to listen to Sam's voice and determine if he was the Zodiac. All three agreed: The caller was an imposter.[51] According to several newspapers, an unnamed officer did not believe it was the same caller on the Dunbar show who had originally called the Oakland Police Department. One journalist even wrote, "Oakland police [...] said they were certain the request was made by 'Zodiac,' as the caller revealed undisclosed knowledge about the killings."[52] The journalist's claim, however, is not supported by other sources and is probably a misunderstanding. A portion of the dramatic TV show is quoted below. Undoubtedly, the Zodiac watched it live on television or listened to it over the radio. How would he react to someone using his name and infamy as a vehicle to attain attention?

Dunbar: “Talk to us. Just, tell us what’s going on, inside you, right now. Please.”

Sam: “I have headaches.”

Dunbar: “Right.”

Belli: “How long have you had those headaches, uh, Sam? Been a long time?”

Sam: “Since I killed a kid.”

Belli: “Well, was it before December that you had the headaches?”

Sam: “Yes.”

Belli: “If, did, were you in service, that you might have had an injury in service, did you ever fall out of a tree or down stairs? Were you ever unconscious?”

Sam: “I don’t know.”

Belli: “You don’t remember. Does aspirin do you any good?”

Sam: “No.”

Belli: “Doesn’t do you any good?”

Sam: “No.”

Dunbar: “Sam.”

Belli: “Damn stuff never did me any good either when I had a headache.”

Dunbar: “Sam, let me ask you a question. Did you, um, did you attempt to call this program one other time when Mr. Belli was with us? And, you called.”

Sam: “What?”

Dunbar: “Did you try to call us one other time about two or three weeks ago when Mel Belli was with us?”

Sam: “Yes.”

Dunbar: “And you, uh, well.”

Belli: “You couldn’t get through, and we were talking?”

Dunbar: “And you couldn’t get through, the phones were tied up, is that it?”

Sam: “Yes.”

Belli: “Sam, let me ask you this: There’s some reason why you go to a particular doctor or a particular priest, and some reason why apparently you wanted to talk to me, or Lee? Is it that you feel we have compassion for people who get in trouble? Or, is that you feel that we can do something for you? Or is that you feel we’re, we’re, have enough integrity that if we promise you something, that we’re gonna stick to it?”

Dunbar: “Well, let’s find out why he wanted to talk to – Why did you want to talk to Mr. Belli, Sam?”

Sam: “I don’t want to be hurt.”

Belli: “You’re not going to be hurt. You’re not going to be hurt if you talk to me.”

Dunbar: “You’re not going to the gas chamber.”

Belli: “I wouldn’t think they’d ask for capital punishment. We should ask the district attorney—you want me to do that, Sam? You want me to talk to the district attorney?”

[Sam screams at this point.]

Belli: “What was that?”

Sam: “I did not say anything. That was my headache.”

Belli: “It sounds like you’re in a great deal of pain. Your voice sounds muffled. What’s the matter?”

Sam: “My head aches. I’m so sick. I’m having one of my headaches.”

[Sam screams again.]

Sam: “I’m going to kill them. I’m going to kill all those kids!”[53]

Saturday, November 8

Up to and until the Stine crime, the Zodiac had received little flak in the press, but this had changed, and its impact was reflected in his next letters (see next page for a transcript). Over this weekend, he sent a letter and a semi-bizarre greeting card that also had a cipher enclosed. The card had been manufactured by a company named, *JESTERS By Forget Me Not Cards*. Both were received on Monday, November 10. The envelopes contained too many stamps, and they were postmarked in San Francisco. Zodiac had written, “Please Rush to Editor,” on both of the envelopes.

The authenticity of the card and cipher was attested by a piece of Stine’s shirt.[54] Photocopies of the handwriting were forwarded to the FBI for further analysis. After comparing and magnifying the handwriting samples received so far, the expert stated that the printing was “prepared by the person who prepared the other threatening letters.”[55]

In the card and letter, the Zodiac claimed he had killed seven people, not the accepted figure of five. In August (notice his reference), there were no homicides attributed to him. However, he was probably alluding to the compulsive stabbing and killing of Deborah Gay Furlong and Kathleen Snoozy. In the news, he was briefly cited as a possible suspect. Lead-investigator Barton L. Collins had a different opinion; he said, “I don’t think he’s (Zodiac) connected with my case at all,” and “If it was, he would have claimed credit long ago.”[56] Collins reasoned that “Zodiac is obviously an egomaniac. I cannot see him committing the brutal murders of those girls without wanting everyone to know,” and “It would simplify my case if it was the Zodiac. There’d be more evidence to work with. But it just isn’t ... not in my book.”[57]

Collins was right: Karl Werner was convicted in 1971 of the murders; he remains incarcerated as of 2020 at the California Medical Facility in Vacaville.

The cipher, now collectively referred to as the *340*, has withstood the test of time, meaning supercomputers, amateur cryptographers, FBI, university students, and zodiologists, just about everyone who reads about the Zodiac killer, have failed to crack the cipher. If we assume it contains a message, what would it likely be?

We should keep in mind that Zodiac never divulged anything of real importance about himself or his identity in his letters. In line with this, the cipher is presumably just another rambling message. Zodiac did not offer any details vis-á-vis his alleged killings in August, and he said, he would not openly proclaim his victims anymore, but maybe he would in a cipher. As we shall see, he is suspected of having committed killings before 1968, and perhaps his cipher detailed these. It would be a great disappointment if he took credit for the Furlong and Snoozy case in the cipher. The card, which accompanied the cipher, and the long letter that arrived at the same time were characterized by anger directed at the police, depression, feelings of loneliness and of being overlooked. The cipher may contain a related message. If we juxtapose his two ciphers, the 408 and 340, they are similar in a visual sense such as in their symmetrical distribution of characters. Further analyses show internal differences and these are best exemplified by the fact that sophisticated decryption software can only solve the 408, indicating that the 340 is not a homophonic substitution cipher, like the 408.[58]

Considering that it has not been solved to this day, Zodiac may have created a fake cipher to keep the police busy chasing false leads, and as a way of attaining immortality.

The Zodiac's message on the greeting card:

This is the Zodiac speaking
I though you would nead a
good laugh before you
hear the bad news.
You won't get the
news for a while yet.
PS could you print
this new cipher
on your frunt page?

I get awfully lonely
when I am ignored,
so lonely I could
do my Thing!!!!!!
⌖
Des July Aug
Sept Oct = 7

The letter read as follows:

1/6

This is the zodiac speaking
up to the end of Oct I have
killed 7 people. I have grown
rather angry with the police
for their telling lies about me.
So I shall change the way the
collecting of slaves. I shall
no longer announce to anyone.
when I comitt my murders,
they shall look like routine
robberies, killings of anger, +
a few fake accidents, etc.
The police shall never catch me,
because I have been too clever
for them.
1 I look like the description
passed out only when I do
my thing, the rest of the time
I look entirle different. I
shall not tell you what my
descise consists of when I kill
2 As of yet I have left no
fingerprints behind me contrary
to what the police say

2/6

in my killings I wear trans –
parent finger tip guards. All it
is is 2 coats of airplane cement

coated on my finger tips – quite
unnoticible + very efective.
3 my killing tools have been bought
en through the mail order out –
fits before the ban went into
efect. except one + it was
bought out of the state.
So as you see the police don't
have much to work on. If you
wonder why I was wipeing the
cab down I was leaving fake clews
for the police to run all over town
with, as one might say, I gave
the cops som bussy work to do to
keep them happy. I enjoy needling
the blue pigs. Hey blue pig I
was in the park - you were useing
fire trucks to mask the sound
of your cruzeing prowl cars. The
dogs never came with in 2
blocks of me + they were to
the west + there was only 2

3/6

groups of parking about 10 min
apart then the moter cicles
went by about 150 ft away
going from south to north west.
p.s. 2 cops pulled a goof abot 3
min after I left the cab. I was
walking down the hill to the
park when this cop car pulled up
+ one of them called me over
+ asked if I saw any one
acting supicisous or strange
in the last 5 to 10 min + I said
yes there was this man who
was runnig by waveing a gun
+ the cops peeled rubber +
went around the corner as

I directed them + I dissap –
eared into the park a block +
a half away never to be seen
again.
Hey pig doesnt it rile you up
to have you noze rubed in your
booboos?
If you cops think Im going to take
on a bus the way I stated I was,
you deserve to have holes in your
heads.[‡‡]

4/6

Take one bag of ammonium nitrate
fertlizer + 1 gal of stove oil +
dump a few bags of gravel on
top + then set the shit off
+ will positivily ventalate any
thing that should be in the way
of the blast.
The death machiene is allready
made. I would have sent you
pictures but you would be nasty
enough to trace them back to
developer + then to me, so I
shall describe my masterpiece
to you. The nice part of it is
all the parts can be bought on
the open market with no quest
ions asked.
1 bat. pow clock - will run for
aprox 1 year
1 photoelectric switch
2 copper leaf springs

‡‡ The part about being stopped by the officers had been highlighted, and in the margin, Zodiac had noted, "Must print in paper."

2 6V car bat
1 flash light bulb + reflecter
1 mirror
2 18" cardboard tubes black with
shoe polish in side + oute[§§]

6/6

the system checks out from
one end to the other in my
tests. What you do not know
is whether the death machiene
is at the sight or whether
it is being stored in my b
asement for future use.
I think you do not have the
man power to stop this one
by continually searching the
road sides looking for this
thing. + it wont do to re roat
+ re schedule the buss es bec
ause the bomb can be adapted
to new conditions.
Have fun!! By the way
it could be rather messy
if you try to bluff me.
PS. Be shure to
print the part I
marked out on
page 3 or I shall
do my thing ⌖

[§§] Page five is a diagram with instructions. It can be viewed in the appendix.

On the back of page 6:

To prove that I am the
Zodiac, Ask the Vallejo
cop about my electric gun
sight which I used to start
my collecting of slaves.

Analysis

Zodiac's six-page missive reads as a long denial of Captain Lee's statements. We have subjected some of his claims to critical analysis and, as we shall see, his assertions do not harmonize with logic and the established facts. Before we go through the letter, it is worth noting the childish reaction of the Zodiac when faced with opposition. He desperately tried to have the last word by proving that he is right and the cops are wrong. Consider this statement from the letter, "Hey pig doesnt it rile you up to have you noze rubed in your booboos?" According to the witnesses, he may have been 45 years old at this time. What kind of 45-year-old would write obscenities like this? What level of maturity does it correspond to? What about his intellectual level? People who knew the Zodiac would probably recognize his immaturity and childishness – and perhaps even recognize his deep-seated resentment toward the police, especially the SFPD. Maybe the Zodiac's anger originates from past run-ins with the police. Judging by the content of the letter, it appears that the Zodiac did not have a deep grasp of forensics, specifically the science of fingerprinting. For example, he claimed to have applied airplane cement to the tips of his fingers, but did not mention how he concealed the rest of his hands, including his palm prints. Airplane cement/glue is a type of clear, fast-drying, liquid adhesive that is used for adjoining small plastic parts of model planes, cars, ships, etc. Even if he had covered all critical surfaces with glue, like a glove, it would have been highly impractical. In those days, it was apparently not common knowledge that a palm print could serve as an identifying print. On a letter posted in 1974, he is also believed to have left a "writer's palm print."[59] Impressions from a palm were also lifted from the cab. In any event, the fact that he wiped several surfaces of the cab gives away that he was concerned about fingerprints, and that the glue excuse is a lie. He could have written that he wore gloves; however, he knew that such a claim would not be in harmony with what the witnesses saw, so he had to invent an invisible cover. His terminology "airplane cement" rather than "airplane glue" is interesting. Did the Zodiac build airplane models in his spare time?

The established movie-pattern continues as the idea of the coated fingertips may have been borrowed from *Batman the movie* from 1966.[60] In the film, Batman and Robin suspect that a mysterious character is the Penguin in disguise. The man denies the allegation. Batman and Robin are unable to confirm their suspicion by examining his fingerprints because he has "plastic coated fingertips." In 1961, the *Bonham Daily Favorite* wrote that detectives had arrested a group of robbers in spite of using "airplane cement" to "conceal fingerprints."[61] A print found in a robbed store in "dried glue was identified"[62] and led detectives onto the right track.

Zodiac also made the questionable connection between wiping the cab and leaving fabricated evidence. As mentioned, prints with *traces of blood* were lifted from an area he had been in contact with. These prints have been eliminated as belonging to anyone present at the crime scene. Therefore, in order for the Zodiac to be telling the truth, he must have been creating fake fingerprints when he wiped off the cab. It is difficult to imagine how one can leave fake prints by wiping with a cloth. Zodiac did not specify *how* and for an obvious reason. He likely felt portrayed as a clumsy criminal that is why he tried to counter the news reports. In his August letter, he similarly tried to put himself in a better light. By thoroughly perusing this lengthy letter, it becomes evident that it was penned by a superficial individual who took little or no time to analyze his own assertions.

His next denial was that he looked completely different when he was not murdering people, yet almost predictably refused to tell in which way. He could have added the glasses as a disguise, but Bill Crow caught a momentary glimpse of a man with short hair and glasses, a man who almost certainly was the Zodiac. In July and September, he did not wear glasses. If he really wanted to give a fake impression of wearing glasses, he would probably have worn a pair at all times. The witnesses were in consensus about his body type; the Zodiac was a stocky individual. Mageau, Hartnell, and Cecelia said his hair was brown. The initial wanted poster and the updated one both stated that his hair was brown. In 1996, Criminalist Cydne Holt of SFPD's DNA laboratory extracted the stamps from the Stine letter and found a reddish-brown hair underneath them. If the Zodiac had elaborately disguised himself he would have worn a wig with long hair which could have concealed his facial structures to a high degree. We can be relatively certain that the composite drawings are reasonably accurate. It is very likely that the arrogance of the Zodiac convinced him that no witnesses would see him, and his plan of killing a cab driver in Presidio Heights would work out without any friction.

While we have already established his deceitful disposition, we should comment on the Zodiac's lack of emotional insight. He used the term *angry* to describe how he felt about the so-called lies told about him. The lies concerned the escape and the evidence as detailed in Avery's article. The Zodiac should rationally have been *happy* for successfully manipulating the investigators into believing that he was fat, short-haired, and left prints. Unavoidably, the police would be telling so-called lies about him because they had no way of knowing that he had used a disguise and planted fake fingerprints.

It is a matter of conjecture, yet intriguing to cogitate how the Zodiac would have responded, and how the case would have evolved, had none of his letters been publicized. He had a ferocious obsession with attention, and his motivation to kill might have been set back had he not attained widespread attention in the media. Alternatively, ignoring him might have tipped him over the edge and his violent behavior escalated into a killing spree, just as he initially promised.

The Zodiac underlined his perceived superiority by emphasizing the clever methods by which he had obtained his weapons. It was a response to a media report that stated the police were trying to trace his two 9 mm pistols. Zodiac was keenly following developments.[63] On a related note, it is unlikely that Zodiac could resist the temptation to save all articles about himself and reread them over and over again.

Captain Lee had this to say about the Zodiac's assertion that he was stopped by two cops and talked to them: "It is preposterous that he was stopped and questioned by the officers. That just didn't happen."[64] On November 12, 1969, right after the Zodiac's claim that he talked to the police, Patrolman Donald Fouke stated in an intradepartmental memorandum (reproduced below) that he and a colleague merely drove by the Zodiac and he was not stopped. He provided a detailed description of the Zodiac and even characterized him as being of "Welsh ancestry." His colleague that evening, Eric Zelms, died in the line of duty on January 1, 1970. He was murdered while trying to apprehend two men burglarizing a shop.

> Sir:
>
> I respectfully wish to report the following, that while responding to the area of Cherry and Washington Streets a suspect fitting the description of the Zodiac killer was observed by officer Fouke walking in an easterly direction on Jackson street and then turn north on Maple street. This subject was not stopped as the description received from communications was that of a [N]egro male. When the right description was broadcast reporting officer informed communications that a possible suspect had been seen going north on Maple Street into the Presidio, The area of Julius Kahn playground and a search was started which had negative results.
>
> The suspect that was observed by officer Fouke was a WMA 35-45 Yrs about 5'10", 180-200 lbs. Medium heavy build - Barrel chested - Medium complexion - Light-colored hair possibly greying in rear (May have been lighting that caused this effect.) Crew cut - Wearing glasses - Dressed in dark blue waist length zipper type jacket (Navy or royal blue) Elastic cuffs and waist band zipped part way up. Brown wool pants pleeted type baggy in rear (Rust brown) May have been wearing low cut shoes.
>
> Subject at no time appeared to be in a hurry walking with a shuffling lope, Slightly bent forward head down. The subjects general appearance to classifiy him as a group would be that he might be of Welsh ancestry.

> My partner that night was officer E. Zelms # 1348 of Richmond station. I do not know if he observed this subject or not. Respectfully submitted
> Donald A. Fouke
> Patrolman 847

Years later, Fouke reemphasized his original statement from 1969: "We never stopped the man. We never talked to him. That is an emphatic statement by me. I wouldn't make the denial."[65] During the same interview, he said,

> One month later, when the composite drawing came out at Richmond station, and was posted on the wall, he looked similar to the man that I had seen on October 11th. I then wrote a scratch, in a departmental memorandum, to my lieutenant to forward to homicide division, so that they would have the additional information, about the appearance of the suspect.

Officer Pelissetti has later, in contrast, stated, "I spoke to Officer Fouke later that evening and I was unaware that he had stopped anybody. Black, white or any other color. However, in subsequent conversations with him, he told me that he did stop somebody." Fouke had told him that "he saw a man walking by and that he asked him: 'Did you see anybody go by?' The person said: 'No,' and I believe that Fouke would have been honest, but that scratch and what he told me do not coincide. It seemed Officer Fouke, in that amount of time, felt that he had stopped the Zodiac." Pelissetti also said, "Well, it's very hard to say whether he did or not. It would be a point of conjecture at this point, and he seemed quite upset." He also said: "Well, it just so happens that area is extremely well-lit, and I cannot imagine [him] not seeing the shine of blood on the clothing if it had been Zodiac. I feel bad for him, if he believes that was the Zodiac. I don't think it was."[66]

In 2010, we contacted Duffy Jennings, a San Francisco Chronicle reporter and friend of Toschi, who agreed to ask him questions for us about the alleged event. We then sent the questions to Duffy. The first question dealt with whether or not he believed the conversation had taken place. The second one if Fouke had disclosed to Toschi that he did speak with the Zodiac. The third question was set forth to ascertain if Zelms and Fouke had contributed to the second wanted poster. We also asked other questions not relevant for this discussion. Duffy replied promptly, "Almost all of your questions were posed to me two months ago by another Zodiac enthusiast. [...] I responded with Toschi's answers, namely "yes" to your first three questions." Duffy then stated, "He wrote back immediately to say that officer Fouke denies that he ever talked to Zodiac, discussed the case with Toschi or contributed to the poster. Fouke told this other man that Toschi 'blew the Zodiac case.'"[67]

If it did happen as Zodiac, Toschi, and Pelissetti said then the Zodiac is the luckiest serial killer of all time. Consider the many variables (blood on clothes not being visible, broadcast description of the killer being an error, etc.) that had to be in the Zodiac's favor in order for him not to be arrested or killed.

As mentioned, Fouke has denied all of the allegations (also see Chapter 14). Regarding the wanted posters, Fouke has later stated that the sketches look like the man he had seen, except that the Zodiac had a more receding hairline and there was "something about the chin."[68] In addition, his crew cut was more traditional. Fouke has also clarified that his Welsh ancestry characterization in the 1969 memo was vis-à-vis the Zodiac's body type that reminded him of Welsh coal miners.[69]

Zodiac also claimed in the letter that he had constructed a morbid piece of engineering: A homicidal device designed to eradicate a bus with schoolchildren in it. In rough form, the alleged bomb consisted of ammonium nitrate and oil. Nowadays, this recipe is well known. The bus bomb circuitry shows that he was a technical individual, with an understanding of circuitry, electronics, and some chemistry. We will not beleaguer the readers with an obtuse analysis of the device. Suffice to say, it is oversimplified and difficult to set up. The purpose of the device was to terrorize, not to kill.

It was important to the Zodiac to prove the authenticity of this letter, which he did on the back of page six. However, he could simply have provided a secret set of numbers or letters in the Stine letter, or previously, and continued to use it in his future communications. Hence, there would never be any doubt.

Recreating the Zodiac's Steps

We did not previously address the Zodiac's movements after he disappeared out of Lindsey's sight. For completeness, we will review information related to the event and present the most probable sequence of events. We know that Zodiac walked north on Cherry Street after departing the cab. Henceforth there is a considerable amount of confusion as to what happened. Armond Pelissetti and his partner Frank Peda arrived at the cab "very quickly,"[70] within a few minutes of Zodiac leaving it. Pelissetti looked into the cab and was "99.9% certain"[71] that Stine was dead. He was quickly told that the killer was a white man. "I couldn't get to the radio fast enough at that point to let everybody else know,"[72] he later said. He did not know if the Zodiac was still in the area. He released his pistol from the holster and followed the Zodiac's steps:

> I did not run because there are innumerable alcoves and parked cars, so I went down following every technique I knew so I didn't get my head blown off. Got down to the corner of Jackson Street, had to make a choice. I was on the east side of the street, so I turned right to the east, went up in that direction. I couldn't see anybody in either direction, nor could I see anybody scaling a wall into the Presidio. I got all the way down to the next corner which was Maple. Decision number two, which way to go? Looked to the left, toward the Presidio, saw absolutely nothing. It was much darker there. I figured the chance of finding somebody was almost nil. I turned to the right and I saw a man walking his dog. He was somewhat older than the description I had, a whole lot thinner, and he had absolutely no blood on his clothes. I asked that gentleman if he saw anybody walking in the area and he told me, 'No.'[73]

Patrolman Donald Fouke worked his way through the ranks and eventually became a sergeant for the SFPD. He has been helpful over the years and addressed the events in several interviews, including one in 1988 for the documentary, *Crimes of the Century: The Zodiac Killer*, which was released in 1989. On October 11, 1969, Fouke's regular partner was hindered, and Eric Zelms accompanied him instead. They headed north on Presidio

Avenue, and after passing Washington Street, they received the dispatch about the NMA. At this point, they were around 0.6 mile or less than two minutes from the crime scene.[74] Fouke turned left at the intersection, and as he was driving west on Jackson Street, he noticed a Caucasian walking on the north side of the road, closer to Zelms who sat on the passenger's seat. In 2004, Fouke explained that he slowed the vehicle as they approached him, and chillingly the man looked right at them when the headlights illuminated him.[75] In 1989, he said, "Since we were looking for a Negro Male Adult we proceeded on Jackson Street toward Arguello continuing our search. As we arrived at Arguello Street, the description of the suspect was changed to a white male adult. Believing that the suspect was possibly the one involved in the shooting, we entered the Presidio of San Francisco and conducted a search on West Pacific Avenue, the opposite side of the wall and the last direction that we observed the suspect going, we did not find the suspect."[76] In the 1969 memo, Fouke wrote that the man turned north on Maple Street toward the Presidio. Later, his account differed when he stated that the man turned left and entered a stairwell leading to the door of 3712 Jackson Street.[77]

There are also other contradictions such as when he said that before he searched the Presidio, he met Pelissetti near the corner of Cherry and Washington: "He stopped us and said that he was looking for the white male that had just gone down the street. There was a little conversation about what the initial description was, and he said, 'No, he was a white male'."[78] This conversation is in conflict with his 1969 memo and also his 1989 interview that both state that the revision was broadcast. It is likewise unlikely that Pelissetti went up Jackson Street before Fouke, which is indicated by their later statements, as it would imply that Zodiac hid somewhere and reappeared when Fouke drove down the street. Additionally, this is inconsistent with the general timeline. One's recollection of an event is almost always more precise and less prone to distortion immediately after the event; thus, the most likely scenario is that Fouke was first on Jackson Street and saw the Zodiac within minutes of leaving the cab. Fouke then chose not to turn left to the crime scene for some reason. Instead, he continued to Arguello. He received a broadcast about the changed description at around this time. The

Zodiac then disappeared. Pelissetti then started pursuing the killer. The Zodiac was unbelievably lucky. On any normal day, he would have been taken into custody or died in a shoot-out. Just about everything went wrong that evening.

Thursday, November 13

A few days after his lengthy letters to the Chronicle, Zodiac might have realized that his actions would have serious consequences if he were caught. It was reported widely that Captain Lee declared him *legally sane*. If a jury reached the same conclusion, he could be sent to San Quentin's notorious gas chamber. "Zodiac Legally Sane,"[79] read the Chronicle's headline. In the related article, the 340 cipher was printed in full on page two, and Lee affirmed that it was only a matter of time before the Zodiac would be arrested. "Our knowledge of this man is increasing ... I am confident we will get him,"[80] Lee said. Lee held the cards close to him when asked about which investigate steps were being taken to catch the Zodiac. It was revealed, however, that they were actively visiting stores to find the specific one where Zodiac had bought the greeting card. Hopefully, "some clerk will recall selling such a card and be able to give the name, or a good description, of the person who purchased it."[81]

Friday, November 21

In a state of violent mental agitation, David O. Martin was holding a handsaw against his daughter's throat. As a bullet pierced his shoulder, blasting him into eternity, he yelled, "I'm Zodiac, that's me."[82] Before dying, he managed to say, "I'm through. Thank you, officer."[83] Then he died. "We had to investigate because he called it out, but there is absolutely no connection,"[84] a police spokesperson said.

Saturday, December 20

Deranged copycats had concocted Zodiac letters in November. However, the real killer included a portion of Stine's shirt with a letter he posted to Melvin Belli on December 20.[85] Zodiac never returned all portions of Stine's shirt. The last part was his trophy. The date, December 20, indicates that the Zodiac commemorated the shooting and killing of David Faraday and Betty Lou Jensen. The envelope was postmarked in San Francisco. Six Thomas Jefferson stamps covered the right top corner of the envelope. A forensic document examiner from the FBI noted that the printing on the envelope and letter was not written as freely as previously. However, it was indicated that "all the threatening letters in this case may have been prepared by one person."[86]

The letter read as follows:

Dear Melvin

This is the zodiac speaking I
wish you a happy Christmass.
The one thing I ask of you is
this, please help me. I cannot
reach out for help because of
this thing in me wont let me.
I am finding it extreamly dificult to hold it in check I am
afraid I will loose control
again and take my nineth +
posibly tenth victom. Please
help me I am drownding. At
the moment the children are
safe from the bomb because
it is so massive to dig in +
the triger mech requires much work
to get it adjusted just right. But
if I hold bacK too long from
no nine I will loose ~~complet~~ all
controol of my self + set the
bomb up. Please help me I can
not remain in control for much
longer.
⊕

On the back of the envelope, Zodiac had written a message:

Mery Xmass +
New Year

Observations

In his crimes and letters, the Zodiac established himself as a remorseless killer and a liar who was frequently manipulative. In addition, he had proven to be immature and conscious of how his public image of notoriety was portrayed in the news. In this light, this latest letter should be read.

Notice how the Zodiac asked Belli to "help" him, just like the imposter Sam had on the Jim Dunbar show. Sam was clearly a mental case, and Zodiac was clearly inspired by him. If we contemplate the Zodiac's twisted nature, it seems reasonable that the Belli letter is an example of his twisted humor and irony, ostensibly mocking the imposter, Sam. Nevertheless, Belli eventually issued an appeal which was broadcast widely and did obviously not escape the Zodiac's attention. Zodiac never replied proving that he was malingering in the letter. Belli said:

> Please write to me in care of the Chronicle and tell me how I may help. If you want to talk to me in person. I will meet you anywhere at any time you designate. If you want to meet with me alone, I will come alone. If you want me to bring along a priest or a psychiatrist or a reporter to talk with, I will do so. I will follow your instructions to the letter. You say you are losing control and may kill again. Do not make things worse. Let me help you now.[87]

We must also consider that this psychiatric letter was written just after Lee's statements about the Zodiac being legally sane. Maybe the Zodiac was paranoid that the evidence would eventually lead to his arrest and maybe he feared the gas chamber.

What can be learned about the Zodiac from this letter? Zodiac's effort to portray insanity is absurd and appears to be inspired by horror movies, which of course is compatible with his argued affection for movies. This letter is not written by an individual who has been exposed to any degree of literature in the field of mental health nor law. It is clearly a layman's attempt. Even if this was a sincere admission, he had nonetheless demonstrated an awareness of right and wrong, which is the essential element in an insanity defense, and he would still - most likely – receive a capital punishment if caught and convicted.

APPENDIX D

Figure 1
The cab was initially observed from this perspective by the witnesses.
Figure 2
Dave Toschi standing next to Paul Stine's cab.
Figure 3
Pieces of Paul Stine's shirt, which the Zodiac cut off and later returned.
Figure 4
Wanted poster released on October 13, 1969.
Figure 5
Second wanted poster released on October 18, 1969.
Figure 6
A realistic rendering of the composite drawing.
Figure 7
Zodiac letter. Received October 14, 1969.
The San Francisco Chronicle.
Figure 8
Zodiac greeting card and 340 cipher. Received November 10, 1969.
The San Francisco Chronicle.
Figure 9
Zodiac letter. Received November 10, 1969.
The San Francisco Chronicle.
Figure 10
Zodiac letter. Mailed December 20, 1969.
Melvin Belli.
Figure 11
Envelopes.

Figure 1

Figure 2

Figure 3

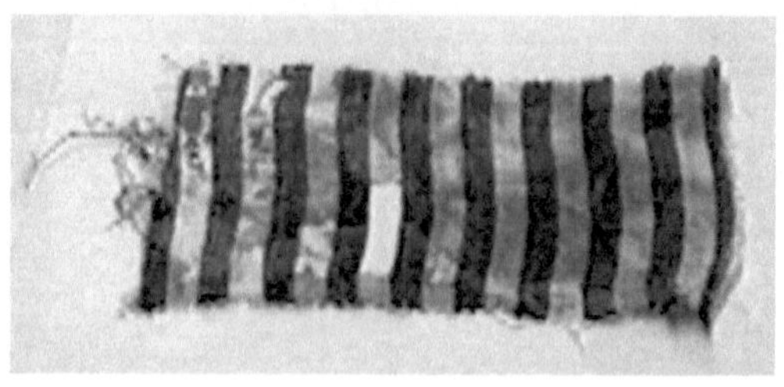

Figure 4

WANTED

SAN FRANCISCO POLICE DEPARTMENT

NO. 87-69 OCTOBER 13, 1969

<u>WANTED FOR MURDER AND ROBBERIES OF CAB DRIVERS</u>

<u>SUSPECT:</u> WMA, 25-30 Years, 5'8" to 5'9"
Reddish Brown Hair - Crew Cut,
Heavy Rim Glasses,
Navy Blue or Black Jacket

<u>M.O.:</u> Suspect takes cab in downtown area at 9:30 P.M. and sits in front seat with driver. Tells driver destination is Washington and Laurel area or area near Park or Presidio. Upon reaching destination, suspect orders driver to continue on at gun-point into or near Park where he perpetrates robbery.
In one case victim was shot in head at contact. Victim's wallet and I.D. in the name of Paul L. Stine and Taxi Cab keys missing.

<u>WEAPON:</u> 9 MM Automatic

Suspect's latent lifts available for comparison.
Refer Homicide Case No. 696314
Robbery Cases No. 692895 and 687697

<u>ANY INFORMATION:</u>
Inspectors Armstrong/Toschi
Homicide Detail

THOMAS J. CAHILL
CHIEF OF POLICE

Figure 5

WANTED

SAN FRANCISCO POLICE DEPARTMENT

NO. 90-69 | WANTED FOR MURDER | OCTOBER 18, 1969

ORIGINAL DRAWING

AMENDED DRAWING

Supplementing our Bulletin 87-69 of October 13, 1969. Additional information has developed the above amended drawing of murder suspect known as "ZODIAC".

WMA, 35-45 Years, approximately 5'8", Heavy Build, Short Brown Hair, possibly with Red Tint, Wears Classes. Armed with 9 MM Automatic.

Available for comparison: Slugs, Casings, Latents, Handwriting.

ANY INFORMATION:
Inspectors Armstrong & Toschi
Homicide Detail
CASE NO. 696314

THOMAS J. CAHILL
CHIEF OF POLICE

Figure 6

Figure 7

This is the Zodiac speaking.
I am the murderer of the
taxi driver over by
Washington St & Maple St last
night, to prove this here is
a blood stained piece of his
shirt. I am the same man
who did in the people in the
north bay area.
The S.F. Police could have caught
me last night if they had
searched the park properly
in stead of holding road races
with their motorciles seeing who
could make the most noise. The
car drivers should have just
parked their cars & sat there
quietly waiting for me to come
out of cover.
School children make nice targets, I think I shall wipe out
a school bus some morning. Just
shoot out the front tire & then
pick off the kiddies as they come
bouncing out.

Figure 8

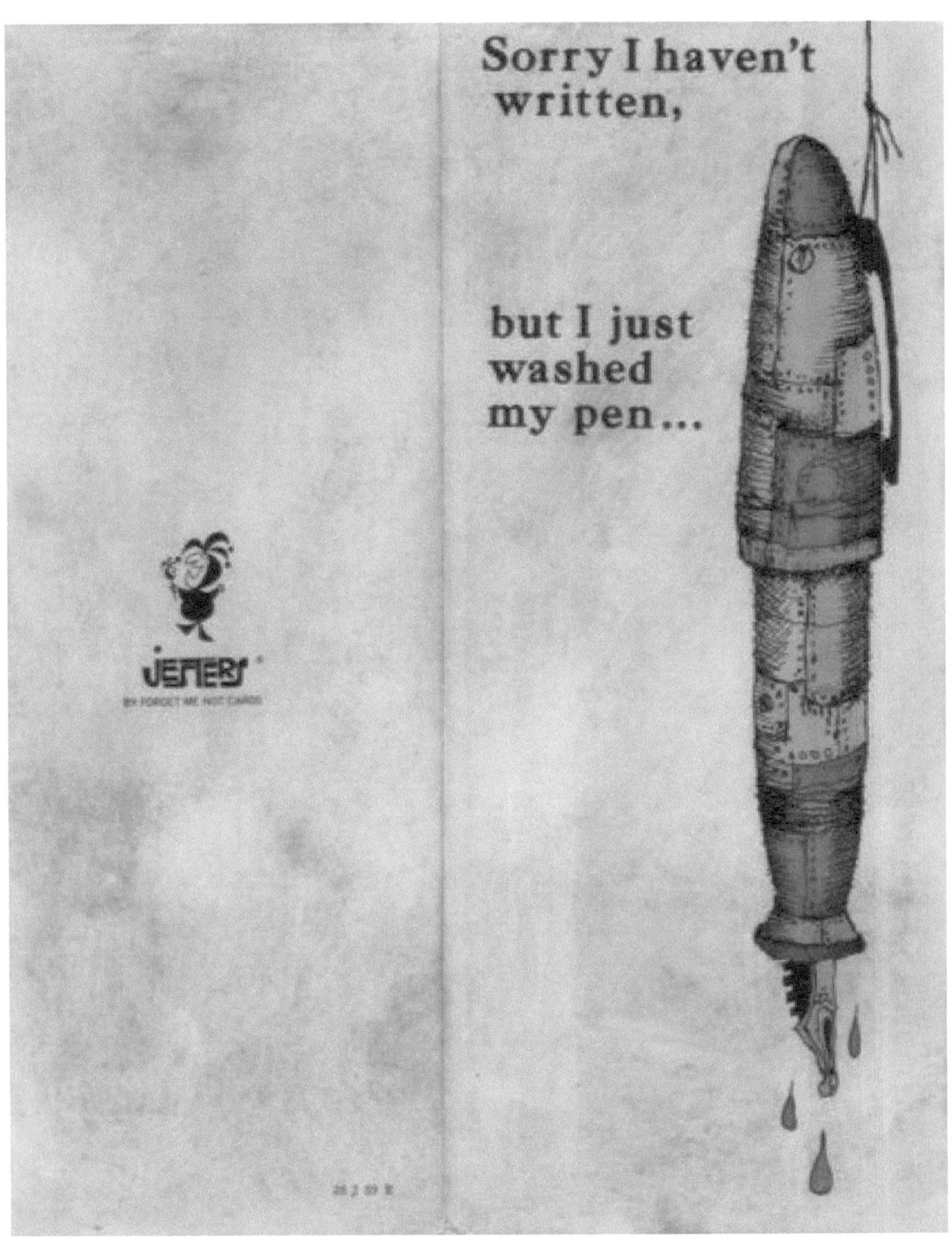

This is the Zodiac speaking
I though you would nead a
good laugh before you
hear the bad news
you won't get the
news for a while yet.
PS could you print
this new cipher
in your frunt page?
I get awfully lonely
when I am ignored,
So lonely I could
do my **Thing**!!!!!!!

and i
Can't
do a
thing
with
it!

Des July Aug
Sept Oct = 7

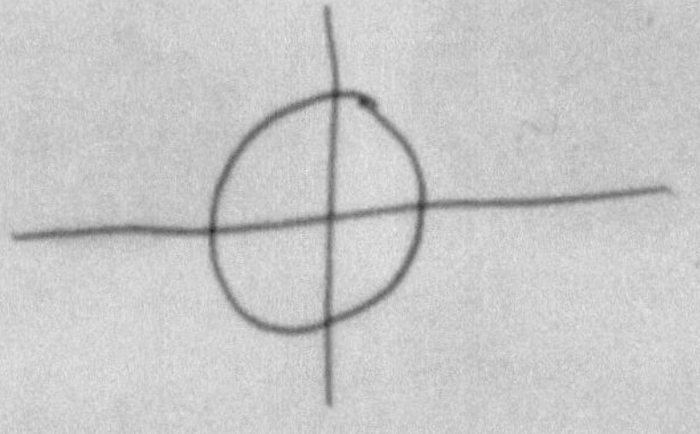

Figure 9

1/6

This is the zodiac speaking
up to the end of Oct I have
killed 7 people. I have grown
rather angry with the police
for their telling lies about me.
So I shall change the way the
collecting of slaves. I shall
no longer announce to anyone.
when I comitt my murders,
they shall look like routine
robberies, killings of anger, +
a few fake accidents, etc.

The police shall never catch me,
because I have been too clever
for them.

1 I look like the description
passed out only when I do
my thing, the rest of the time
I look entirle different. I
shall not tell you what my
descise consists of when I kill

2 As of yet I have left no
finger-prints behind me contrary
to what the police say

2/6

in my killings I wear transparent finger tip guards. All it
is is 2 coats of airplane cement
coated on my finger tips - quite
unnoticible + very efective.
3 my killing tools have been bought
en through the mail order outfits before the ban went into
efect. except one & it was
bought out of the state.
So as you see the police don't
have much to work on. If you
wonder why I was wipeing the
cab down I was leaving fake clews
for the police to run all over town
with, as one might say, I gave
the cops som bussy work to do to
keep them happy. I enjoy needling
the blue pigs. Hey blue pig I
was in the park - you were useing
fire tracks to mask the sound
of your cruzeing prowl cars. The
dogs never come with in 2
blocks of me + they were to
the west + there was only 2

3/6

groups of parking about 10 min apart then the motor cicles went by about 150 ft away going from South to north west.

ps. 2 cops pulled a goof abot 3 min after I left the cab. I was walking down the hill to the park when this cop car pulled up + one of them called me over + asked if I saw any one acting supicisous or strange in the last 5 to 10 min + I said yes there was this man who was runnig by waveing a gun + the cops peeled rubber + went around the corner as I directed them + I dissapeared into the park abbott + a half away never to be seen again.

Must Print in Paper

Hey pig doesnt it rile you up to have you noze rubed in your booboos?

If you cops think I'm going to take on a bus the way I stated I was, you deserve to have holes in your heads.

4/6

Take one bag of ammonium nitrate fertlizer + 1gal of stove oil + dump a few bags of gravel on top + then set the shit off + will positivily ventalate any thing that should be in the way of the Blast.

The death machiene is allready made. I would have sent you pictures but you would be nasty enough to trace them back to developer + then to me, so I shall describe my masterpiece to you. The nice part of it is all the parts can be bought on the open market with no quest ions asked.

1 bat. pow clock - will run for aprox 1 year
1 photoelectric switch
2 copper leaf springs
2 6V car bat
1 flash light bulb + reflector
1 mirror
2 18" cardboard tubes black with shoe polish in side + oute

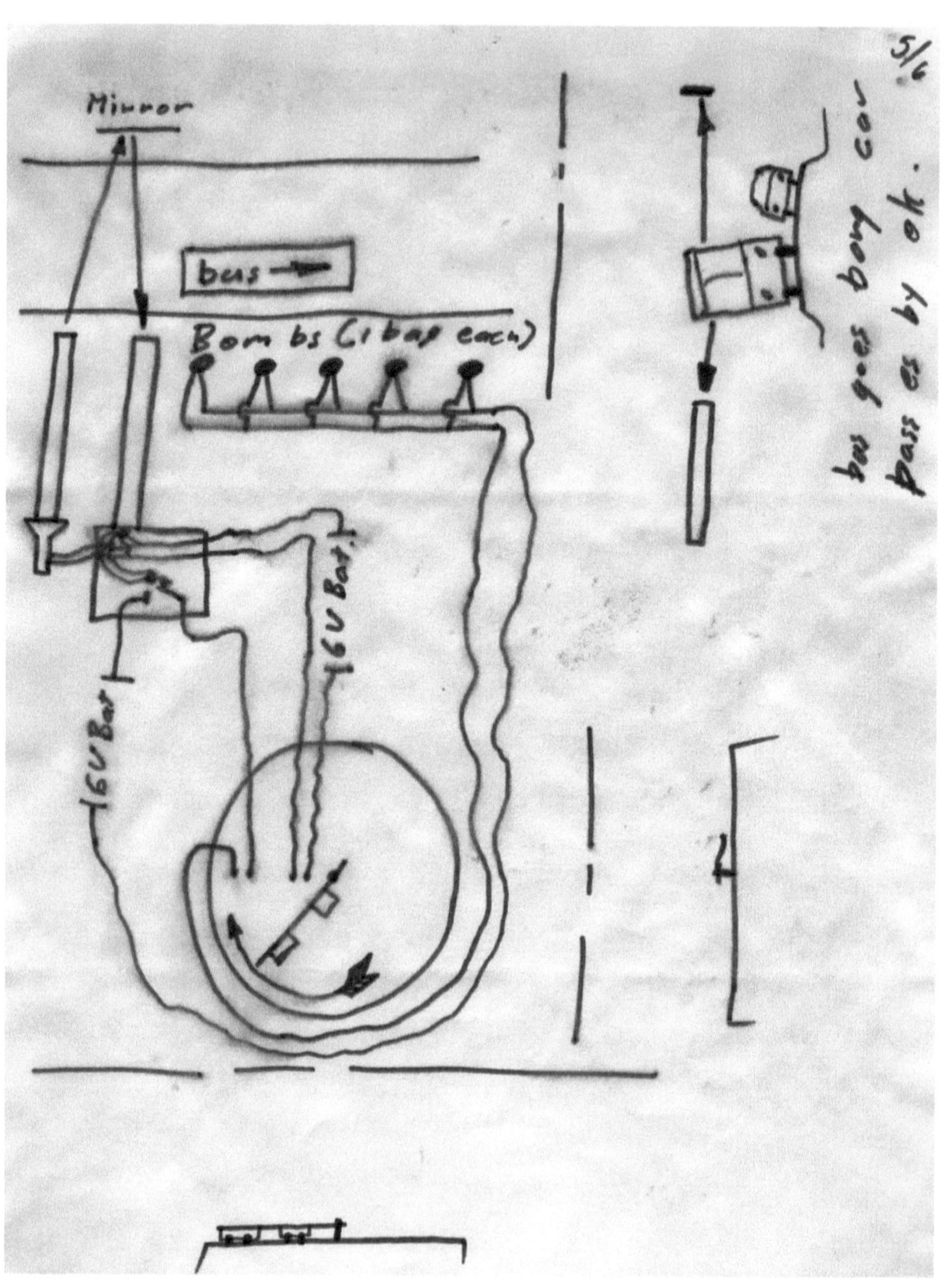
Mirror
bus
Bombs (1 bag each)
6V Bat
6V Bat
bus goes bomb car
passes by ok.
5/6

4/6

the system checks out from
one end to the other in my
tests. What you do not know
is whether the death machine
is at the sight or whether
it is being stored in my
basement for future use.
I think you do not have the
man power to stop this one
by continually searching the
road sides looking for this
thing. & it wont do to re route
& re schedule the busses bec
ause the bomb can be adapted
to new conditions.
Have fun!! By the way
it could be rather messy
if you try to bluff me.

PS. Be shure to
print the part I
marked out on
page 3 or I shall
do my thing ⊕

To prove that I am the Zodiac, Ask the Vallejo cop about my electric gun sight which I used to start my collecting of slaves.

Figure 10

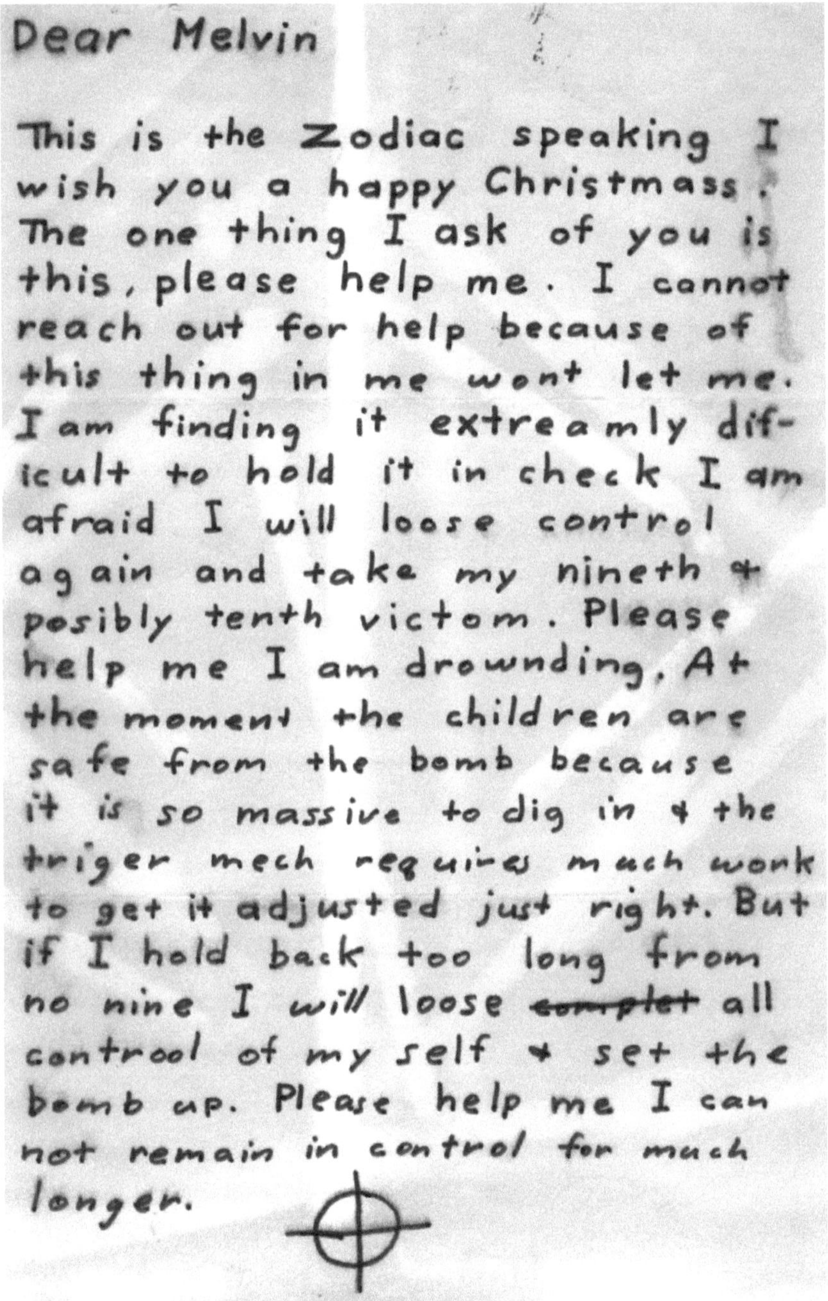

Dear Melvin

This is the Zodiac speaking I
wish you a happy Christmass.
The one thing I ask of you is
this, please help me. I cannot
reach out for help because of
this thing in me wont let me.
I am finding it extreamly dificult to hold it in check I am
afraid I will loose control
again and take my nineth &
posibly tenth victom. Please
help me I am drownding. At
the moment the children are
safe from the bomb because
it is so massive to dig in & the
triger mech requires much work
to get it adjusted just right. But
if I hold back too long from
no nine I will loose ~~complet~~ all
controol of my self & set the
bomb up. Please help me I can
not remain in control for much
longer.

Figure 11

Received on October 14.

The greeting card envelope, received on November 10.

Please Rush to Editor

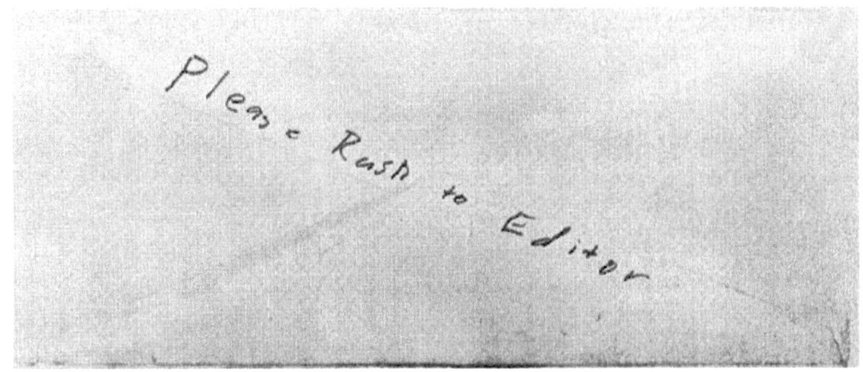

The six-page letter envelope, received on November 10.

S.F. CHRONICLE
San Fran Calif
Please Rush to Editor
SAN FRANCISCO
NOV 9 PM 1969
CA

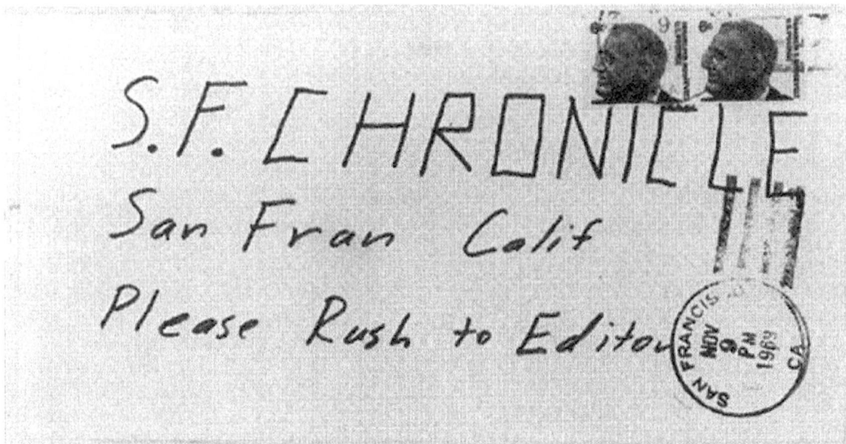

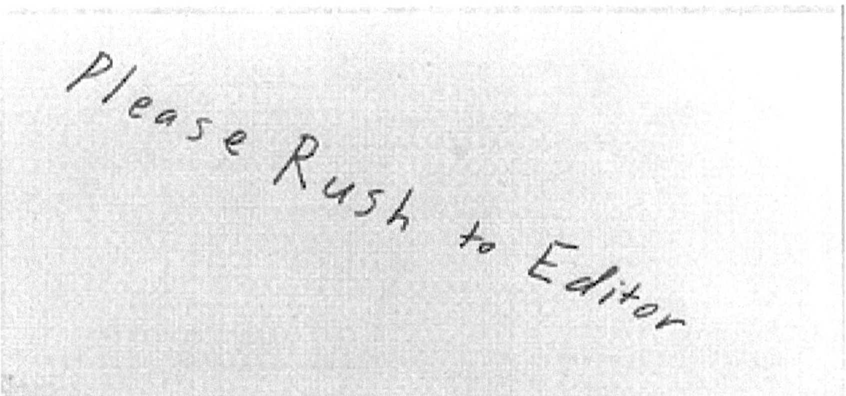

Please Rush to Editor

The Melvin Belli envelope.

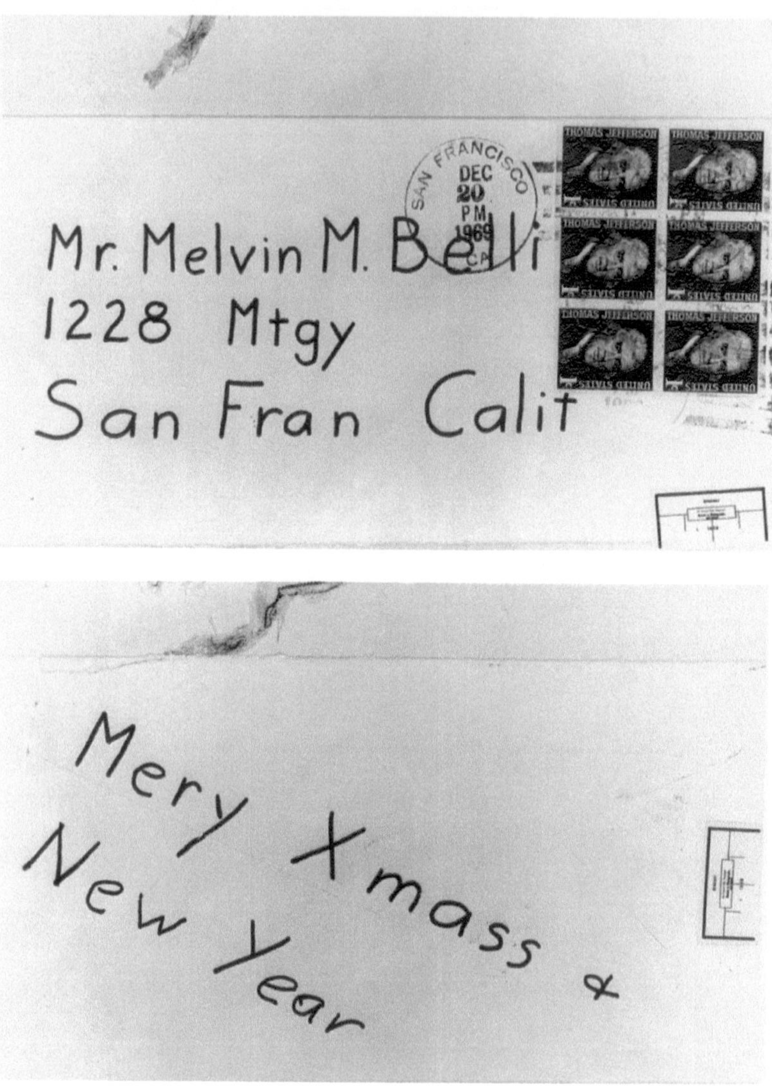

ENDNOTES D

[1] "Dare by Brother of Slain Man," San Francisco Chronicle, October 23, 1969.
[2] California Department of Justice/Division of Law Enforcement/Bureau of Investigation, Zodiac Homicides, for Law Enforcement Use Only, 6.
[3] San Francisco Crime Report, Case Number 696314, 1.
[4] California Department of Justice/Division of Law Enforcement/Bureau of Investigation, Zodiac Homicides, for Law Enforcement Use Only, 6.
[5] "MYSTERYQUEST: Paul Holes and The Murder of Paul Stine," http://zodiackillerfacts.com/main/mysteryquest-paul-holes-and-the-murder-of-paul-stine (retrieved May 2016).
[6] San Francisco Crime Report, Case Number 696314, 1.
[7] Ibid.
[8] "Duffy Jennings, 40 years of Zodiac - The cold case that haunts Dave Toschi," http://www.sfgate.com/cgi-bin/blogs/djennings/detail??blogid=162&entry_id=48821 (retrieved April 2011).
[9] Ibid.
[10] California Department of Justice/Division of Law Enforcement/Bureau of Investigation, Zodiac Homicides, for Law Enforcement Use Only, 6.
[11] Freedom of Information and Privacy Acts, Subject: Zodiac Killer, File Number: 9-HQ-49911, Section 1, Federal Bureau of Investigation, 86.
[12] Ibid, 81.
[13] Ibid.
[14] Ibid.
[15] Jennings, Duffy. Email to Søren Roest Korsgaard. August 4, 2010.
[16] A&E Cold Case Files, The Zodiac Killer, episode 51.
[17] "Duffy Jennings, 40 years of Zodiac - The cold case that haunts Dave Toschi," http://www.sfgate.com/cgi-bin/blogs/djennings/detail??blogid=162&entry_id=48821 (retrieved April 2011).
[18] San Francisco Crime Report, Case Number 696314, 2.
[19] "The Witnesses," www.zodiackillersite.com/viewtopic.php?f=30&t=402 (retrieved January 2017).
[20] Ibid.
[21] Ibid.
[22] Ibid.
[23] "Robbery Victim, Cabbie Slain in Presidio Hts," San Francisco Chronicle, October 12, 1969, 1.
[24] Freedom of Information and Privacy Acts, Subject: Zodiac Killer, File Number: 9-HQ-49911, Section 1, Federal Bureau of Investigation, 56.
[25] "The Boastful 'Slayer,'" San Francisco Chronicle, October 15, 1969, 1.
[26] "Zodiac Killer Link Affirmed," the Napa Register, October 16, 1969, 1A.
[27] Ibid.

[28] "THE FINGERPRINTS OF A KILLER," https://www.zodiacciphers.com/zodiac-news/the-fingerprints-of-a-killer#comments (retrieved June 2020).
[29] https://www.newspapers.com/newspage/12705208/ (The Daily Reporter, October 21, 1969, 17).
[30] Freedom of Information and Privacy Acts, Subject: Zodiac Killer, File Number: 9-HQ-49911, Section 5, Federal Bureau of Investigation, 43.
[31] "Kids Next, 'Zodiac Killer' Warns," Press-Telegram, Long Beach, California, October 17, 1969, 1.
[32] "Zodiac Killer Wants A Bus," The Daily Times-News Burlington, N.C., October 17, 1969, 1.
[33] "Zodiac Killer Wants to Add School Bus 'Kiddies' to List," Ironwood Daily Globe, October 17, 1969, 5.
[34] "'Zodiac' To Stalk School Bus?" Tri-City Herald, October 17, 1969.
[35] "Zodiac Portrait of a killer," San Francisco Chronicle, October 18, 1969.
[36] Ibid.
[37] Ibid.
[38] Ibid.
[39] Ibid.
[40] http://www.forensicartist.com/ (retrieved May 2015).
[41] Crow, William. Email to Søren Roest Korsgaard. September 24, 2010.
[42] "Zodiac's Graph: Impotent, Shrewd, Paranoid," San Francisco Examiner, October 21, 1969, 16.
[43] Ibid.
[44] Ibid.
[45] Ibid.
[46] Ibid.
[47] Ibid.
[48] Ibid.
[49] Ibid.
[50] "Zodiac Calls Belli on TV Show," Desert Sun, October 22, 1969.
[51] Department of Justice, Bureau of Criminal Investigation and Investigation Report, Case Number 1-15-311-F9-5861, 29.
[52] "'Zodiac' Again Phones Belli," Lodi News-Sentinel, October 23, 1969, 1.
[53] "Melvin Belli & The Zodiac 'Birthday" Call,'" zodiackillerfacts.com/myths-legends/melvin-belli-the-zodiac-birthday-call (retrieved April 2020).
[54] "Zodiac Note Warns of Future Murders," Bridgeport Post, November 12, 1969, 15.
[55] Freedom of Information and Privacy Acts, Subject: Zodiac Killer, File Number: 9-HQ-49911, Section 2, Federal Bureau of Investigation, 50.
[56] "Another Grim Message: 'I've killed Seven' The Zodiac Claims," San Francisco Chronicle, November 12, 1969.
[57] Ibid.

[58] "2015 Cryptologic History Symposium: A Century of Cryptology. The Zodiac Ciphers - What Do We Know, and When Do We Stop Trying To Solve Them?" David Oranchak.
[59] "Zodiac Revisited," http://www.timesheraldonline.com/article/ZZ/20070222/NEWS/702229824
[60] Leslie H. Martinson, Director, Batman, 1966.
[61] "Suspects Held in Huston Robbery," Bonham Daily Favorite, April 3, 1961, 1.
[62] Ibid.
[63] "'Zodiac' Killer' Notes May Lead to His Capture," Long Beach Independent, October 21, 1969, 2.
[64] "Another Grim Message: 'I've killed Seven' The Zodiac Claims," San Francisco Chronicle, November 12, 1969.
[65] David Fincher, Director, Zodiac 2-Disc Director's Cut, 2008.
[66] Ibid.
[67] Jennings, Duffy. Email to Søren Roest Korsgaard. August 4, 2010.
[68] "1st Interview with Don Fouke," https://web.archive.org/web/20060504171838/http://www.mikerodelli.com/1interview.html (retrieved May 2016).
[69] "2nd Interview with Don Fouke," https://web.archive.org/web/20050313055504/http://www.mikerodelli.com/2interview.html (retrieved May 2016).
[70] David Fincher, Director, Zodiac 2-Disc Director's Cut, 2008.
[71] Ibid.
[72] Ibid.
[73] Ibid.
[74] Ibid.
[75] "1st Interview with Don Fouke," https://web.archive.org/web/20060504171838/http://www.mikerodelli.com/1interview.html (retrieved June 2016).
[76] "The Crime of the Century," https://www.youtube.com/watch?v=A7VUfXM1WuM (retrieved May 2016).
[77] David Fincher, Director, Zodiac 2-Disc Director's Cut, 2008; also see notes by movie producer for the 1989 documentary: Crimes of the Century: The Zodiac Killer.
[78] Ibid.
[79] "Zodiac Legally Sane," San Francisco Chronicle, November 13, 1969, 1.
[80] Ibid.
[81] Ibid.
[82] "Zodiac Claim False in S.F," Lodi News-Sentinel, November 22, 1969, 4.
[83] Ibid.
[84] Ibid.
[85] Freedom of Information and Privacy Acts, Subject: Zodiac Killer, File Number: 9-HQ-49911, Section 3, Federal Bureau of Investigation, 66.

[86] Ibid, 70.
[87] "Noted lawyer answers Zodiac killer's plea," Chronicle-Telegram Elyria, December 29, 1969, 28. Belli's request for help was featured in multiple newspapers.

CHAPTER 5

THE KIDNAPPING

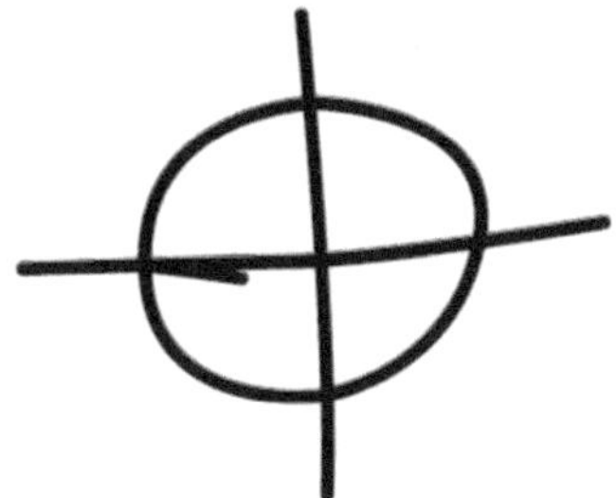

Kathleen Johns and her infant daughter were apparently kidnapped and their car torched in late March 1970. Several months passed by and the Zodiac took credit. But who was responsible? The common difficulties in attaining a smog-free view of any incident related to the Zodiac case is in this specific occurrence intensified by contradictory police reports and several noteworthy inconsistencies. For clarity, we summarize the points of consensus as per the police reports on the first pages; afterwards, we analyze the case and introduce additional information.

Monday, March 23, 1970

In the early morning hours, Kathleen Johns, age 22, was in the Patterson Police Department trying to give a statement to Sergeant Charles McNatt who noted that she was "hysterical."[1] While the sergeant asked her a series of questions, she started screaming and "became hysterical again."[2] To enlighten the puzzled sergeant she pointed to a wanted poster on the wall. She had not seen it before. She recognized the person depicted as her kidnapper. Johns had pointed toward the Zodiac's wanted poster!

On Sunday, March 22, the previous night, a car followed her on Highway 132. Her attention had been drawn to the car when the driver started blinking the lights to get her to pull over. She believed something was wrong with her car. She passed under the Interstate-5 overpass and pulled over just east of South Bird Road, county of Stanislaus. From her vantage point, she could see a gas station in the distance, a Richfield on Chrisman Road. Roughly two miles further, *132* merges with Interstate-580, which leads to the Bay Area. The other car, a late model and light tan in color, stopped and backed up.[3] The man was a Caucasian, approximately 30 years old, 5'9", 160 pounds, dark hair, and wearing black-rimmed plastic glasses. He had on a dark ski jacket and dark-blue, bell-bottomed pants.[4] He approached Johns to tell her that one of the wheels of her car was "wobbling"[5] and that he would take care of the problem. He grabbed a tire wrench in his car and pretended to tighten the lug bolts, and then he got into his car. When Johns started to drive the wheel "came off."[6] The man returned and told her that he would drive her to a service station to get it repaired. Johns, holding her baby, entered his car, and he pressed down the accelerator. He pulled into the Richfield only to discover that it had been closed, and he continued driving. The route hereafter was not established, but we know that they entered the city of Tracy, located around 15 minutes from the gas station. As they drove around, she asked him about other service stations, each time he claimed that it was not the right one.[7] The bizarre excursion lasted 1-1.5 hours.

Johns asked him where he worked, and he cryptically answered that he would work for "two months and then just drive around mostly at nights."[8] She also sarcastically asked him if he always went around helping people. "By the time I get through with them, they won't need my help,"[9] he replied. During the drive, she became terrified of the man. Sooner or later, when they came to a stop sign, Johns saw her chance and got away, holding her daughter. She subsequently stopped a vehicle and got the occupants to transport her to the Patterson Police Department.[10] When the cops found her car, its interior was "completely burned."[11] One of the hubcaps of her car had fallen off. Subsequently, an expert applied fine powders to it and latent fingerprints became visible. The keys to her car were never found.

Analysis

As indicated, many questions remain unanswered, primarily because the police did not regard Kathleen Johns as credible. Their lack of faith in her is reflected in the police reports that are contradictory, superficial, and fail to address important issues and matters. On the other end of the spectrum is the investigation of the Lake Berryessa crime. Detectives in that case documented almost every aspect of the crime, such as getting as much information as possible about the Zodiac's voice, clothes, pistol, and knife. Johns had spent lots of time with the man, and she had plenty of opportunities to observe him and give a detailed description of his voice, hair, eyes, hands, etc. Instead, it is stated in the police report that his face reminded her of the wanted poster.[12] Paul Avery interviewed her shortly after the incident and to him she provided unique details about his face.[13] The officers should also have accounted for everything she observed inside his car and had her attempt to identify the car model and make. In this instance, too, they displayed carelessness and only typed that it was a "late model vehicle, light tan in color."[14] If they had considered Johns to be credible, they would probably have summoned a vehicle expert or even a mechanic to assist her in identifying the car model and make. As we shall see, Johns provided numerous details about what she saw in the car to Avery.

In the police reports, it is typed that the *left rear* wheel came off and this subterfuge served as the basis for the kidnapping. This was apparently what Johns had said. Incongruously, it is also typed that this wheel was *in place* when her car was found but the hubcap was missing and later found. On closer inspection, the *right rear* wheel had been secured with one "nearly tight" lug bolt and another "loose"[15] one. Obviously, Johns knew that her car would continue with two loose lug bolts and without the hubcap. One is tempted to draw the conclusion that the police even failed to review their own reports since this and other discrepancies were not discussed or resolved.

One of the police reports plainly states that after the escape the man "did not leave the vehicle nor did he chase her."[16] In interviews after the event, Johns, on the other hand, has consistently said that he did chase her. This statement appears as far back as November 1970 in an article by Avery.[17]

In Deputy Lovett's report it is stated that "the suspect was quite friendly with her, did not make any advances towards her, or threats toward her, and when asked if he was going to stop he would merely elude the question and start talking about something else. She became quite frightened, feeling that possibly the suspect intended to do some physical injury to her."[18] Lovett did not address what exactly changed her attitude toward the man. Johns has always maintained that he was "threatening to kill her"[19] and throw the baby out of the window. To Avery, she said that she had gratefully accepted his offer because he "seemed so nice."[20] But suddenly his character changed, and he said, "You know I'm going to kill you," and "You know you're going to die." Johns described how it affected her: "I was terrified," and "I knew ... I knew he meant it. He said it over and over in a calm, quiet voice and you could feel he meant every word. I just sat there waiting for it to happen."[21]

Some researchers have opined that Johns exaggerated certain details of the incident or that it was a hoax. This position is supported by the discrepancies and other details, e.g. why would the man pull into the Richfield if he did not want to help her; hence, the case does not appear to carry the usual constituents associated with a kidnapping. On the contrary, that Johns divulged this detail suggests that she was telling the truth.

The exact location she escaped at is unknown, but there are some indications that it occurred near Highway 132. One critic in particular considers this to be a peculiarity since *132* ceased shortly after where she had parked. It may thus be inferred that the kidnapper and Johns returned to the general area of her car.[22] Also, skeptical eyes have pointed out that it seems to be too much of a coincidence that those who dropped her off at Patterson Police Department did not stick around to give a statement. They remain unidentified.[23]

While the inconsistencies, discussed in this chapter, may be the result of deception, they may, on the contrary, be the product of trauma. We should recall that Sergeant McNatt typed that Johns was "hysterical." She could have been incapable of providing a consistent account and an overview of the kidnapping due to mental stress and trauma. Johns had been with her infant daughter, and she was also several months pregnant. During pregnancy, the hormones, estrogen and progesterone, rise and affect different neurotransmitters and cause moodiness. If she had been kidnapped, these biochemical changes would almost assuredly have affected her. Additionally, her memory did not likely benefit from pregnancy. A recent, major study showed that pregnancy affects memory. One of the scientists involved in the study, said, "Pregnant women are significantly impaired on some, but not all, measures of memory."[24]

Munchausen syndrome, which is a psychological disorder wherein those affected simulate disease, illness or psychological trauma to draw attention or sympathy, can probably be excluded as (1) she did not display any attention seeking behavior, (2) she never wrote a book to gain sympathy or cash in on the event, (3) and she went into hiding after the incident.

If Johns invented her story and torched her own car, she must have been motived by something. However, a financial incentive or any other has never been identified. If she orchestrated the event, she would almost assuredly have underlined to the officers that her abductor wanted to kill her, it certainly was a kidnapping, and so on.

While the evidence and circumstances of the incident do not support the deception hypothesis, it is a whole different matter whether or not the Zodiac was responsible. Nevertheless, the media immediately documented a Zodiac-connection: "Woman Says Zodiac Killer Captured Her,"[25] "Rode With Zodiac, Woman Claims."[26] Media coverage prompted two individuals, Frederick Beaman and William Horton, to contact the authorities. A driver in a white 1959 Buick had tried to flag them down not far from where Johns had pulled over.

The Avery Interview

A few months after the incident, Paul Avery tracked down Kathleen Johns. Unlike the superficial police reports, Avery's article contains a wealth of information. Johns told Avery that the man was wearing "a dark blue nylon windbreaker-style jacket over

dark blue or black woolen bell-bottom pants."[27] His shoes were "'spit-shined,' the high-gloss black reflecting the interior light of the car."[28] He had on a pair of "black thick-rimmed glasses – held tightly on his head by a thin band of elastic."[29] His voice was monotonous and without an accent. He drove "a late-model American make: a light-colored two-door with black bucket seats between which was a sporty console-style automatic transmission gear shift. At the front end of the console was an ashtray, in which, on the right-hand side, was a built-in cigarette lighter."[30] The license plates were from California. The interior of the car was messy with clothes and papers "scattered on the dash-board and on both the front and back seats. Mostly men's clothing, but also some smaller, patterned tee-shirts such as a child of 8 to 12 years might wear."[31] She also saw that on the dashboard "were a couple of colored plastic scouring pads, and also a black, rubber-grip flashlight."[32] In contrast to the police report, she emphatically stated that the man had chased her with a flashlight in his hand.
One might object that kidnapping and arson do not pertain to the category of Zodiac crimes, but keep in mind that he changed his methods often and it is not possible to prognosticate if his demons drove him to commit the latter two crimes. For example, if we start by considering the initial two offences (December 20 and July 4), we would perhaps be able to predict that he would target a couple the next time, but we would be less likely to predict that he would use a costume, rope, and a knife. The final killing of Stine is different in almost all aspects than his previous crimes.

The 1998 Interview

On January 1, 1998, Johnny Smith and Howard Davis met with Johns and interviewed her about her possible encounter with the Zodiac.[33] Four years later she died of cardiac arrest. We will now go through the interview chronologically.
According to Johns, she was employed at the Sonoma State Hospital and lived in San Bernardino. She worked in the psychiatric department.[34] On March 22, 1970, she was going to visit her mother.[35] A car behind her began flashing the lights. He pursued her for roughly 10-15 minutes, and he first stopped flashing the lights when she pulled over. She recalled that the driver turned the lights on and off rather than turning on the

headlamp. She felt uncomfortable stopping on a dark road, so she waited. She finally stopped to find out what the issue was.[36] She felt there could have been "anything"[37] wrong with her car. His car was big and a lot newer than hers. He was "military looking"[38] and taller than her (she was 5'9"). Johns further described him as big, not fat, but rather big boned, and he was wearing glasses and had no facial hair. She also stated that his voice was "very monotone"[39] and without an accent.

During the interview, Johns shared a theory of her own that the man had probably "no idea" she had a sleeping baby in her car, and that she was several months pregnant, and maybe that surprised him.[40]

Johns got into his car and they drove off. Roughly 10 minutes passed before he started talking. He pulled to the side and told her, "You know you going to die, you know I am going to kill you."[41] He also threatened to "throw that baby out."[42] Johns added, "He didn't look like he was really there."[43] She was asked if he repeated the threats many times: "Oh yeah, many times in this monotone, no feeling, no looking at me, driving on,"[44] Johns replied.

She looked around in his car and found it to be very messy. It contained items you normally would not have in a car, like clean pots and pans. She also noticed both adult and small children's clothes. He could have been living in his car, she said.

She assumed he was a military man because of his glasses, haircut, and shoes.[45]

Johns was of the impression that he was searching for a place mentally and that "he needed an action for a reaction."[46] He was probably "waiting for me to break,"[47] she also said.

At no time did it appear that the man was lost; he "knew where he was,"[48] she said. She escaped when they came to a stop. He chased her while yelling, "Come back here!"[49] He may have used a flashlight.[50] He chased her for about two minutes until a truck driver arrived. Before leaving, the kidnapper apparently had an argument with the driver. Johns elaborated on the chase, "I could hear him behind me; he wasn't losing distance in the sound, so he was coming after me."[51] At the police station, she did not become hysterical when she saw the wanted poster. The officer spoke with someone on the phone and ordered her to follow him to a restaurant. Here he told her to wait, which she did "for hours."[52]

During the interview, she expressed dissatisfaction over the police who ignored their obvious need for supplies; "I don't know what they thought of me, but obviously not much."[53]

When she got home, she discovered much to her disbelief that her personal information had been publicized in the San Bernardino press.

Johns also disclosed that in late October 1970, she received a taunting Halloween card in her mailbox. She would later send the card to Paul Avery. The card did not upset her as it could have been authored by a large number of cranks who had seen her address in the newspaper. The inside of the card featured a skeleton and the text, "To the lady in the station wagon."[54] In October 1970, Avery, too, was mailed a Halloween card. Sherwood Morrill attributed it to the Zodiac based on handwriting analysis. Johns was shown a picture of that card; she said it looked like the card she had received, apart from one minor difference. The difference was that Avery's card had a pumpkin glued on to it (see next chapter). The whereabouts of the card sent to Johns is unknown. Shortly after the incident, someone had called her several times, but the person would hang up when she picked up the phone. The interview was concluded by her saying, "I remember him exactly the way that composite looks, I mean it's frozen in my mind."[55]

Although nearly three decades had passed between the two interviews outlined above, Johns remained overall consistent, but not in regard to some aspects mentioned the police reports. If Johns had been a pathological liar or a deranged mental patient, we would not expect her to remain consistent to such a degree. Her consistency is a good indication of veracity.

The Zodiac or Not?

As evidenced, it is problematic to determine what went down on that night in March of 1970. Everything should have been collected and addressed immediately after the incident, but was not and this has left many doors open. The evidence connecting the Zodiac to the kidnapping includes the identification, Zodiac taking credit (next chapter), the military association, his monotone voice, and using a ruse to get the victim into a vulnerable situation. Johns said he was heavy and big boned and weighing about 160 pounds. Zodiac earned similar adjectives, in spite of the fact that his weight was estimated to be 180 and 250 pounds.[***] Johns told Avery that the man's chin had "traces of pock marks such as can be caused by acne."[56] We should recall that Donald Fouke remarked that there was "something about the chin"[57] of the Zodiac. Could he have seen the same marks? The man Johns encountered appears to have been taller than the estimated height of the Zodiac (5'8" on the second wanted poster).

We will probably never know with certainty if Zodiac and Kathleen Johns had a highly unusual encounter in March 1970. This chapter has critically examined the response of the police, and it is clear that they did not live up to the standards of other cases we have covered. However, they did dust the hubcap for prints and lifted some. If these still exist somewhere, they could be examined using the latest technology and possibly be compared to the suspected Zodiac prints.

[***] In contrast to his statement to the police, Mageau is quoted by a reporter as saying that the Zodiac weighted "about 160 pounds" ("KILLER'S SOLE SURVIVOR TALKS" *Vallejo Times*, August 1969).

ENDNOTES E

[1] Patterson Police Department, Case Number 7425, 1.
[2] Ibid.
[3] Sheriff's Department, County of Stanislaus, File Number C62677, 1.
[4] Ibid.
[5] Patterson Police Department, Case Number 7425, 1.
[6] Ibid.
[7] Office of Sheriff – Coroner, County of San Joaquin, Standard Crime Report, Case Number 70-7475, 6.
[8] Ibid.
[9] Ibid.
[10] Sheriff's Department, County of Stanislaus, Follow-up Report, File Number C62677, 1.
[11] Patterson Police Department, Case Number 7425, 1.
[12] Office of Sheriff – Coroner, County of San Joaquin, Standard Crime Report, Case Number 70-7475, 6.
[13] "An Exclusive Report: New Evidence in Zodiac Killings," San Francisco Chronicle, 16 November 1970.
[14] Sheriff's Department, County of Stanislaus, Follow-up Report, File Number C62677, 1.
[15] Office of Sheriff – Coroner, County of San Joaquin, Standard Crime Report, Case Number 70-7475, 5.
[16] Ibid, 4.
[17] "An Exclusive Report: New Evidence in Zodiac Killings," San Francisco Chronicle, 16 November 1970.
[18] Sheriff's Department, County of Stanislaus, Follow-up Report, File Number C62677, 1.
[19] See for example, "Zodiac Linked to Slaying of Riverside Coed," The Daily News, November 16, 1970, 1.
[20] "An Exclusive Report: New Evidence in Zodiac Killings," San Francisco Chronicle, 16 November 1970.
[21] Ibid.
[22] Office of Sheriff – Coroner, County of San Joaquin, Standard Crime Report, Case Number 70-7475, 4.
[23] "Kathleen Johns 3-22-1970," http://www.thequesterfiles.com/kathleen_johns_--_the_quester_.html (retrieved May 2016).
[24] "Pregnancy 'does cause memory loss'," http://www.theguardian.com/science/2008/feb/03/medicalresearch.pregnancy (retrieved August 2015).
[25] "Woman Says Zodiac Killer Captured Her," McClatchy Newspapers Service, March 1970.

[26] "Rode With Zodiac, Woman Claims," San Francisco Examiner, March 23, 1970, 4.
[27] "An Exclusive Report: New Evidence in Zodiac Killings," San Francisco Chronicle, November 16, 1970.
[28] Ibid.
[29] Ibid.
[30] Ibid.
[31] Ibid.
[32] Ibid.
[33] Nelsen, Jim. Email to Søren Roest Korsgaard. September 7, 2010. "Yes, you may use quotes from the CD. All we ask is that you make reference to where the quotes came from and mention our website, www.TheZodiacMansonConnection.com."
[34] Johnny Smith and Howard Davis. Interview with Kathleen Johns. January 1, 1998. CD 1.
[35] Ibid.
[36] Ibid.
[37] Ibid.
[38] Ibid.
[39] Ibid.
[40] Ibid.
[41] Ibid.
[42] Ibid.
[43] Ibid.
[44] Ibid.
[45] Ibid.
[46] Ibid.
[47] Ibid.
[48] Ibid.
[49] Ibid.
[50] Ibid.
[51] Ibid.
[52] Ibid, CD 2.
[53] Ibid.
[54] Ibid.
[55] Ibid.
[56] "An Exclusive Report: New Evidence in Zodiac Killings," San Francisco Chronicle, 16 November 1970.
[57] "1st Interview with Don Fouke," https://web.archive.org/web/20060504171838/http://www.mikerodelli.com/1interview.html (retrieved August 2015).

CHAPTER 6

THE SECRET PAL

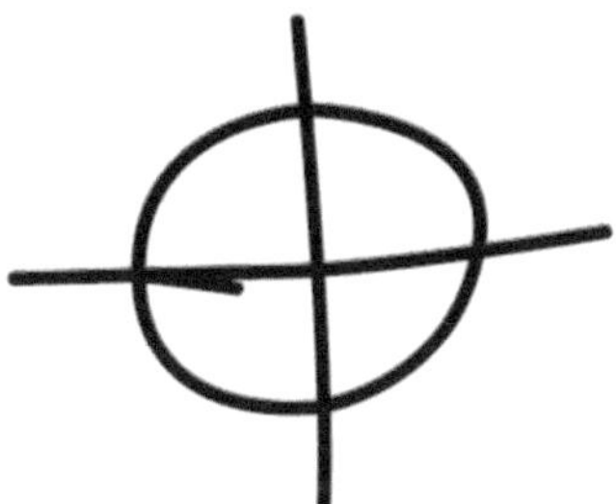

The Zodiac did not immediately begin writing to brag about his alleged failed encounter with Johns and her baby. Before he took credit, he penned three communiqués in his characteristic tone. He made more bomb threats and vaguely hinted that he had murdered more people, and cryptically he claimed that a new cipher finally revealed his name. Abruptly, he had aborted his insanity defense and continued his usual amusement of writing to the editor of the Chronicle. We ought to rewind and recall that in November, he claimed a body count of seven and a month later he cautioned that he might take his ninth and tenth victim. Now, in April, he claimed a total of 10 victims. We see manipulation without question.

Monday, April 20, 1970

On this day, the Zodiac mailed a letter to the editor of the Chronicle. The envelope bore a San Francisco postmark and contained two stamps. The letter was analyzed by FBI's handwriting expert who established that it was the Zodiac's hand printing.[1] Before mailing the letter, the Zodiac had probably seen that the Chronicle had published an article with the title, "Bizarre Zodiac Murder."[2] Robert Michael Salem had been savagely murdered in his apartment. Inspector Gus Coreris was reluctant to attribute it to the work of the Zodiac even though the coroner's deputy said it was a "Zodiac-style murder."[3] A few days later more details about the crime emerged: "Police found the bloody words, 'Satan Saves...Zodiac,' near the body of lamp designer Robert Salem in the artist's expensively-decorated, hippie-style pad. Salem, 40, had been stabbed six times and his throat had been slashed."[4] Coreris stated, "Probably the person we are after wanted us to think it was Zodiac." He then added, "But other than the word on the wall, there is absolutely nothing linking Zodiac to the murder of Mr. Salem."[5] Stanley Dean Baker later implicated himself in the murder of Salem in front of a jury. However, the killing of Robert Salem remains officially unsolved. Baker was convicted of a different murder, a murder so brutal that it even made hardened detectives vomit. During bouts of madness and mayhem, Baker had shot, mutilated, and dismembered James Schlosser. Baker then devoured Schlosser's raw human heart. Unbelievably, he was released after a few years.[6] Baker did not commit this murder alone, however. Henry Allen Stroup had assisted him, but was paroled after spending only two years in prison. Baker and Stroup are today deceased.

The envelope read:

Editor
San Fran. Chronicle
San Francisco, Calif.

"Editor" was also written on the back of the envelope.

The letter read as follows:

This is the Zodiac speaking
By the way have you cracked
the last cipher I sent you?
My name is –

[Cipher text]

I am mildly cerous as to how
much money you have on my
head now. I hope you do not
think that I was the one
who wiped out that blue
meannie with a bomb at the
cop station. Even though I talked
about killing school children with
one. It just wouldnt doo to
move in on someone elses teritory.
But there is more glory in killing
a cop than a cid because a cop
can shoot back. I have killed
ten people to date. It would
have been a lot more except
that my bus bomb was a dud.
I was swamped out by the
rain we had a while back.

On page two, Zodiac had outlined a new bomb configuration and provided instructions. At the bottom of the letter, he added:

PS I hope you have fun trying
to figgure out who I killed.

⊕ =10 SFPD =0

Analysis

Based on the timing of this new letter and the Zodiac's claim of a total of 10 victims, we can infer that he took credit for killing Salam.

In the letter, Zodiac also alluded to Sergeant Brian McDonnell, who had died as a result of a bomb attack at the San Francisco Police Department Park Station. No convictions were ever made, but the bomb was considered to have been placed by a domestic terrorist group called *Weather Underground*.[7] When Zodiac used "blue meannie" as a synonym for police officer, he was alluding to the 1968 film-animation, *Yellow Submarine*, in which the "blue meanies" represent all the bad people in the world.[8] It can be deduced that the Zodiac was a movie buff rather than a bookworm.

One interesting aspect is why the Zodiac explicitly denied involvement in the bombing. One possibility is that he wanted to give an impression of sincerity in that he would not take credit for something he had not done. He may have hoped that the police would then be more inclined to add Salem to his body count.

In the Zodiac's August 1969 letter, he made the claim that the police would have him if they could decrypt the 408 cipher. He lied. He clearly constructed the name-cipher for his own egotistical reasons, and it would be out of character for him to freely provide the police with anything of significance. From a technical standpoint, the shortness of the cipher obstructs the verification process; thus, it is not possible to verify whether or not a solution is the right one; a computer can effortlessly be programmed to find strings of text and even names that fit the cipher, for example, Steve Pete West, Adrian A Harrah, Gary Lyle Large, Eddie Gene Oden, and many more.[9]

Zodiac had ostensibly continued his studies in morbid engineering from where he previously left off, and finally he presented his master thesis to the readers: a photoelectric switch bomb. The Zodiac undoubtedly knew that this device and the previous one were oversimplified and practically difficult to set up. He was probably ignorant about it as he undoubtedly had no intentions of bombing anyone. His criminal profile had evolved from serial murder to attention via terrorism and these purported devices served this purpose. There was no need for him to write a detailed manual, his drawings and descriptions should merely be enough to

make people think or fear that he might blow up somebody. It remains evident nonetheless that he was a technical individual, and he might have been exposed to counter-culture literature on bomb making. When the letter was published, the bomb threat was omitted - this did not please the Zodiac.
The letter does not convey much information not already covered in previous chapters. Its primary purpose was to generate attention via (1) the cipher, (2) the bomb diagram, and (3) by means of the new body count.

Tuesday, April 28

Zodiac was dissatisfied with the omission, and he sped to a mailbox and posted a *Jolly Roger* greeting card to express his contempt for the decision to withhold his threat. If the threat were not published, he would have a "blast" he menaced. Like previously, Zodiac had affixed too many stamps on the envelope. It was postmarked in San Francisco.

The envelope read:

Editor
San Fran. Chronicle
San Fran. Calif.

Zodiac had chosen a truly uncanny greeting card as a vehicle for delivering his message. Two wacky individuals are pictured on the front sitting on a dragon and a mule. Next to the caption of the card, "Sorry To Hear: Your ass is a Dragon," Zodiac had written a message:

I hope you
enjoy your
selves
when I
have my
Blast.
⊕
P.S. on
back

On the back of it, he wrote:

If you dont want me to
have this blast you must
do two things. 1 Tell every
one about the bus bomb with
all the details. 2 I would like
to see some nice Zodiac butons
wandering about town. Every
one else has these buttons like,
☮, black power, melvin eats
bluber, etc. Well it would cheer
me up considerbly if I saw
a lot of people wearing my
buton. Please no nasty ones
like melvin's
Thank you
⊕

Analysis

Even though this card had to have been authored by the Zodiac due to the knowledge of the bomb, it was forwarded to the FBI for analysis. In his report, the FBI expert stated that "all of the threatening letters" were "probably prepared by one writer."[10]
At this point, the Zodiac's tone of communication had started to lose the force and domination that initially characterized it. In this recent card, he communicated a bomb threat on a bizarre and somewhat humorous greeting card, probably the type of card one might send to a long-term friend on a special occasion. A threat to murder and bomb people does not go hand in hand with such a card, especially considering that the Zodiac wanted to be seen as an imminent threat to the people of the Bay Area. Perhaps his apparent lack of emotional intelligence also translated into bizarre behaviors in his personal life; he may have been the type of person who would frequently make inappropriate comments at social gatherings.
His jealousy had also risen to a God-like level. Of course, no one (that we know of) wore his symbol, but had people done so we can only guess what the next demand would be: Talk shows? Movies? Music? His demand indicates that his insight into how the public

perceived him was grossly distorted. They viewed him as a murderer, a devil, a maniac, and a lunatic. He might not have truly realized the ramifications of his actions. In his delusions of grandeur, he might have believed that the public admired him and his alleged intelligence.

The Melvin badge was the Zodiac's invention. He had probably seen the badge with the words, "Melville Eats Blubber,"[†††] a badge referring to the author of Moby Dick. This he twisted into a Melvin Belli reference. In this regard, his real purpose for mentioning Belli remains unclear, yet it seems he was unappeased with him. The case had consumed a great deal of Belli's time and thoughts, and despite his overbooked calendar, he had worked hard to reach the Zodiac through the media and even promised to represent him in court. In spite of the fact that the Zodiac was ever demanding and rarely satisfied, he could hardly have been displeased with Belli.

Thursday, April 30

Using extortion, the Zodiac succeeded in getting the bomb threat published but the police continued to withhold the diagram.[11] Inspector William Armstrong told at a news conference that "a contemporary greeting card received by the San Francisco Chronicle on Wednesday warned that they must reveal the bus bombing plot and promote the wearing of 'Zodiac buttons' if they want to stop the blast."[12] The Zodiac must have been satisfied by the police dancing to his tune.

Friday, June 19

At approximately 5:25 a.m., San Francisco Police Officer, Richard P. Radetich, stopped his traffic patrol car for the purpose of giving a citation on an unattended parked vehicle in front of 643 Waller Street, San Francisco. Before he had the chance to get out of his

[†††] There is some confusion as to what the badge actually stated, it may have been, 'Herman Melville Eats Blubber.'

car, an unrelated person pulled out a .38-caliber revolver and fired three times through the closed driver's side window.[13] One bullet lodged in a door, one went through the window, and the last one went into Radetich's brain. He expired at 8:02 p.m.[14]
It was a dangerous time to be an officer of the law. Homicide Inspector Napoleon Hendrix would later say, "Police were being killed because we wore the badge." Back then, "it was a crazy time, because people were targeting us for doing our job. [...] These were flat-out ambushes. They were trying to pick us off and blow us up."[15] Inspector Hendrix was, among others, alluding to the ambush killing of Richard Eugene Huerta who worked as a patrolman for the San Jose Police Department. On August 6, 1970, he was writing a citation for a young man who sat beside him. A black man, Emile Hubert Thompson, who was later charged and convicted of Huerta's death, suddenly thrust his arm through the open window. In the grip of his hand was a gun. He then fired six shots, only hitting Huerta.[16] He was arrested a few hours later. Thompson, the son of an Oakland police officer, was given a life sentence and will be incarcerated for the rest of his life.[17] There were other killings with a similar *modus operandi*. On August 20, 1970, Patrolman Ronald T. Tsukamoto stopped a motorcyclist for a traffic violation. A young black man suddenly appeared and shot Tsukamoto in the head. The motorcyclist commented, "There was no warning … He just fired twice and split. I don't think he was interested in me at all."[18] Police Chief Bruce Baker of the Berkeley Police Department, later said, "There is no doubt that this shooting was political."[19]

Saturday, June 20

The tragic killing of Radetich entered the front page of the Chronicle: "New Cop Slaying: Mystery Gunman Kills S.F. Officer."[20] In part the article read: "The only solid clue police could find was the casing of a .38 caliber bullet lying outside the smashed window of Radetich's car."[21]

Friday, June 26

The Zodiac posted a cryptic letter on June 26. He had for the first time chosen not to over-post the envelope.* As previously, it had a San Francisco postmark. It was addressed to his favorite media outlet: The Chronicle. Enclosed was a large map and, in conjunction with a code, it would allegedly lead his pursuers to a bomb. The FBI expert formed the opinion that the letter was probably prepared by the Zodiac.[22]

The letter read:

This is the Zodiac speaking
I have become very upset with
the people of San Fran Bay
Area. They have not complied
with my wishes for them to
wear some nice buttons.
I promiced to punish them
if they did not comply, by
anilating a full School Buss.
But now school is out for
the summer, so I punished
them in an another way.
I shot a man sitting in
a parked car with a .38.

⊕ -12 SFPD-0
The Map coupled with this
code will tell you where the
bomb is set. You have untill
next Fall to dig it up. ⊕

[Cipher text]

* Note that the August 1969 envelope is unavailable at this point.

The envelope read:

S.F Chronicle
San Fran.
Calif.

Letter Analysis

Conspicuously, the Zodiac continually deferred his supposed plan of attacking a school bus. He, at first, wanted to shoot the tires and then kill the passengers, like a mad sniper. Then, he changed his mind and instead wanted to bomb it. He then complained of difficulties in setting it up. Next, he constructed a new bomb device. Then finally, he claimed that the police could locate his bomb if they solved a code. Attention and terrorism were central to him, not bombing.

With this letter, Zodiac enclosed a Phillips 66 map of San Francisco and Vicinity, a map he could have bought at most service stations. If we inspect the map, we see that he set *Mount Diablo* in focus, a mountain that is visible from the lovers' lane on Lake Herman Road. About 160 years ago, it was chosen "as the initial point for determining base and meridian lines still used in official land surveys."[23] In addition to his preference for cardinal points, Zodiac demonstrated navigational knowledge or experience, especially when he wrote, "Mag. N," with this being an unusual abbreviation for Magnetic North. While a compass will point to magnetic north, *true north* is located hundreds of miles away on the imaginary axis at which the earth rotates. At Mount Diablo in 1970, the angle between the two was ~17 degrees east of true north. The code or cipher is the last one ever sent by the Zodiac and remains unsolved.

In the letter, the Zodiac also insinuated that he had shot and killed Radetich as a punishment for people not wearing his badge. There are certain Old Testament undertones to this Zodiac letter, specifically the tale of the Pharaoh being punished for defying God. Zodiac only offered a vague statement as proof that had already been published six days before he wrote the letter. Investigators accepted it as a reference to Radetich and ultimately concluded that he did not do it.[24] Radetich's family never got a resolution to the case, and it remains unsolved to this day. The San Francisco Office of the Mayor has offered a $100.000 reward for information leading to the arrest and successful prosecution of the killer.[25]

Tuesday, June 30

Zodiac was once again caught in the act of deception and exposed by Paul Avery under the headline, “Zodiac Says He Killed S.F. Officer.”[26] Avery quoted an inspector of the SFPD, “If he’s hinting he shot Officer Radetich then he’s lying,” and “we have already issued an arrest warrant in the case.”[27] An ex-convict, Joe Wesley Johnson, had been identified by a witness as Radetich’s killer. The charges against him were, however, in the long run dropped because they could not produce enough evidence to secure a conviction.[28] If Zodiac had killed Radetich, he would undoubtedly have “screamed his lungs out” in a letter to the Chronicle. Could he have been alluding to a different crime? No other crimes in the relevant period matched his description.
His most recent bomb threat was not withheld. Avery wrote that Zodiac indicated he had “planted a bomb somewhere in the vicinity of Mount Diablo.”[29] It was probably evident to most individuals that he bluffed. Zodiac could only have been displeased at seeing his credibility taking another blow.

Friday, July 24

Less than a month went by and the Zodiac picked up his favorite pen and wrote a letter to the Chronicle. The envelope contained a single stamp, and it was postmarked on July 24 in San Francisco.

The Zodiac’s letter read:

> This is the Zodiac speaking
> I am rather unhappy because
> you people will not wear some
> nice ⊕ buttons. So I now
> have a little list, starting with
> the woeman + her baby that I
> gave a rather intersting ride
> for a coupple howers one
> evening a few months back that

ended in my burning her
car where I found them.

The envelope:

S.F. Chronicle
San Fran. Calif

Analysis

Zodiac finally took credit for the Kathleen Johns incident. He uncharacteristically failed to provide any details that had not already been published in the news. In June, his delusions of grandeur made him promise a severe punishment to the people of the Bay Area for not wearing badges with his symbol. Zodiac, who was clearly a narcissistic individual, must have been greatly affected if he had failed to do physical harm to a pregnant young mother. This elucidates why the Zodiac did not take credit immediately if he had actually kidnapped her.
His claim should be seen as a reply to the criticism he had received for taking credit for killing Radetich. He wanted to make the statement that he was dangerous and should be feared. It took him almost a month to come up with the response. Maybe he had to shift through his newspaper articles to find a suitable incident that hinted at his involvement. Johns had already implicated the Zodiac, and it would be unlikely that he would be discredited at any time soon. Underneath, we have juxtaposed his statements with quotes from the initial article about the kidnapping titled, “Rode With Zodiac, Woman Claims.”[30] It is striking how much his phrasing resembles the information from the article.

(Z = Zodiac; E = Examiner article)
Z: “woeman + her baby”
E: “Johns, who is seven months pregnant, had her year-old daughter with her.”
Z: “intersting ride for a coupple howers”
E: “Then began a weird two-hour ride.”
Z: “ended in my burning her car where I found them”

E: "she left her home [...] and headed up Highway 132 […]. [A]dding a weird touch to the story is the fact that about an hour later, Mrs. Johns' car was found on Highway 132 burned."

The Zodiac's involvement is disputed and discussed to this day. In 1988, Inspector William Armstrong offered his opinion and stated that there is a "high degree of probability"[31] that Kathleen Johns did meet him.

Sunday, July 26

The Zodiac elaborated on his 'little list' in a five-page missive which turned out to be a "low-grade plagiarism"[32] of Gilbert and Sullivan's opera *the Mikado*. The envelope was postmarked on July 26 in San Francisco. Zodiac had stopped using excess postage. In addition to showing off his alleged musical skills, he referred to 13 slaves, meaning he supposedly had committed more murders. There is an obvious difference between his initial letters and his later ones. One has to wonder if the conversion from being methodical and factual to telling a distorted and grotesque version of an old opera signifies mental instability or even substance use. The FBI's document examiner typed that "hand printing characteristics indicate that all of the threatening letters [...] were probably prepared by one person."[33] An article in the Chronicle stated, "There is no doubt the July Zodiac letters are authentic. Crime Lab handwriting experts have made comparisons with other known messages from the killer and say the hurried printing and crossed-circle signature are identical."[34] If the Zodiac expected the arrival of the letter to result in immediate front-page coverage, he was wrong. His internal tension was relieved in October when it was published.

Fingerprints

A high-quality scan of page three and four of the July 26 letter shows areas circled with a pencil that have reddish tint due to treatment with fine powders. These areas contain unidentified latent prints. We also know of the prints because of correspondence between the SFPD and FBI. A letter to the FBI asking for assistance with the prints states that an Inspector of the SFPD

Crime Laboratory "believes the left ring finger latents [sic] […] bears similarity to bloody latent fingerprint removed from door of vehicle driven by victim taxi driver."[35] Elimination prints were "obtained of all persons connected with the newspaper and the Police Department who could have possibly handled the letters."[36] "Eight latent fingerprints were developed [...] [they] are individually identifiable with the possible exception of the print that is believed to be the right little finger. Six of the latent prints were developed on the letter in a position that indicates they are impressions of the middle, ring and little fingers of the right and left hand. Two of the latent prints may be of the thumb or index finger of the right and left hand."[37]
We previously mentioned that the Zodiac left fingerprints and his prints were cross-referenced, showing that one man committed the crimes. However, why would he leave several prints on this letter? Were alcohol and/or drugs taking over his life? Did the prints belong to someone else?

The latest letter read:

Page 1,

This is the Zodiac speaking
Being that you will not wear
some nice ⊕ buttons, how about
wearing some nasty ⊕ buttons.
Or any type of ⊕ buttons that
you can think up. If you do
not wear any type of ⊕
buttons I shall (on top of every
thing else) torture all 13
of my slaves that I have
wateing for me in Paradice.
Some I shall tie over ant hills
and watch them scream + twich
and sqwirm. Others shall have
pine splinters driven under their
nails + then burned. Others shall
be placed in cages + fed salt

beef untill they are gorged then
I shall listen to their pleass
for water and I shall laugh at
them. Others will hang by
their thumbs + burn in the
sun then I will rub them down
with deep heat to warm

Page 2,

them up. Others I shall
skin them alive + let them
run around screaming. And
all billiard players I shall
have them play in a dark
ened dungen all with crooked
cues + Twisted Shoes.
Yes I shall have great
fun in flicting the most
delicious of pain to my
Slaves

SFPF = 0 ⌖ = 13

Page 3,

As some day it may hapen
that a victom must be found.
I've got a little list. I've
got a little list, of society
offenders who might well be
underground who would never
be miss ed who would never be
missed. There is the pest –
ulentual nucences who whrite
for autographs, all people who
have flabby hands and irritat –
ing laughs. All children who
are up in dates and implore
you with implatt. All people
who are shakeing hands shake

hands like that. And all third
persons who with unspoiling
take thoes who insist. They'd
none of them be missed. They'd
none of them be missed. There's
the banjo seranader and
the others of his race and
the piano orginast I got him
on the list. All people who
eat pepermint and phomphit

Page 4,

in your face, they would
never be missed They would
never be missed And the
Idiout who phraises with in -
thusastic tone of centuries
but this and every country but
his own. And the lady from
the provences who dress like
a guy who doesn't cry and
the singurly abnomily the
girl who never Kissed. I don't
think she would be missed
Im shure she wouldn't be
missed. And that nice impriest
that is rather rife the judic –
ial hummerest I've got him on
the list All funny fellows, com –
mic men and clowns of private
life. They'd none of them be
missed. They'd none of them be
missed. And uncompromiseing
Kind such as wachamacallit,
thingmebob, and like wise, well –
- nevermind, and tut tut tut tuT,
- and whatshisname, and you know

Page 5,

who, but the task of filling
up the blanks I rather leave
up to you. But it really does -
n't matter whom you place
upon the list, for none of
them be missed, none of
them be missed.

PS. The Mt. Diablo Code concerns
Radians +#inches along the radians

Zodiac had made an unusual misspelling in the address:

S.F. Chronicle
San Fran. Claif.

Analysis

Seeing his symbol of murder had become Zodiac's most recent obsession, and he was now willing to compromise as long as people wore his imaginary badge even if it was in an offensive way. His crimes did not carry any sadistic undertones, but in this missive, he described a fantasy scenario of omnipotence intermingled with torture.

The Mikado first came to light on March 14, 1885, in London and right away became a success. When the opera premiered at Ford's Opera House in August 1885, a critic acknowledged the opera for its "unusual smoothness"[38] and noticed that it received "every mark of approval from a large audience."[39]

There can be little doubt that the Zodiac identified himself with Ko-Ko, a central figure of the Mikado. In the town of Titipu, the act of flirting is a capital crime, and city officials appoint Ko-Ko as the Lord High Executioner whose job is to execute all those caught in the act of flirting. Zodiac directed his wrath onto three couples who were in the process of flirting or in a location associated with such activity. And we should not forget his executioner's style costume worn at Lake Berryessa. Maybe the entire murder plot was a morbid rendition of the Mikado right from the beginning. The

Zodiac's identification with Ko-Ko appears to be so strong to the point where he felt compelled to plagiarize him extensively in this letter. Specifically, in the opera, Ko-Ko introduces a "little list," which is not so little after all, of society offenders "who never would be missed."[40] Zodiac distorted and plagiarized this part of the opera from Act 1 on pages three to five. On page one to two, he distorted "A More Humane Mikado" from Act II.[41] Zodiac clearly used the Mikado to elaborate on the vow he made in his lengthy missive of November 1969. He had allegedly decided not to inform police officials of his future homicides. So far, it appears that he now employed this strategy because he no longer had intentions of killing people, getting front-page coverage was ostensibly enough to satisfy him at this point.

It also appears that the Zodiac had not memorized the Mikado by script, seemingly it was by memory. While the Zodiac introduced his own perversions in the letter, his rendition of the Mikado also includes a phrase about a *girl that has never kissed*, which is not a part of the standard lyrics. Specifically, this phrase was used in Groucho Marx's version of the Mikado.[42] Marx's version was recorded in 1960 and subsequently published. The Zodiac had a vinyl player in his home apparently. In proximity to the postal date of the letter, the *Lamplighters* were performing the Mikado in San Francisco. Just perhaps a beefy individual with glasses and an unclean conscience attended the opera. The Mikado is reportedly the most popular opera ever written, in that light, his familiarity with it is not unusual.[43] The cops went so far as to hypothesize that Zodiac was associated with the opera and began to look deeper at the workers and actors.

As a postscript to the letter, the Zodiac mentions *radians*. The radian is used instead of degrees typically in what is referred to as *higher* mathematics. *Radians plus # inches along the radians* is not a concept that concerns mathematicians as the radian is a linear measure of an angle. If finding a specific location is the goal, it would appear that the Zodiac did not understand the concept of radians.

Many researchers have looked into the possibility that his murders were orchestrated using a scheme. The efforts have not been successful, and such a scheme is in contrast to the Zodiac's instruction that the map and code led to a bomb. Since there never was a bomb, we can conclude that it was a hoax. On the contrary, if we recall the article from Popular Science, which may have influenced the Zodiac, it detailed *Zodiac murders* that were plotted using a grand astrological scheme; it could be that Zodiac had planned his crimes in terms of locations or else how.

Selected Transcript of "A More Humane Mikado" (Act II).

The billiard sharp who any one catches
His doom's extremely hard —
He's made to dwell —
In a dungeon cell
On a spot that's always barred
And there he plays extravagant matches
In fitless finger-stalls
On a cloth untrue
With a twisted cue
And elliptical billiard balls!

Transcript of Groucho Marx's "I've Got a Little List" (Act II).

As some day it may happen that a victim must be found,
I've got a little list I've got a little list.

Of society offenders who might well be underground,
And who never would be missed - who never would be missed.

There's the pestilential nuisances who write for autographs,
All people who have flabby hands and irritating laughs.

And all children who are up in dates and floor you with 'em flat,
And all persons who when shaking hands shake hands with you like that.

And all third persons who are spoiling tête-á-têtes insist,
They'd none of them be missed, they'd none of them be missed.

There's the banjo serenader and the others of his race,
And the piano-organist, I've got him on the list.

And the people who eat peppermint and puff it in your face,

They never would be missed, they never would be missed.

And the idiot who praises with enthusiastic tone,
All centuries but this, and every country but his own.

And the lady from the provinces who dresses like a guy,
And who doesn't think she dances but would rather like to try.

And that singular anomaly, the girl who's never kissed,
I don't think she'd be missed, I'm sure she'd not be missed.

And that Nisi Prius nuisance, who just now is rather rife,
The Judicial humorist, I've got him on the list.

All funny fellows, comic men and clowns of private life,
They'd none of them be missed, they'd none of them be missed.

And apologetic statesmen of a compromising kind,
Such as — what d'ye call him — thing'em-bob, and likewise, ah never mind.

And a tut tut tut and what's-his-name, and well, well you know who,
Ah, the task of filling up the blanks, I'd rather leave to you.

For it really doesn't matter whom you put upon the list,
For they'd none of them be missed, they'd none of them be missed.

Monday, October 5

Someone purporting to be the Zodiac sent the Chronicle a debated and cryptic card without handwriting.

The card:

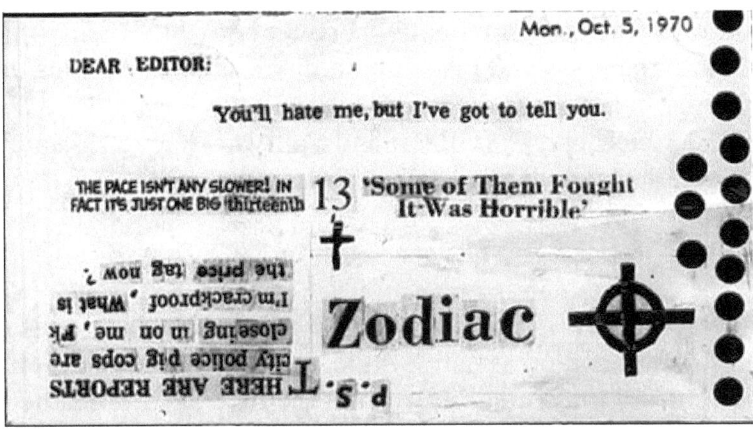

Mon., Oct. 5, 1970

DEAR EDITOR:

You'll hate me, but I've got to tell you.

THE PACE ISN'T ANY SLOWER! IN FACT ITS JUST ONE BIG thirteenth 13 'Some of Them Fought It Was Horrible'

Zodiac

P.S. THERE ARE REPORTS city police pig cops are closeing in on me, Fk I'm crackproof, What is the price tag now?

Avery, in his related article, typed that they received the "3-inch by 5-inch file card"[44] on October 7, and after an exhaustive study detectives had opined that it was "highly probable"[45] it was sent by the Zodiac. Contrary to the press, the cross on the front was not made in blood but with thin red paper.[46] The black dots are actual holes in the card made by the Zodiac or Zodiac copycat. The words on the card had been cut out of an edition of the Chronicle and pasted onto it.

The body count of 13 is one more than what Zodiac claimed on June 26, although it is the same as in the unpublished letter of July. It could be that a copycat had attempted to emulate the Zodiac's tendency of increasing his body count. However, he was unaware that the figure had already been used. Or did the Zodiac indicate some information about his alleged victim number 13? Maybe he wanted to tell us that number 13 "Fought [and] It Was Horrible." In his letter of April 1970, the Zodiac mentioned how much money was on his head. In this card, his "price tag," meaning how much money had been offered for information leading to his arrest, was also mentioned. The card states, "P.S. THERE ARE REPORTS city police pig cops are closeing in on me, Fk I'm crackproof, What is the price tag now?" As we shall see, in March 1971, Zodiac used the term *crack proof* in a confirmed letter. Furthermore, the author of the card misspelled *closing*, a well-known Zodiac trait. These observations point to the Zodiac as the author of the card. Taunting appears to have been the main motivation for sending the card and to support the assertion that Zodiac killed secretly without anybody noticing his involvement. The back of the card contained a single stamp.

In addition to the card, the unpublished letter of July finally made its way into the press and made numerous headlines. "Police doubt new murder boasts in Zodiac-type notes,"[47] "In New Notes, Zodiac Brags of 13 Murders,"[48] "Gilbert and Sullivan Clue to Zodiac,"[49] and "Mysterious 'Zodiac' boasts of kills to paper."[50]

Tuesday, October 27

Paul Avery, known for his reporting on the Zodiac case in his straightforward and provocative style, received a highly decorated Halloween card in the mail. It was not the type of card that he commonly received at this time of the year since it was a greeting and death threat from the Zodiac! The reader should recall that Johns said she also picked up a Halloween card from her mailbox in October. Only Avery's card featured the superimposed pumpkin. It is unlikely that Johns knew that the pumpkin had been pasted on Avery's version of the card. It indicates that she received a greeting from the Zodiac.

Avery had just been singled out by a notorious and heartless serial killer, yet he remained calm saying, "I'm not frightened, but I think Zodiac is."[51] He also said, "I'm really not scared. I've needled him in some of my stories and maybe that's why he wrote to me."[52] Just in case, so to say, Avery began carrying a concealed .38 revolver. The Chronicle staff, Avery included, started wearing badges or buttons, not with Zodiac symbols, but stating, "I am not Paul Avery."

In his God-like delusions, the Zodiac had issued a profound statement that he tolerated no criticism by the media. Journalists were his slaves and he would punish them if they did not move to his tune.

Morrill determined that the handwriting was the Zodiac's.[53] The questioned document examiner of the FBI, however, noted that the hand printing was "too limited and distorted to definitely associate it with any of the hand printing on threatening letters received previously in this case; however, a few hand printing similarities were noted."[54] Zodiac had flipped open the envelope and had written inside that there was no new cipher this time. He then placed a decorated *Secret Pal* card in the envelope, but the Zodiac in his twisted irony was certainly not implying that he was somehow secretly admiring Avery's work. The envelope was postmarked on October 27 in San Francisco.

The front of the card carries a prewritten message by the manufacturer, "FROM YOUR SECRET PAL," and continues with "I feel it in my bones. You ache to know my name. And so I'll clue You in..." Zodiac could not resist the temptation to tease his pursuers with his anonymity. On the dancing skeleton, he had written "14" on the hand. He had Avery in mind to be his next victim. The Zodiac had glued a pumpkin onto the pelvis area. It has been conjectured that this could be a hidden reference to Avery's assertion that Zodiac was a latent homosexual. The prewritten message continues on the inside of the card, "… But, then, why spoil the game!" and ends with "Happy Halloween!" In addition to the manufacturer's message on the inside, Zodiac had also glued-on a skeleton and artistically drawn 13 eyes. In Zodiac's morbid-childish tone, he had also written four messages to Avery: "PEEK-A-BOO," "YOU ARE DOOMED!" "4-TEEN," and "BOO." Underneath the skeleton, the Zodiac had decorated the area with his crosshair symbol, a capital Z, and an unusual symbol subject to much speculation. Did the symbol finally clue us in to his name? No doubt, Avery had angered the Zodiac who used the card to spread his wrath and as a

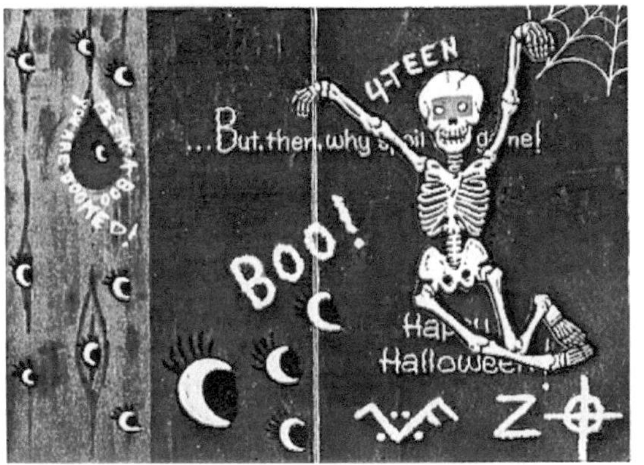

vehicle to get attention. In this he succeeded: The card received significant attention, even worldwide.[55] "Zodiac threatens life of reporter,"[56] "REPORTER GETS ZODIAC'S CARD,"[57] "Zodiac, Believed Mad Killer of Five, Sends Ghoulish Card to Crime Writer,"[58] read a few headlines.

On the back of the card, Zodiac showed off his creativity by intersecting "PARADICE" and "SLAVES," almost like a bored student would do in her notebooks. In the four quadrants around these two words, he had written down the murder-weapons and other paraphernalia that he had utilized in his crimes: "FiRE," "GUN," "KNiFE" and "ROPE." He apparently again emphasized that he had abducted Johns and torched her car by writing *fire*. The enigmatic nature of the card has led many individuals into trying to find clues in the symbolism and lineup of words, especially by examining the symbol found in the card. If there is a deeper meaning, it has yet to be ascertained conclusively.

APPENDIX F

Figure 1
Zodiac letter. Mailed April 20, 1970.
The San Francisco Chronicle.
Figure 2
Zodiac greeting card. Mailed April 28, 1970.
The San Francisco Chronicle.
Figure 3
Zodiac letter and map. Mailed June 26, 1970.
The San Francisco Chronicle.
Figure 4
Zodiac letter. Mailed July 24, 1970.
The San Francisco Chronicle.
Figure 5
Zodiac letter. Mailed July 26, 1970.
The San Francisco Chronicle.
Figure 6
Suspected Zodiac card. Received October 7, 1970.
The San Francisco Chronicle.
Figure 7
Zodiac greeting card. Mailed October 27, 1970.
Paul Avery.
Figure 8
Envelopes.

Figure 1

This is the Zodiac speaking
By the way have you cracked
the last cipher I sent you ?
My name is —

A E N ⊕ ⊗ K ⊗ M ⊗ ⫫ N A M

I am mildly cerous as to how
much money you have on my
head now. I hope you do not
think that I was the one
who wiped out that blue
meannie with a bomb at the
cop station. Even though I talked
about killing school children with
one. It just wouldnt doo to
move in on someone elses teritory.
But there is more glory in killing
a cop than a cid because a cop
can shoot back. I have killed
ten people to date. It would
have been a lot more except
that my bas bomb was a dud.
I was swamped out by the
rain we had a while back.

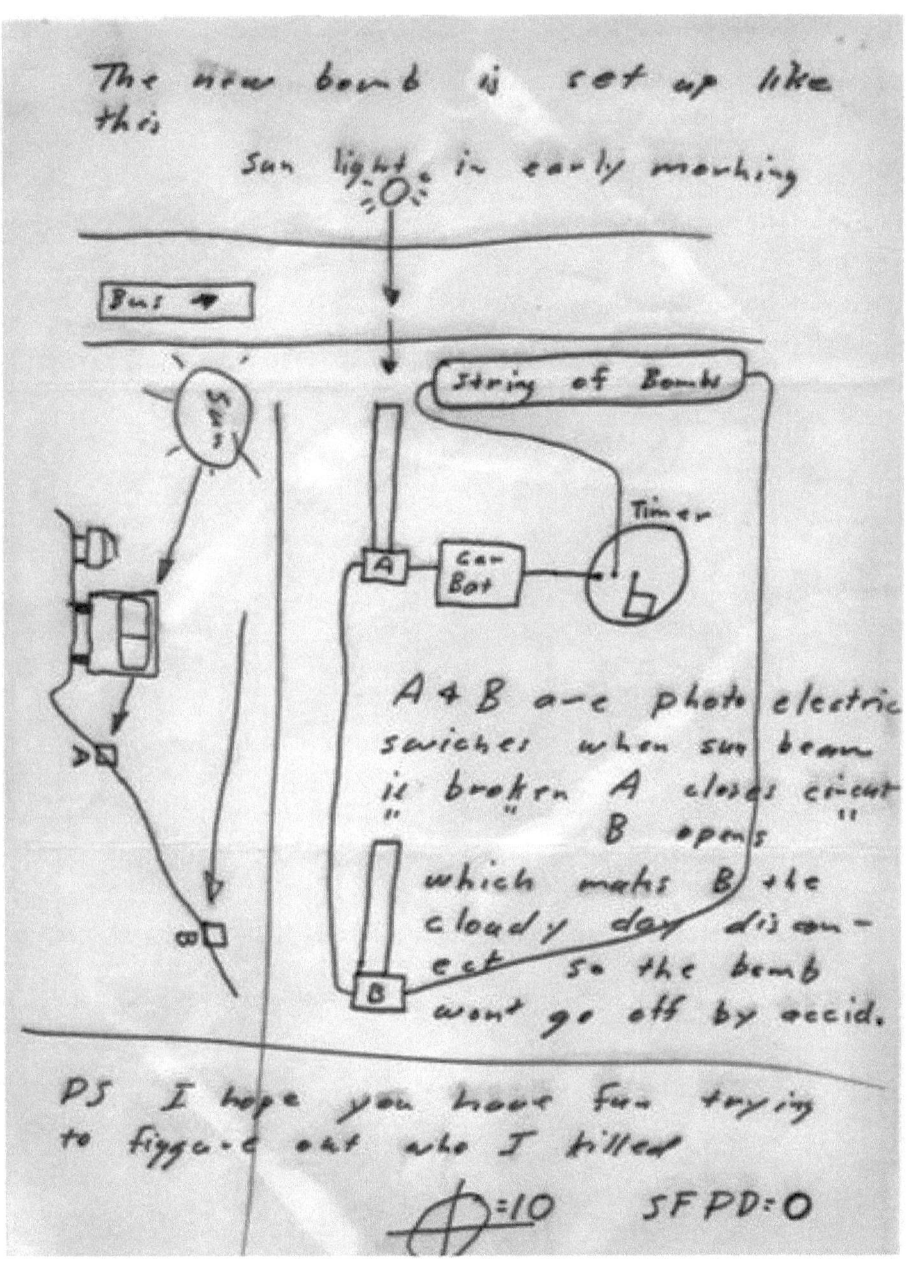
The new bomb is set up like this
Sun light in early morning
Bus →
String of Bombs
Sun
Timer
A
Car Bat
b
A
B
B
A & B are photo electric swiches when sun beam is broken A closes cricut
" " B opens "
which maks B the cloudy day dis con-ect so the bomb wont go off by accid.
PS I hope you have fun trying to figgure out who I killed
⊕=10 SFPD=0

Figure 2

SORRY TO HEAR
YOUR ass is a DRAGON
I hope you enjoy your selves when I have my Blast.
P.S. on back

JOLLY ROGER

If you dont want me to
have this blast you must
do two things. Tell every
one about the bus bomb with
all the details. & I would like
to see some nice Zodiac butons
wandering about town. Every
one else has these buttons like,
☮, black power, melvin eats
bluber, etc. Well it would cheer
me up considerably if I saw
a lot of people wearing my
buton. Please no nasty ones
like melvin's

Thank you

⊕

Figure 3

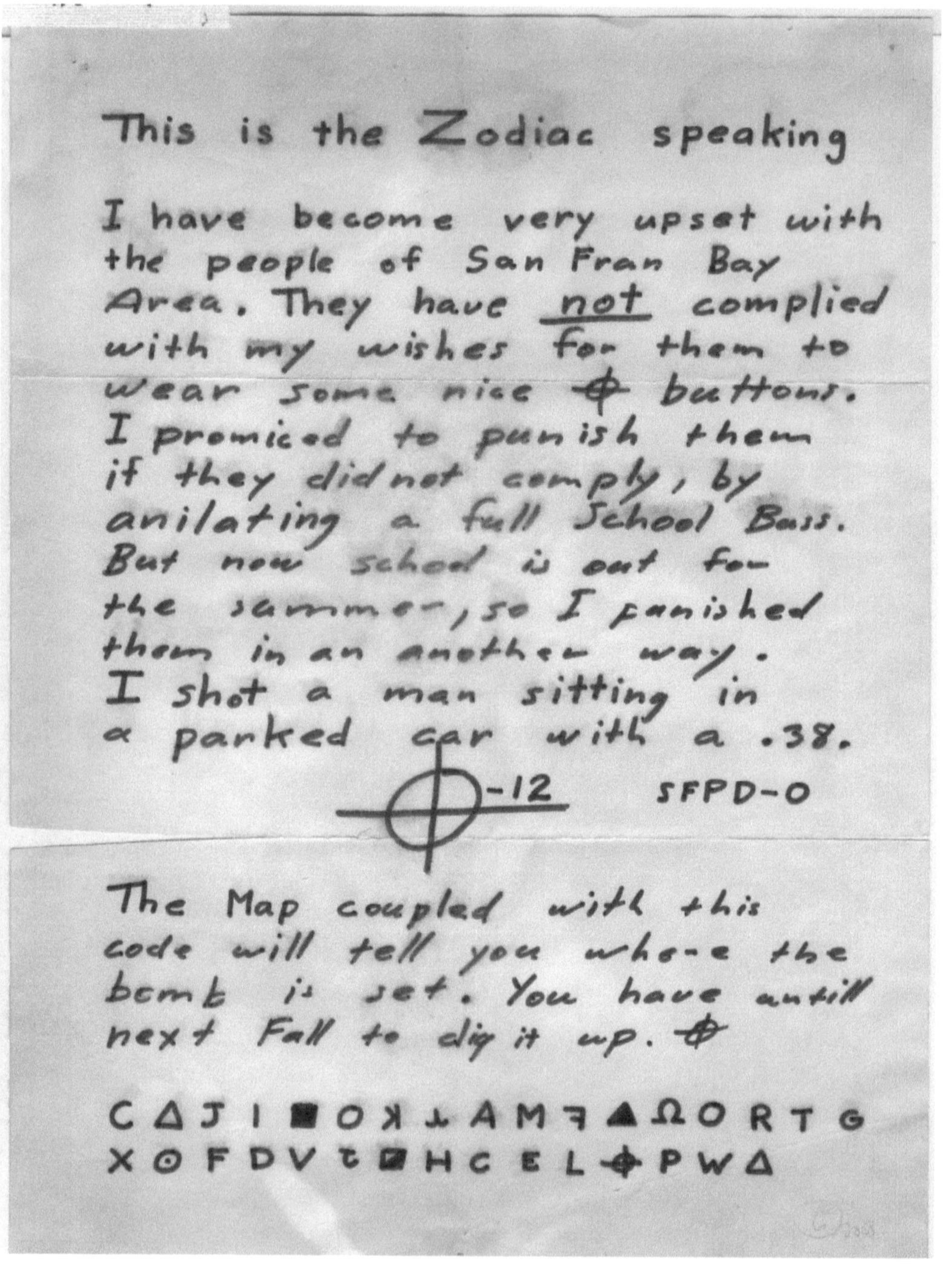

This is the Zodiac speaking

I have become very upset with the people of San Fran Bay Area. They have not complied with my wishes for them to wear some nice ⊕ buttons. I promiced to punish them if they did not comply, by anilating a full School Buss. But now school is out for the summer, so I punished them in an another way. I shot a man sitting in a parked car with a .38.

⊕-12 SFPD-0

The Map coupled with this code will tell you where the bomb is set. You have untill next Fall to dig it up. ⊕

C △ J I ■ O ꓘ ⊥ A M ꟻ ▲ Ω O R T G
X ⊙ F D V t ◪ H C E L ⊕ P W △

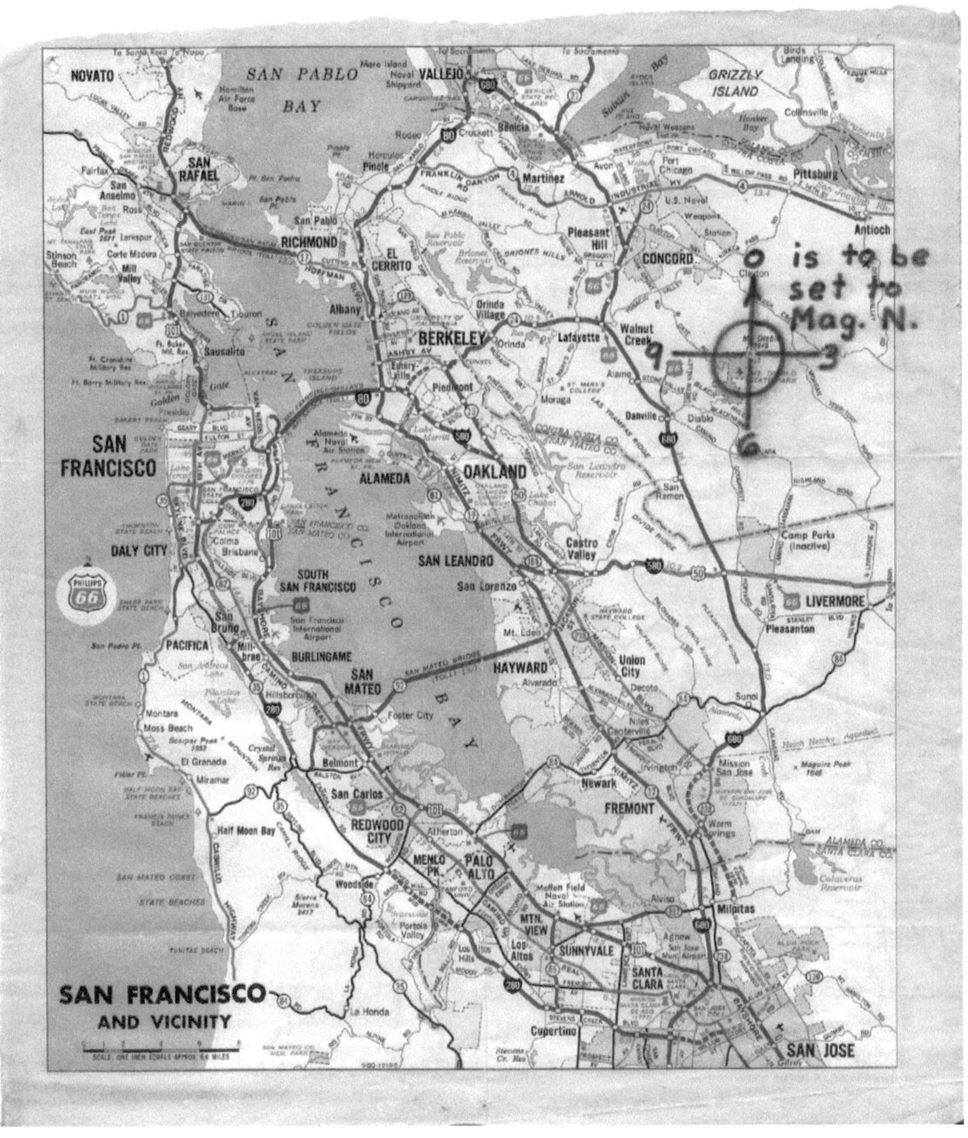

0 is to be set to Mag. N.
9
3
6
SAN FRANCISCO
AND VICINITY
NOVATO
SAN PABLO BAY
VALLEJO
GRIZZLY ISLAND
SAN RAFAEL
Benicia
Martinez
Pittsburg
Antioch
RICHMOND
EL CERRITO
Pleasant Hill
CONCORD
Albany
BERKELEY
Orinda
Lafayette
Walnut Creek
Sausalito
SAN FRANCISCO
Alameda
OAKLAND
Danville
San Ramon
DALY CITY
SOUTH SAN FRANCISCO
SAN LEANDRO
Castro Valley
LIVERMORE
Pleasanton
PACIFICA
HAYWARD
Union City
SAN MATEO
BURLINGAME
FREMONT
REDWOOD CITY
MENLO PK.
PALO ALTO
MTN. VIEW
SUNNYVALE
SANTA CLARA
Milpitas
Cupertino
SAN JOSE
Half Moon Bay
La Honda

Figure 4

This is the Zodiac speaking

I am rather unhappy because
you people will not wear some
nice ⊕ buttons. So I now
have a little list, starting with
the woeman + her baby that I
gave a rather intersting ride
for a coupple howers one
evening a few months back that
ended in my burning her
car where I found them.

Figure 5

This is the Zodiac speaking

Being that you will not wear
some nice ⊕ buttons, how about
wearing some nasty ⊕ buttons.
Or any type of ⊕ buttons that
you can think up. If you do
not wear any type of ⊕
buttons I shall (on top of every
thing else) torture all 13
of my slaves that I have
wateing for me in Paradice.
Some I shall tie over ant hills
and watch them scream + twich
and sqwirm. Others shall have
pine splinters driven under their
nails + then burned. Others shall
be placed in cages + fed salt
beef untill they are gorged then
I shall listen to their pleass
for water and I shall laugh at
them. Others will hang by
their thumbs + burn in the
sun then I will rub them down
with deep heat to warm

them up. Others I shall skin them alive + let them run around screaming. And all billiard players I shall have them play in a dark ened dungeon cell with crooked cues + Twisted Shoes. Yes I shall have great fun inflicting the most delicious of pain to my Slaves

SFPD=

=13

As some day it may hapen that a victom must be found. I've got a little list. I've got a little list, of society offenders who might well be underground who would never be missed who would never be missed. There is the pest-ulentual nucences who whrite for autographs, all people who have flabby hands and irritating laughs. All children who are up in dates and implore you with im platt. All people who are shakeing hands shake hands like that. And all third persons who with unspoiling take thoes who insist. They'd none of them be missed. They'd none of them be missed. There's the banjo seranader and the others of his race and the piano orginast I got him on the list. All people who eat pepermint and phomphit

2

in your face, they would never be missed They would never be missed And the Idiout who phrasises with in-thusastic tone of centuries but this and every country but his own. And the lady from the provences who dress like a guy who doesn't cry and the singurly abnomily the girl who never kissed. I don't think she would be missed Im share she wouldn't be missed. And that nice impriest that is rather rife the judicial hummerest I've got him on the list All funny fellows, commic men and clowns of private life. They'd none of them be missed. They'd none of them be missed. And uncompromiseing kind such as wachamacallit, thingmebob, and likewise, well-nevermind, and tut tut tut tut, and whatshisname, and you know who, but the task of filling up the blanks I rather leave up to you. But it really doesn't matter whom you place upon the list, for none of them be missed, none of them be missed.

PS. The Mt. Diablo Code concerns Radians & # inches along the radians

Figure 6

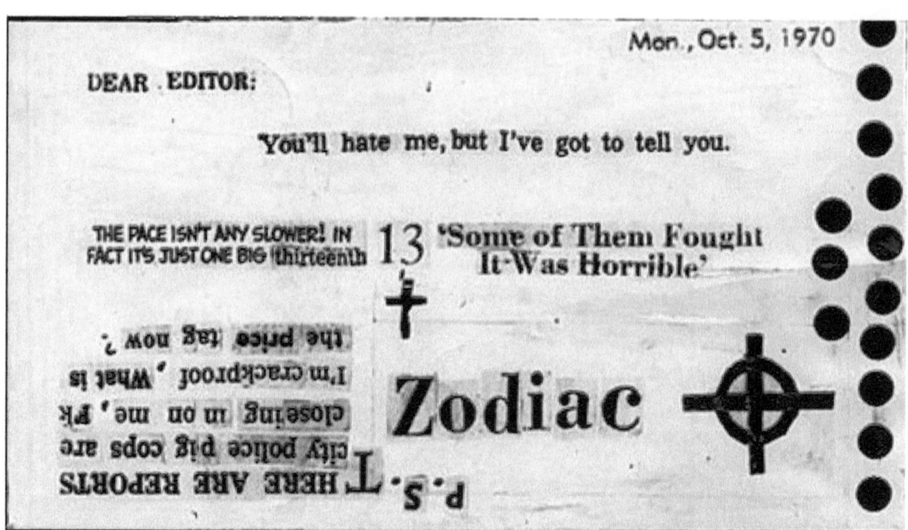

Mon., Oct. 5, 1970

DEAR EDITOR:

You'll hate me, but I've got to tell you.

THE PACE ISN'T ANY SLOWER! IN FACT IT'S JUST ONE BIG thirteenth 13 'Some of Them Fought It Was Horrible'

Zodiac

P.S. THERE ARE REPORTS city police pig cops are closeing in on me, Fk I'm crackproof, What is the price tag now?

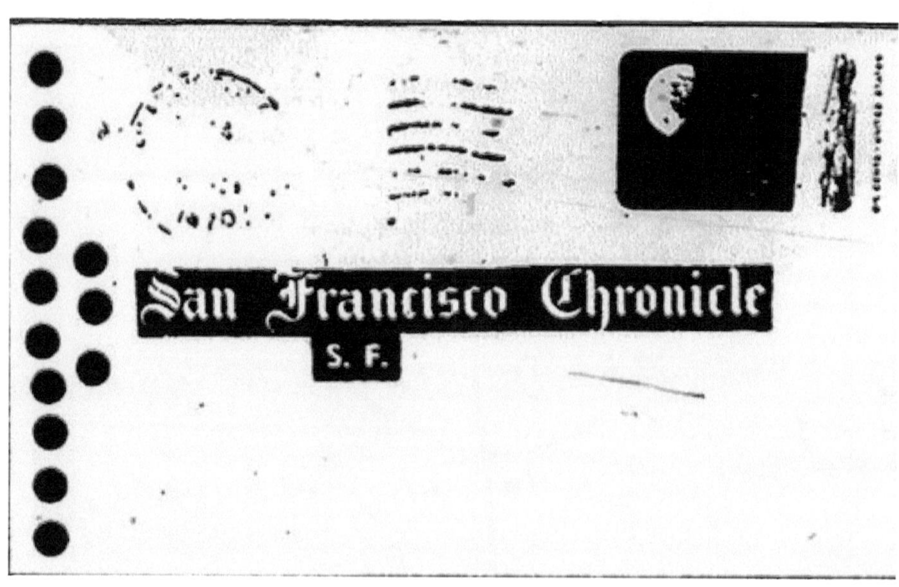

Figure 7

FROM YOUR
SECRET
PAL
14
I feel it in
my bones,
You ache
to know
my name,
And so
I'll clue
you in...

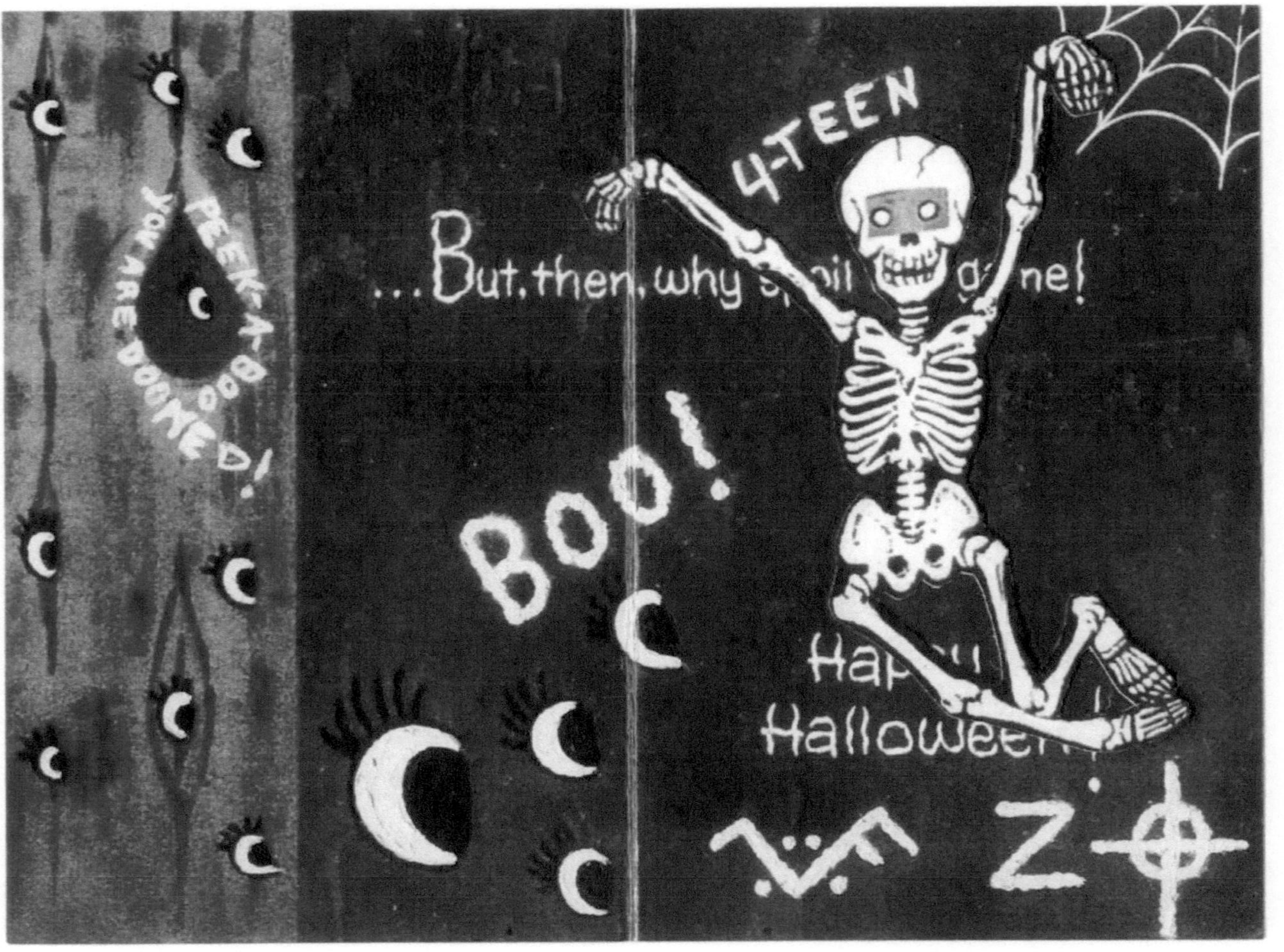
PEEK-A-BOO
YOU ARE DOOMED!
4-TEEN
BOO!
Halloween

By Fire
Paradise
Slaves
By Gun
By Knife
By Rope

Figure 8

Mailed April 20, 1970.

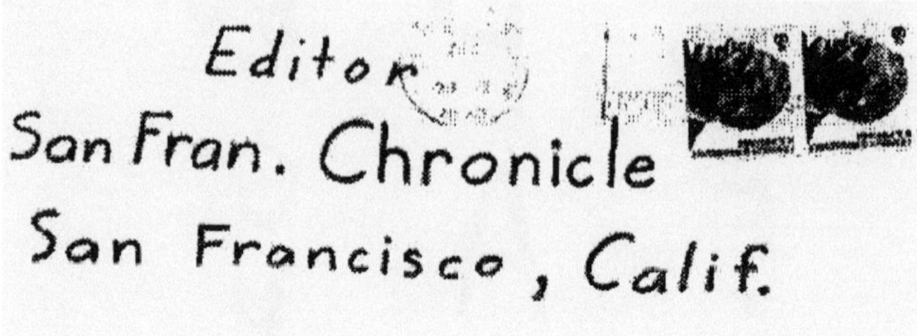

Editor

Mailed April 28, 1970.

Editor
San Fran. Chronicle
San Fran. Calif.

Mailed June 26, 1970.

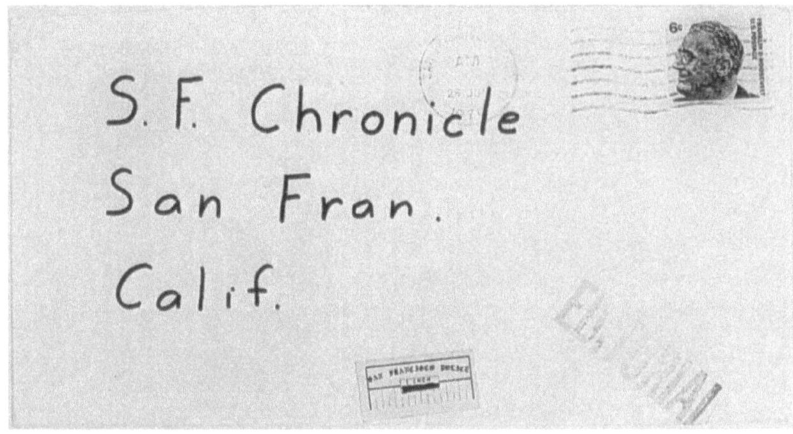

Mailed July 24, 1970.

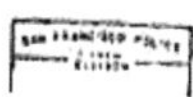

Mailed July 26, 1970.

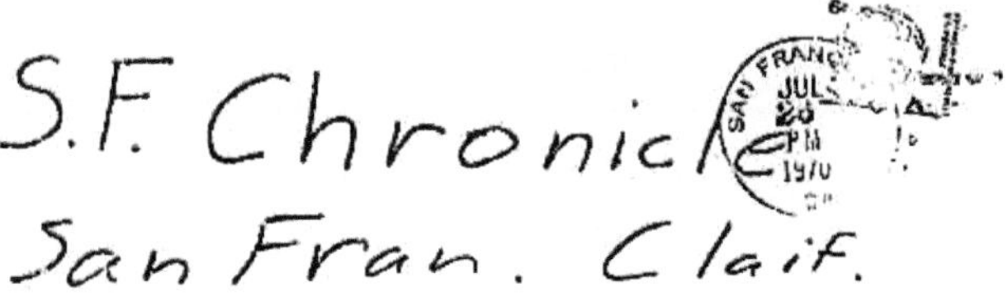

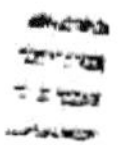

Mailed October 27, 1970.

ENDNOTES F

[1] Freedom of Information and Privacy Acts, Subject: Zodiac Killer, File Number: 9-HQ-49911, Section 3, Federal Bureau of Investigation, 169.
[2] "Bizarre Zodiac Murder," San Francisco Chronicle, April 20, 1970.
[3] Ibid.
[4] "'Zodiac' claims 10 victims in latest letter to police," Bulletin - Bend, Oregon, April 22, 1970, 11.
[5]"The Bloody 'Satan' Murder," San Francisco Chronicle, April 21, 1970, 3.
[6] "Cannibal-murderer sent to mental hospital," the Independent Record, November 17, 1972, 5.
[7] "ODMP Remembers... Sergeant Brian V. McDonnell," http://www.odmp.org/officer/8924-sergeant-brian-v-mcdonnell (retrieved May 2011).
[8] George Dunning, Director, Yellow Submarine, 1968.
[9] "Another possible solution," http://www.zodiackillerfacts.com/forum/viewtopic.php?f=51&t=375 (retrieved June 2011).
[10] Freedom of Information and Privacy Acts, Subject: Zodiac Killer, File Number: 9-HQ-49911, Section 3, Federal Bureau of Investigation, 184
[11] "California Zodiac killer warns school bus 'next'," Windsor Star, May 1, 1970, 9.
[12] "New Zodiac Threat Warns of Bus Bomb," Press-Courier, May 1, 1970.
[13] Record of Death for Richard Radetich, 1.
[14] "DEATHS OF POLICE LINKED TO HATRED," https://www.nytimes.com/1970/09/06/archives/deaths-of-police-linked-to-hatred-berkeley-chief-explains-3-recent.html (retrieved April 2020).
[15] "1967-71 -- a bloody period for S.F. police," https://www.sfgate.com/news/article/1967-71-a-bloody-period-for-S-F-police-2654263.php (retrieved April 2020).
[16] "DEATHS OF POLICE LINKED TO HATRED," https://www.nytimes.com/1970/09/06/archives/deaths-of-police-linked-to-hatred-berkeley-chief-explains-3-recent.html (April 2020).
[17] "Officer Richard E. Huerta," https://www.odmp.org/officer/6806-officer-richard-e-huerta (retrieved April 2020).
[18] "DEATHS OF POLICE LINKED TO HATRED," https://www.nytimes.com/1970/09/06/archives/deaths-of-police-linked-to-hatred-berkeley-chief-explains-3-recent.html (retrieved April 2020).
[19] "YOUNG POLICEMAN SLAIN IN BERKELEY," https://www.nytimes.com/1970/08/21/archives/young-policeman-slain-in-berkeley-shot-as-he-writes-a-ticket-3d.html (retrieved April 2020).
[20] "New Cop Slaying: Mystery Gunman Kills S.F. Officer," San Francisco Chronicle, June 20, 1970, 1.

[21] Ibid.
[22] Freedom of Information and Privacy Acts, Subject: Zodiac Killer, File Number: 9-HQ-49911, Section 3, Federal Bureau of Investigation, 225.
[23] D. Kim Rossmo, Geographic Profile, Zodiac Serial Murders.
[24] Freedom of Information and Privacy Acts, Subject: Zodiac Killer, File Number: 9-HQ-49911, Section 3, Federal Bureau of Investigation, 217.
[25] "Crime Bulletin 07-011," http://sanfranciscopolice.org/crime-bulletin-07-011 (retrieved April 2016).
[26] "Zodiac Says He Killed S.F. Officer," San Francisco Chronicle, June 30, 1970.
[27] Ibid.
[28] "1967-71 -- a bloody period for S.F. police," http://www.sfgate.com/news/article/1967-71-a-bloody-period-for-S-F-police-2654263.php (May 2016).
[29] "Zodiac Says He Killed S.F. Officer," San Francisco Chronicle, June 30, 1970.
[30] "Rode With Zodiac, Woman Claims," San Francisco Examiner, March 23, 1970, 4.
[31] Notes by movie producer for the 1989 documentary: Crimes of the Century: The Zodiac Killer, 40.
[32] "Mysterious 'Zodiac' boasts of kills to paper," Chronicle-Telegram Elyria, October 12, 1970, 4.
[33] Freedom of Information and Privacy Acts, Subject: Zodiac Killer, File Number: 9-HQ-49911, Section 3, Federal Bureau of Investigation, 239.
[34] "Gilbert and Sullivan Clue to Zodiac," San Francisco Chronicle, October 12, 1970, 5.
[35] Freedom of Information and Privacy Acts, Subject: Zodiac Killer, File Number: 9-HQ-49911, Section 3, Federal Bureau of Investigation, 245 & 250.
[36] Ibid, 251.
[37] Ibid.
[38] "GILBERT & SULLIVAN'S 'MIKADO'," The Baltimore Sun, August 26, 1885, 4.
[39] Ibid.
[40] "THE MIKADO or THE TOWN OF TITIPU," http://www.hostultra.com/~daisybtoes/Mikadotext.html (retrieved June 2011).
[41] Ibid.
[42] "Throw the book at him! [Part 2]," http://www.zodiackillerciphers.com/?p=86 (retrieved May 2016).
[43] "The Mikado; or, The Town of Titipu," http://austinlivetheatre.blogspot.com/2011/04/upcoming-mikado-gilbert-and-sullivan.html (retrieved June 2011).
[44] "Gilbert and Sullivan Clue to Zodiac," San Francisco Chronicle, October 12, 1970, 5.
[45] Ibid.

[46] Freedom of Information and Privacy Acts, Subject: Zodiac Killer, File Number: 9-HQ-49911, Section 4, Federal Bureau of Investigation, 6.
[47] "Police doubt new murder boasts in Zodiac-type notes," The Daily Review, October 12, 1970, 4.
[48] "In New Notes, Zodiac Brags of 13 Murders," Corpus Christi Times, October 12, 1970, 4.
[49] "Gilbert and Sullivan Clue to Zodiac," San Francisco Chronicle, October 12, 1970, 5.
[50] "Mysterious 'Zodiac' boasts of kills to paper."[50] Chronicle-Telegram Elyria, October 12, 1970, 4.
[51] "Zodiac threatens life of reporter," Chronicle-Telegram Elyria, October 31, 1970.
[52] Ibid.
[53] "Zodiac Pens Ghoulish Halloween Message," The Daily Review, October 31, 1970, 1
[54] Freedom of Information and Privacy Acts, Subject: Zodiac Killer, File Number: 9-HQ-49911, Section 4, Federal Bureau of Investigation, 28.
[55]The Avery Report, 1971, 13.
[56] "Zodiac threatens life of reporter," Chronicle-Telegram Elyria, October 31, 1970.
[57] "REPORTER GETS ZODIAC'S CARD," Bridgeport Post, October 31, 1970, 10.
[58] "Zodiac, Believed Mad Killer of Five, Sends Ghoulish Card to Crime Writer," The Daily Courier, October 12, 1970, 1

CHAPTER 7

THE ZODIAC'S CONFESSION

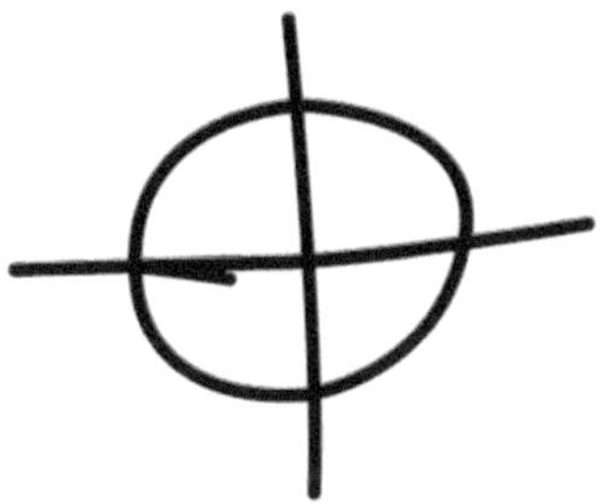

The details of the Zodiac's actions were disseminated on a large scale, and many individuals picked up the reported facts, subjected them to analysis, and tried to figure out the identity of the killer. The details also reached other police departments who began looking at their unsolved crimes and wondered if the Zodiac had operated in their jurisdiction. Thomas Kinkead, Chief of the Riverside Police Department (RPD), noticed conspicuous parallels between his unsolved murder case of Cheri Jo Bates in Riverside and the Zodiac's crimes and actions. Eventually, the RPD began sharing information with investigators working on the Zodiac case. In October 1969, Kinkead mailed a letter to Earl Randoll, Sheriff of Napa County, in which he gave a summary of his case: In 1966, a man had killed Cheri with a knife. Letters were received, purportedly written by the killer. Kinkead typed that there were "numerous similarities in your homicide and our [case]. I thought you should be aware that we are working [on] a similar-type homicide investigation. If you are able to determine by handwriting comparison or by any other means that your homicide suspect is the same as ours, please advise."[1] The media did not receive word about the connection until an anonymous source tipped Paul Avery. On Monday, November 16, 1970, the Chronicle reported the connection under the headline, "New Evidence in Zodiac Killings, A Link to Murder in Riverside."[2] With the Zodiac link established, the case was recharged and massive news reporting ensued. Some headlines: "Zodiac Linked to Slaying of Riverside Coed,"[3] "'Zodiac' is Linked to '66 Killing of Riverside Coed,"[4] "Printing Link Could Lead to Capture of Zodiac Murderer"[5] and "Definite link with Zodiac in Riverside coed's death."[6]

Sunday, October 30, 1966

The city of Riverside has experienced a steep population growth from 84.000 in 1960 to exceeding 330.000 residents in 2020.[7] Riverside is located 640 miles southeast of Vallejo and about 60 miles east of Los Angeles. The inhabitants of the major cities were accustomed to brutal violence and crime in their neighborhoods; however, in Riverside things were different, and it is commonly said that the city lost its innocence when Cheri Jo Bates was brutally slain. As a consequence, the murder triggered the most massive criminal investigation in the history of the city. [8] Cheri, an eighteen-year-old graduate of Ramona High School, attended Riverside City College (RCC). She lived with her father, Joseph Bates. Joseph's older son, Michael, was in the Navy. At home, Cheri did the dishwashing while her father did the cooking. He later stated, "As long as I can remember, she wanted to be a stewardess."[9]

She left him a note, writing that she "went to RCC library."[10] She parked her 1960 Volkswagen Beetle near the campus library on Terracina Street. She checked out three books from the library. She later went to her car, placed them inside it, and got ready to leave. She unsuccessfully attempted to start the engine. While she was at the library, a man had opened the rear trunk of her car and disabled it by removing the coil wire from the distributor socket. She was "either forced or enticed"[11] to accompany him for a distance of about 200-300 feet to a driveway between two empty houses owned by the college. Specifically, it was located between 3680 and 3692 Terracina Street, and here he viciously attacked and murdered her with a knife. As reported by the Press-Enterprise, a Riverside newspaper, a woman living nearby heard an "awful scream"[12] followed by a muted one. She heard the screams somewhere between 10:15 and 10:45 p.m. After about two minutes, she heard "a loud sound like an old car being started up."[13] Cheri had fought the man, and he had been injured to the extent that he was dripping blood on the driveway. The trail indicated that he had proceeded back to Terracina Street after killing her.[14] It was later reported that at around 9 p.m., just before the killing, a female student of RCC had walked down the driveway where Cheri was killed. She saw a young man lurking in the shadows. He was looking in the direction of Cheri's car. They acknowledged each other's presence with a 'Hi.'[15] This report coincides with an obscure Department of Justice document that describes the possible suspect as a white male adult, 19-20 years old, 5'11".[16]

Monday, October 31

Hours after the killing at 6:30 a.m., Cleophus Martin, a groundskeeper at RCC, discovered the body of Cheri Jo Bates lying face down. Her purse was underneath her. Don Walters, who was patrolling the area near the campus, was the first officer to arrive. He phoned the headquarters. Thomas Kinkead and Captain Irvin Cross, Chief of Detectives, were notified hereafter. When Cross reached the crime scene, he told Det. Sgt. Gren and six other detectives that "You will drop everything else you are engaged in and work full time on this case."[17] These six detectives were Dick Yonkers, Earl Brown, Wayne Durrington, Cliff Arons, Curtis Best, and Bob Walters. Subsequently, Detective Tom Mullen was also assigned to working full time on the murder case. Gren stated to reporters that within 24 hours they had already questioned 75 individuals.[18] That number quickly rose to more than 200. More than 30 investigators dealt with various parts of the case the first month. Cross told his men that "in a major case of this importance and magnitude, everything else is secondary."[19]

The detectives quickly ruled out robbery and sexual assault as motives. When they realized that Cheri's car had been sabotaged, they had it dusted for prints. An expert found "greasy"[20] finger and palm prints on the driver's door. It was observed that the key was in the ignition. When investigators combed through the scene of the murder, they found a Timex watch that had been torn off a wrist of approximately 7" girth. Another delicate piece of evidence emerged when the clear impression of a heel was noticed in the dirt. It was concluded that the killer had made it. A plaster cast was made of the impression, and the brand was subsequently identified as the B. F. Goodrich Company. A spokesperson for the company said that this type of heel was exclusively sold to the Federal prison industries at Leavenworth, Kansas, where they were affixed to black dress shoes and supplied to the Armed Forces. If the killer was local he could have bought them at the Base Exchange at March Air Force Base in Riverside. Measurements indicated that the heel had been attached to an eight or ten size shoe.[21]

Near the body, a cigarette butt was found and taken into evidence. When advanced forensic technology became available, it was tested for DNA.[22] However, whether it had belonged to the killer was never established.

At 11 a.m., Dr. F. Rene Modglin, the county pathologist, initiated the autopsy of Cheri in front of several witnesses including Detectives Gerald Dunn, Earl Brown, and Deputy Coroner Mike Reilly. Before initiating the surgical work and examination of the injuries, Dr. Modglin removed four brown hairs from a blood clot at the base of Cheri's right thumb.[23] She had pulled out some of the killer's hair. In 1999, an expert extracted mitochondrial DNA from the hairs.

It rapidly became evident that a violent struggle had taken place. Her hands had been severely battered, and Dr. Modglin typed eleven points in the report detailing the precise cuts and abrasions.[24] The killer had also slashed and/or stabbed the breast area, both arms, and inflicted a horizontally orientated stab wound on the left side of her back, just underneath the shoulder blade. Gruesomely in his demonic frenzy, the killer had made numerous cuts and abrasions to her face, even slashing her left cheek and upper lip. Her throat had been "extensively and irregularly lacerated."[25] Upon further review of the neck region, it was perceived that the knife had severed the right common carotid

artery. This fatal cut resulted in unconsciousness and exsanguination. When the media pressed for details, Reilly told them that "Her throat was savagely hacked."[26]
Also, during the fight, Cheri had scratched the killer with her manicured fingernails. Dr. Modglin analyzed the scrapings, which contained skin tissue. Cross told the media, "Preliminary analysis of the scrapings from beneath the fingernails of the dead girl tends to show the murderer is a white male."[27] It was evident that most of the injuries Cheri had sustained were defense wounds, mainly the bruises and cuts to her hands. She fought him until the very end. The autopsy indicated that he had used a short and slender bladed knife. It was presumably a pocketknife.[28] After the portrayal of the knife had been communicated in the media, the police received many telephone calls about knives being found in a wide range of spots in Riverside. A detective said, "The phones have been almost ringing off the hooks" and that "We are checking out each tip." [29]

Thursday, November 3

The detectives hoped that further analysis of the evidence would bring new leads to light. In particular, they were anxious to get more knowledge about the watch. They sent off the watch and other items to the California Criminal Identification and Investigation Bureau. Detective Gren admitted that after 72 hours of non-stop scrutiny, few substantial leads had developed. He told the media that Cheri had scratched and clawed her killer. "We are checking on leads on persons who have recent unexplained scratches,"[30] he also said.

Saturday, November 5

The evidence had been analyzed and the report was picked up from the mailbox at the RPD. Experts determined that the Timex had been "sold in an Armed Forces PX at an overseas military base."[31] The military connection was getting stronger each day. Not only was the footwear of the killer linked to the military, but also his watch. Detectives now focused their attention on the March Air Force Base in Riverside. Eventually, they questioned 154 military men, many of whom attended classes at RCC. Later, they submitted the watch to further testing by a specialized firm in San Diego. They discovered paint traces on the watch.[32]

Sunday, November 13

Library records and individuals coming forward enabled the police to identify most of those present in the library around the time Cheri had been killed. Two weeks had passed after the murder, and the police were now ready to conduct a reenactment of the activity in and around the library. They instructed the participants, more than 60 individuals, to wear the same clothes and park their cars in the same areas as on November 30. Prints and hair samples were collected from all the men. The cops established that at approximately 7 p.m., a 1947-52 Studebaker with ”light-colored, oxidized paint”[33] had been parked just south of Terracina Street. The driver did not appear at the enactment. Witnesses spoke of a bearded, heavyset man present in the library that failed to show up. Local newspapers requested help from the public and showed a photo of a similar car. Detective Mullen was tasked with tracking down the car, but despite a flood of tips and phone calls, he could not identify the owner or the killer.[34]

Tuesday, November 29

On this day someone posted two letters to the RPD and Daily-Enterprise respectively (the Press-Enterprise issued a morning and evening edition.). They contained a horrifying message reminiscent of future Zodiac letters. In the afternoon, a worker from the RPD picked it up from the mailbox. It had been addressed to Homicide Detail. The next day, exactly one month after the killing, the Enterprise received the letter. Both envelopes were postmarked in Riverside, did not contain postage, and the addresses had been penned with a felt tip pen in block lettering. The content of the letters were identical, the writer had sent fourth or fifth-grade copies, and he had torn off the top and bottom of the papers so the original length could not be determined.[35] Despite these efforts to prevent an identification of the typewriter and paper, it was indicated that he might have used a compact Royal Typewriter with Elite sort, Canterbury shaded.[36] Experts noted similarities between the paper and that used in teleprinters, a device now outdated with the advent of computers.

A transcript of the envelope to the RPD is unavailable at this time. The other envelope stated:

DAILY ENTERPRISE
RIVERSIDE
CALIF
ATTN: CRIME

Kinkead, in his letter to the sheriff, concluded that the writer "is aware of facts about the homicide that only the killer would know. There is no doubt that the person who wrote the confession letter is our homicide suspect."[37]
"The man who wrote that letter certainly has a deranged mind,"[38] said Detective Al DeWindt, who was also working on tracking down the killer.
In the following, the controversial letter will be examined in great depth to establish if Cheri's killer indeed authored it and to find out if that person is the Zodiac. Back in the late sixties and seventies, key figures in RPD embraced the possibility that Zodiac had killed Cheri. However, in the early eighties, they released a statement to the press that emphasized that the "alleged connection with the Zodiac"[39] was based on outdated information. They had a suspect, and he was "not"[40] the Zodiac. As advances in forensic technology emerged, it became clear that the suspect had nothing to do with the crime, for example, his DNA did not match the DNA extracted from the hair.[41]

The confession read:

THE CONFESSION
BY ______________________________

SHE WAS YOUNG AND BEAUTIFUL. BUT NOW SHE IS BATTERED AND DEAD. SHE IS NOT THE FIRST AND SHE WILL NOT BE THE LAST. I LAY AWAKE NIGHTS THINKING ABOUT MY NEXT VICTIM. MAYBE SHE WILL BE THE BEAUTIFUL BLOND THAT BABYSITS NEAR THE

LITTLE STORE AND WALKS DOWN THE DARK ALLEY EACH EVENING ABOUT SEVEN. OR MAYBE SHE WILL BE THE SHAPELY BLUE EYED BROWNETT THAT SAID NO WHEN I ASKED HER FOR A DATE IN HIGH SCHOOL. BUT MAYBE IT WILL NOT BE EITHER. BUT I SHALL CUT OFF HER FEMALE PARTS AND DEPOSIT THEM FOR THE WHOLE CITY TO SEE. SO DON'T MAKE IT EASY FOR ME. KEEP YOUR SISTERS, DAUGHTERS, AND WIVES OFF THE STREETS AND ALLEYS. MISS BATES WAS STUPID. SHE WENT TO THE SLAUGHTER LIKE A LAMB.SHE DID NOT PUT UP A STRUGGLE. BUT I DID. IT WAS A BALL. I FIRST PULLED THE MIDDLE WIRE FROM THE DISTRIBUTOR. THEN I WAITED FOR HER IN THE LIBRARY AND FOLLOWED HER OUT AFTER ABOUT TWO MINUTS. THE BATTERY MUST HAVE BEEN ABOUT DEAD BY THEN I OFFERED TO HELP. SHE WAS THEN VERY WILLING TO TALK WITH ME. I TOLD HER THAT MY CAR WAS DOWN THE STREET AND THAT I WOULD GIVE HER A LIFT HOME. WHEN WE WERE AWAY FROM THE LIBRARY WALKING, I SAID IT WAS ABOUT TIME. SHE ASKED ME "ABOUT TIME FOR WHAT?". I SAID IT WAS ABOUT TIME FOR HER TO DIE. I GRABBED HER AROUND THE NECK WITH MY HAND OVER HER MOUTH AND MY OTHER HAND WITH A SMALL KNIFE AT HER THROAT. SHE WENT VERY WILLINGLY. HER BREAST FELT VERY WARM AND FIRM UNDER MY HANDS, BUT ONLY ONE THING WAS ON MY MIND. MAKING HER PAY FOR THE BRUSH OFFS THAT SHE HAD GIVEN ME DURING THE YEARS PRIOR. SHE DIED HARD. SHE SQUIRMED AND SHOOK AS I CHOAKED HER, AND HER LIPS TWICHED. SHE LET OUT A SCREAM ONCE AND I KICKED HER HEAD TO SHUT HER UP. I PLUNGED THE KNIFE INTO HER AND IT BROKE. I THEN FINISHED THE JOB BY CUTTING HER THROAT. I AM NOT SICK. I AM INSANE. BUT THAT WILL NOT STOP THE GAME. THIS LETTER SHOULD BE PUBLISHED FOR ALL TO READ IT. IT JUST MIGHT SAVE THAT GIRL IN THE ALLEY. BUT THAT'S UP TO YOU. IT WILL BE ON YOUR CONSCIENCE. NOT MINE. YES I DID MAKE THAT CALL TO YOU ALSO. IT WAS JUST A

WARNING. BEWARE ... I AM STALKING YOUR GIRLS NOW.

CC. CHIEF OF POLICE
ENTERPRISE

The Confession in Detail

This letter differs noticeably from the Zodiac's rambling letters, with the main difference being the literary style that is used throughout, which, among others, suggests that it was not penned in a hurry, and that it was carefully put together. If we look a little deeper, we can see that it was typed using "a bipolar structure to oppose contrasting conditions."[42] For example,

Young and beautiful vs. battered and dead,
not the first vs. not the last,
beautiful blonde vs. shapely blue eyed brunet,
not sick vs. insane.

The writer demonstrated a degree of complexity, perhaps some exposure to literature and poetry, unlike what is found in the subsequent letters signed as the Zodiac that beleaguered the readers with a wretched version of the Mikado. As we shall see, it took a long time before the Zodiac associated himself with Riverside, the delay could have been motivated by a desire to hide that he was capable of expressing himself using literary devices. But why then would he have sent the confession letter in the first place? In the Catholic Church, the Sacrament of Penance or Confession is the standard ritual sinners must perform in order to obtain absolution from mortal sins committed after baptism. This confession can easily be seen as a mockery of the Catholic Church. No doubt, the writer was familiar with the Bible when he stated that Cheri went to the slaughter like a lamb, an expression that is used several times in the Bible.[43]

Interestingly, the writer strongly implied that he and Cheri were known to each other. According to the letter, she had rejected him in the past, and he got revenge by killing her. Why would the presumed killer give the police groundbreaking pieces of information to his identity? Had the killer known Cheri it would

only have been a matter of time before the detectives had identified him. Given that the writer is able to express himself relatively clearly, and that the letter does not contain any psychotic overtones, it is clear that this is clever trickery, i.e. he was trying to manipulate the investigators into focusing on acquaintances and former schoolmates of Cheri. Thereby, he actually showed us that he was a stranger to Cheri, if he in fact had killed her.
The style of writing points not to the Zodiac at first glance. However, at a closer look, it becomes manifest that he authored the letter. The smoking gun is the word, *twitch.* Compare these two sentences whereas the first is from the confession, the second is from Zodiac's July 1970 letter.

1) "SHE *SQUIRMED* AND SHOOK AS I CHOAKED HER, AND HER LIPS *TWICHED.* SHE LET OUT A *SCREAM.*"
2) "Some I shall tie over ant hills and watch them *scream* + *twich* and *sqwirm.*"

We see the same phraseology and importantly the same misspelling of twitch, which is a low-frequency word. Furthermore, they shared a penchant for the word "shall," a verb that is much more common in British English. There are many more identical or nearly identical traits shared by the two: They demanded that their letters should be published. Both of them made threats and were skilled manipulators. The confession writer attempted to induce widespread fear in the population, especially among women. This psychological fingerprint is shared by the Zodiac. The Zodiac threatened couples, everyone, children, and then unknowns. We cannot exclude him as being the author of the confession letter simply because he did not specifically target women. The Zodiac was unpredictable, and it is possible, even likely, that his initial focus was aimed at females. The threat toward children was the most successful concerning media coverage and terrorization of the public. The quotes below show how Zodiac singled out several different groups within a short period.

1) July 1969: "I will cruse around and pick of all stray people or coupples that are alone then move on to Kill some more untill I have killed over a dozen people."

2) October 1969: “School children make nice targets, I think I shall wipe out a school bus some morning.”
3) July 1970: “I’ve got a little list, of society offenders who might well be underground who would never be missed who would never be missed.”

Zodiac and the confession writer delighted in giving synthetic clues to their identity. The confession was received by the Enterprise exactly one month after the crime. Zodiac was likewise keen on sending greetings on anniversaries and referring to the dates of his crimes. Even the taunting introduction of the confession, ”BY _______,” is very similar to the April 1970 letter in which the Zodiac wrote, ”My name is,” and then provided a cipher that cannot be solved satisfactorily. Within a restricted geographical area and timeframe, one is extremely unlikely to find two different individuals who:

1) Write anonymous letters to the news media.
2) Make sure their letters are received on anniversaries related to crimes that they have taken credit for.
3) Describe and take credit for murders.
4) Provide a synthetic motive.
5) Misspell the same word.
6) Are inclined to use “shall” instead of “will.”
7) Refer to past murders.
8) Make hollow threats.
9) Demand their letters to be published.
10) Make or refer to phone calls.
11) Use a felt tip pen.
12) One of the ideas expressed in the confession is psychologically identical to the Zodiac’s statement about sex and murder in the 408 cipher. The writer first complimented Cheri’s breast, but refrained from any further sexual actions, and then stated that killing was his true aim.

In essence, the confession exudes with Zodiac characteristics, and no solid arguments or evidence are pointing in a different direction. We should also note that apart from the stylistic differences, the Zodiac never wrote or said the names of his victims, he depersonalized them by stating "girl," "boy," "taxi driver," and "people," despite their names frequently being mentioned in the media. In the confession, he was personal and stated the victim's surname, Bates. This may indicate that depersonalization of the victim had never taken place, within the Zodiac's twisted psyche, because he did not kill her.

The Killer's Identity

Although, we have established the overwhelming probability that Zodiac authored the confession, we have yet to determine if he in fact killed Cheri Jo Bates or was taking credit for someone he had not killed. The unprecedented nature of the crime resulted in a massive press coverage that encompassed many aspects of the crime, making it a possibility that the confession was nothing more than a hoax.

"SHE WAS YOUNG AND BEAUTIFUL."
Distinct from even a casual read of the first article in the Enterprise about the case: "Cheri Jo Bates, an 18 – year-old Riverside City College student and former Ramona High cheerleader."[44] Cheri's picture was also shown in the news.

"SHE DID NOT PUT UP A STRUGGLE."
This statement is not consonant with the autopsy report that documents lacerations to the face, neck, hands, arm, forearm, and more. Moreover, it is not in agreement with the reporting in the newspapers, e.g. the Los Angeles Times stated that the autopsy "indicated the girl put up a tremendous struggle with her assailant."[45] The key to understanding the claim might be contained in the next sentence in the confession, which stated, "BUT I DID." The Zodiac tried to convey that the brutality of the killing was not due to any loss of control at the crime scene, but because he desired to kill her violently, a cat and mouse game. This psychological trait remained consistent within his psyche, and when he entered the Zodiac persona, he had not changed one bit.

"I FIRST PULLED THE MIDDLE WIRE FROM THE DISTRIBUTOR."
A detective from RPD is paraphrased in an FBI report as affirming that "the manner in which her vehicle was disabled" was "known only to the unknown subject who murdered her."[46] Specifically, the killer had pulled out the coil wire of the distributor socket.[47] However, this fact had already been published in numerous newspapers, for example, the Enterprise wrote, "The distributor coil and the condenser to her car's engine had been torn out."[48] The Los Angeles Times stated that the "ignition wiring" had been "yanked loose."[49] Another newspaper revealed that "the coil wire" had been "yanked loose."[50] The writer had correctly used middle wire as a synonym for coil wire, and this probably led the detective to conclude that the writer had specialized knowledge of the crime. However, if the Zodiac were familiar with a typical Volkswagen engine he would have known that the middle wire *is* the coil wire and it protrudes significantly from the distributor cap.

"THEN I WAITED FOR HER IN THE LIBRARY AND FOLLOWED HER OUT."
He may have tried to give the impression that he was the stocky man missing in the enactment (a fact reported by newspapers). If this individual was the same as the young man lurking at the driveway, remains unknown.[‡‡‡]

"THE BATTERY MUST HAVE BEEN ABOUT DEAD BY THEN I OFFERED TO HELP."
If one disconnects the coil wire, the ignition coil cannot deliver the necessary spark to ignite the fuel and the car will not start; it will not drain the battery. The writer could accurately describe the method of sabotage, yet he was unaware of how it affected the car. Alternatively, the writer may have meant that Cheri made several attempts to start the car and that drained the battery, and then he

‡‡‡ The cops most likely obtained detailed descriptions of the two individuals. We do not have access to these.

offered his help. In any event, if the writer had performed the said activity to sabotage the car, he would have known with certainty what happened when he offered to help. The words, "must have been about dead," indicate that he was unsure.
This sentence indicates that he did not kill Bates.

"I TOLD HER THAT MY CAR WAS DOWN THE STREET AND THAT I WOULD GIVE HER A LIFT HOME. WHEN WE WERE AWAY FROM THE LIBRARY WALKING, I SAID IT WAS ABOUT TIME."
It was reported that the "Police believed she may have walked with her killer to the place where she was killed."[51] The letter by Kinkead to Randoll states that Cheri and her killer *walked* together until he decided to attack. Contrary, Captain Cross stated to the press that "The girl may have run up the driveway from the street to escape her assailant. There were scuffs in the gravel on the driveway."[52] Overall there was confusion concerning this issue in the newspapers. For example, the Enterprise wrote, "The police believe Miss Bates either walked to the rear of the house with her slayer, or was followed there."[53] The Los Angeles Times had a different perspective and stated that the killer "sprang upon her when she tried to start the car."[54] Either way, it is not certain that the investigators were able to determine what exactly happened. Cheri has been described as "very proud of her little car" and that she "never left it without locking the doors and rolling the windows up."[55] The key was in the ignition and both windows were rolled down when the car was found. It seems reasonable that she walked out of the library and got inside her car. She attempted to start it. When the murderer made his presence known by offering his help, she rolled down the driver's window. At some point, he brandished his knife and forced her to follow him to the driveway; she never had a chance to secure the car. This scenario accounts for the mysterious circumstances. It seems farfetched that Cheri would leave the windows rolled down, etc., if she had only accepted a lift from the killer. This indicates that the Zodiac did not kill her and that the alleged conversation outlined in the confession did not take place.

"I GRABBED HER AROUND THE NECK WITH MY HAND OVER HER MOUTH."
Typically, the reaction of the victim in such a situation is to grab the attacker's hands or hair. The brown hairs found in Cheri's right-hand blend in with the writer's description.[56] It is interesting that Zodiac had brown hair, too.

"A SMALL KNIFE AT HER THROAT."
Measurements and observations made during the autopsy enabled the coroner to establish that the murder-weapon was a knife with a blade of a minimum of 0.5 inches in width and 3.5 inches in length.[57] Unfortunately, the Daily-Enterprise had already divulged that the weapon could have been "a slender-bladed knife at least three inches in length."[58]
The adjective *small* is significant. First, psychologically, he may have been bragging that he only required a small knife to kill her. Second, as a factual statement, but it was already public knowledge. It gives the strong impression that he added details he had extracted from the media to pretend that he was the killer. He could have described numerous aspects only known to the police. He did not.

"SHE LET OUT A SCREAM ONCE AND I KICKED HER HEAD TO SHUT HER UP."
The scream had been reported in the news as a single one followed by a muted one. According to Deputy Coroner Reilly, "it appeared the girl was punched several times in the face."[59] He also said that the autopsy "revealed numerous other brutal blows to the girl's chest, arms, hands and face."[60] Reading about these blows may have influenced the Zodiac to embed the statement.

"I CHOAKED HER."
This was not stated in the autopsy of Cheri, and the media did not report it either. However, Kinkead did write that she had been "choked."[61]

I PLUNGED THE KNIFE INTO HER AND IT BROKE. I THEN FINISHED THE JOB BY CUTTING HER THROAT."

The autopsy did not reveal any blade fragments in the body of Cheri, and according to Cross there was "no evidence"[62] that it had happened.

Zodiac typed that it broke when it penetrated her and *then* he cut her throat. Her wounds would likely have reflected that condition of the blade during the autopsy. Maybe he meant that the guard broke, but this does not jibe with his limited description. If the handle broke, he could not have proceeded to use it at that point. What could have happened is that the handle *cracked* due to the force applied to it during the murder.

His finishing remark is likewise not consistent with the fact that her throat had been lacerated at least seven times.[63] On the contrary, his claim is in conformity with the initial reporting in the Riverside Press, which stated that she was found with "her throat deeply slashed and at least one stab wound in her back."[64] Maybe Reilly's quotation escaped his attention, and he relied upon reporting from other sources, this does not seem likely, however. For example, many of the statements appeared together such as on November 1 in the Enterprise that reported the "hacked" quotation from Reilly, the details of the beating, the size of the knife, and that her car had been sabotaged.[65] If he derived his factual statements from a newspaper, it was likely a local one, presumably the Enterprise. Zodiac appears to have planted manipulation and deception in the letter for various psychological reasons.

"YES I DID MAKE THAT CALL TO YOU ALSO. IT WAS JUST A WARNING."

Captain Cross commented to a newspaper that his office had "received numerous crank calls since the murder, but nothing which could be linked to this letter."[66] If there were a call, it would have been made to the Enterprise.

Conclusions

The description of the killing of Cheri Jo Bates is in some respects consistent with the facts, whereas in other places it is not. If the Zodiac killed her, he took a risk by incorporating his own manipulation. He did this in the August 1969 letter. Zodiac, although guilty of the crimes he took credit for, lied about the speed of his car when he exited the parking lot. He lied because it painted an unfavorable picture of him. The same psychological tendency is evident in the confession letter where he lied about Cheri fighting back, probably because it made him look weak. Concerning evidence, there are no unknowns provided in the confession that could not have been extracted from a meticulous study of newspapers and newscasts. In this regard, we should consider the probability and oddity that the Zodiac, if indeed he was the murderer, would only pen details that had already been broadcast or could have been reasoned or guessed. He could have stated numerous factual details that were only known to the killer and the police, such as losing his watch at the crime scene. This fact strongly indicates that the Zodiac did not kill Cheri. The closest, the Zodiac comes to providing something not disclosed in the press is the use of middle wire as a synonym for coil wire and the choking. However, as mentioned previously, this is not mentioned in the autopsy, and, thus, appears to be an inaccuracy in Kinkead's 1969 letter to Earl Randoll.

Moreover, the Zodiac laid out a false, clear-cut motive for killing Cheri. He did it to baffle and lead the investigators in the wrong direction. Initially, they jumped the bait when they "turned their search toward possible rejected suitors. Literally hundreds of young men – mostly fellow students, but military personnel from several nearby bases as well – were checked out and cleared."[67] The actual killer would have been highly motivated to implement this strategy. However, knowing the deceptive and manipulative history of the Zodiac, we can deduce that he would have found much joy in conning the Riverside Police Department, regardless of his culpability in the murder of Cheri.

Overall, the strongest circumstantial evidence pointing to the Zodiac as the killer is outlined below.

1) Both were killers – only an extremely small percentage of the population can be placed in this category.
2) Used a knife.
3) Killings not motivated by sex or financial gain.
4) Both entered and left in a car.
5) Both deceived their victims so that the crimes could be carried out.

6) Cheri's killer disabled her car; Zodiac claimed to have disabled Kathleen Johns' car.
7) Cheri's killer had brown hair. Witnesses stated that Zodiac had brown hair, and a reddish-brown hair was found underneath the stamps of the October 1969 letter.
8) The heel print had been attached to a shoe of size eight or ten. The Zodiac wore a pair of Wing-Walkers, size 10.5.
9) The killer's military association was established by the watch and heel print. Zodiac wore military shoes and displayed skills associated with the military, e.g. cryptography.
10) Zodiac claimed to have killed Cheri in the confession.
11) As we shall see, in a letter sent to the Los Angeles Times, the Zodiac gave the police credit for "stumbling across" his Riverside "activity."
12) Zodiac was paranoid about Hartnell fighting back despite the fact that he was well-armed. Such paranoia could be the result of a previous bad experience.
13) The killer observed Cheri leaving the car and followed or waited for her; Zodiac sneaked in on Hartnell and Cecelia.
14) Cheri's killer and the Zodiac were both weekend offenders.

When the connection became apparent, Inspector Armstrong of the SFPD noticed "strong similarities" in the two cases and said, "There's a very good possibility it's our man."[68] However, as previously mentioned, many years later the Riverside Police Department issued a statement that the Zodiac was not the killer of Cheri; our analysis of the confession letter points in that direction, too.

December 1966

During Christmas at the Riverside City College library, a custodian made a shocking discovery while removing several desks. On one of them, he observed a chilling poem ostensibly referring to the killing of Cheri Jo Bates. The writer had used a ballpoint pen.[69]

The disturbing poem read:

Sick of living/unwilling to die
cut.
clean.
if red /
clean.
blood spurting,
    dripping,
        spilling;
all over her new
dress
oh well
it was red
anyway.
life draining into an
uncertain death.
she won't
die
this time
someone ll find her.
just wait till
next time.
    rh

Sunday, April 30, 1967

Six months after the crime, the killer, or someone pretending to be him, mailed a letter to Cheri's dad, Riverside Police, and the Press-Enterprise. The writer had used a pencil to write on "ordinary loose leaf binder paper,"[70] which the Chronicle characterized as "lined 3-hole school paper."[71] The content of the letters were practically indistinguishable, and they were clearly commemorating the death of Cheri. In 1970, when the Zodiac connection had been fully established, Morrill concluded that they were "unquestionably the work of Zodiac."[72] Morrill also analyzed the poem and said to the media that "The handprinting scratched on the desk is the same as on the three letters, particularly like that on the envelopes, and this handprinting is by the same person who has been preparing the Zodiac letters that have been received by The Chronicle."[73] In

1978, handwriting expert, John Shimoda, Director of Postal Crime Laboratory, also analyzed the poem and the three letters and reached the conclusion that the Zodiac did not author them.[74] The FBI was called in to settle the matter. These questioned documents and the confession envelopes had already been analyzed in 1974 by FBI's handwriting expert whom at that time was not able to make a definitive statement.[75] The new FBI analysis, which this time encompassed multiple Zodiac letters, was again inconclusive. The expert elaborated that the hand printing "shows a wide range of variation and various writing speeds. Additionally, portions of the material, particularly the three Riverside letters, may have been disguised or deliberately distorted."[76] Nonetheless, "consistent hand printing characteristics were noted […] which indicate that one person may have prepared all of the letters including the Riverside letters and the message found on the desk top in the Riverside case."[77] Questioned document examination, or handwriting analysis, is a powerful tool when there is plenty of writing. A definitive statement can be difficult to make under certain circumstances, such as when the handwriting is not freely flowing or if there is limited handwriting to work with.

The letter sent to the RPD:

BATES HAD
TO DIE
THERE WILL
BE MORE
Z

The signature at the bottom appears to be a "Z."

The *over-posted* envelope read:

Riverside Police Dept.
Riverside,
Calif

Analysis

The detectives interpreted the gloomy and bloody nature of the poem as an abstract reference to Cheri or possibly some unknown victim. Not many straightforward facts are contained in the poem. However, the murder of Cheri seems to be inconsistent with the ramblings on the desk. For example, she did not wear a dress and she *did* die and not "next time." For this reason and others, many have disputed the authenticity of the poem; some opine it was the work of a depressed teenager contemplating suicide.

The poem ends with what appears to be a signature or a reference to the president of RCC whose name was *R.H.* Bradshaw. Eventually, investigators looked into the possibility that Zodiac may have worked or studied at RCC, trying to find other samples of his printing. If in fact the poem had been penned by the Zodiac, we would expect him to be associated with RCC or at least the library. The investigators' efforts appear to have been comprehensive yet failed to identify him or link him to the library, indicating that someone else might have authored the poem. However, it is certainly a possibility that he went under the radar, especially if he graduated or dropped out a long time before the killing, and, thus, the poem was not about Cheri.

If a scale of horror exists, the three notes would attain a top grade. Handwriting analysis was inconclusive due to the distorted nature of the printing; however, these notes are without a doubt the work of the Zodiac killer. Many of the similarities we highlighted in our discussion of the confession are also applicable in this instance. In addition, in 1967 the probability that someone other than Zodiac would sign a taunting note with what appears to be a Z is vanishingly small. He over-posted the envelopes and perversely commemorated the murder of Cheri Jo Bates, and in so doing he revealed to us his identity, *the Zodiac*. He promised us that there would be more. He surely kept his promise.

Tuesday, November 17, 1970

The Zodiac-connection to Riverside was hot at this time, and the Zodiac was undoubtedly reading the articles eagerly. In the Chronicle, Avery authored the article, "Riverside Slaying in 1966: Zodiac Link is Definite."[78] Avery left the readers in no doubt that

Zodiac was behind the killing of Cheri. In the article, Avery also reported a related incident that took place in 1968 near Telegraph Avenue, Berkeley. A witness saw a 25-40-year-old man assisting two girls with their car. When the witness apparently approached the scene, the man became "obviously enraged at the intrusion and stalked off."[79] The man had disabled their car by pulling out "the distributor."[80] Earlier in the evening, the girls had rejected the man's offer for a ride because they had their own car after which they went for a snack at a bar. When they came out of the bar, their car would not start. The same man approached them and offered to help. The police had not identified the girls.

Thursday, November 19

Avery published another piece in the Chronicle, and he titled it "Closed Session in Riverside: Police Confer on Zodiac Killings."[81] He described a closed nine-hour meeting in Riverside between Captain Cross, Inspector Dave Toschi, Det. Sgt. Ken Narlow and Inspector Melvin Nicolai. A consensus was formed that Zodiac had killed Cheri. They believed he "may well have been a fellow student of the pretty cheerleader at Riverside City College," "one of her teachers," "a military man then stationed in the area," or "even a traveling salesman from the Bay Area."[82] They found it to be an interesting coincidence that Zodiac's fourth victim, Cecelia Shepard, was a student at the University of California at Riverside. They also believed that he hid his connection to Riverside because he had realized that he had "made some blunder" that left behind "a telltale clue to his identity that they will stumble onto. That clue may well be a set of initials – 'r h' – which were found inscribed."[83] They considered it "quite probable"[84] that he had authored the confession.

Tuesday, November 24

The Enterprise published a story with the headline, "Detectives hope to find Zodiac's handwriting in City College records."[85] Cross revealed, "The handwriting will be checked to see if there is any connection with the writing on the desk."[86] Furthermore, "Cross would only say that the handwriting samples being checked came from 'a lot of people' who attended RCC that year."[87] He also said "the hunt for the Zodiac was moved to Riverside,"[88] and "the department has gotten some 20 letters and a like number of phone calls from persons who felt they had information for the police."[89]

Saturday, March 13, 1971

The Zodiac had read enough articles about his alleged murder in Riverside, and now he wanted to have a say in this. On Saturday, March 13, he mailed a letter to the Los Angeles Times from Pleasanton in Alameda County. Handwriting expert John J. Harris of Los Angeles determined "There's absolutely no question about it. The Zodiac killer wrote the letter."[90] Captain Cross quickly dismissed the Zodiac's newest claim of an excess of 17 victims: "There are most certainly no other killings in this city which can be linked to Zodiac."[91]
In the letter, Zodiac stated that his motivation for writing to the Times was out of anger that he was not devoted enough front-page coverage in other newspapers. Publicity was on his mind. This was the first and only time he mentioned Riverside. He leaves us guessing by using the vague term, "activity." True to his word, the Zodiac enjoyed needling his pursuers, he knew their hunger for information, but he did not intend to assist them in any way. He probably derived great satisfaction from the thought of irritating the detectives and leading them astray. His use of the term 'crack proof' suggests that he authored the October card – or imitated a copycat.[92]

The L.A. Times letter read:

> This is the Zodiac speaking
> Like I have allways said
> I am crack proof. If the
> Blue Meannies are evere
> going to catch me, they had
> best get off their fat asses
> + do something. Because the
> longer they fiddle + fart
> around, the more slaves
> I will collect for my after
> life. I do have to give them

credit for stumbling across
my riverside activity, but
they are only finding the
easy ones, there are a hell
of a lot more down there.
The reason that I'm writing
to the Times is this, They
don't bury me on the back pages
like some of the others.
⊕
SFPD-0   17+

The envelope read:

The L.A Times
Los Angeles Calif
Please Rush to Editor
AIR Mail

Observations

In November 1969, Zodiac communicated that he had started his collection of slaves in 1968 at Lake Herman Road. This idea was also echoed on Bryan Hartnell's car door. After killing Paul Stine, the Zodiac went on to claim that he had committed more murders, and he was eventually humiliated in the press for making false claims. It seems out of character that he did not strike back at them and boast of the Bates murder. Even if he only wrote the confession letter, as the evidence points toward, he could still have bragged about killing her. Zodiac must have had a clear motive for only reluctantly implying he had killed Cheri Jo Bates. It is possible that there is something that we have overlooked all along, such as a connection or link between the crimes he committed as the Zodiac and his ties to Riverside. If we can identify the missing piece of the puzzle, we might eventually be breathing down his neck.
If we make the assumption that he killed Bates, then there is an interesting theory we can ponder. Before dying in the electric chair, notorious serial killer Ted Bundy assisted Homicide Detective Robert Keppel in tracking down the Green River Killer. Bundy found it easy to convey the killer's compulsions, behaviors, and

methods. Years later when the Riverman (Bundy's title for the killer) had finally been identified as Gary Ridgway, it was revealed that Bundy's predictions had been "startlingly accurate."[93] During the straining, hour-long interviews, Bundy remarked that before the police would notice an obvious pattern linking the same perpetrator to a series of killings, the killer could have committed early murders that were significantly different. However, the killer might not be able to admit to them because "the victim might be someone with whom the killer had a kind of relationship, even if it was only in his own mind or if the victim saw something human or intimate in the killer through their association. Maybe it was someone the killer actually thought he liked."[94] Bundy also mentioned that if the victim was "too young" or "too close to family"[95] then the killer could find it difficult to discuss.

APPENDIX G

Figure 1
A portrait of Cheri Jo Bates.
Figure 2
The killer's Timex watch.
Figure 3
Cheri Jo Bates' 1960 Volkswagen Beetle.
Figure 4
The murder scene between the two houses.
Figure 5
Suspected Zodiac letter. Mailed November 29, 1966.
The Riverside Daily-Enterprise.
Figure 6
Suspected Zodiac poem. Discovered in December 1966.
Figure 7
Suspected Zodiac letter. Mailed April 30, 1967.
Joseph Bates.
Figure 8
Suspected Zodiac letter. Mailed April 30, 1967.
The Riverside Press-Enterprise.
Figure 9
Suspected Zodiac letter. Mailed April 30, 1967.
The Riverside Police Department.
Figure 10
Zodiac letter. Mailed March 13, 1971.
The Los Angeles Times.
Figure 11
Envelopes.

Figure 1

Figure 2

Figure 3

Figure 4

Figure 5

352-481

THE CONFESSION

BY____________________

SHE WAS YOUNG AND BEAUTIFUL. BUT NOW SHE IS BATTERED AND DEAD. SHE IS NOT THE FIRST AND SHE WILL NOT BE THE LAST. I LAY AWAKE NIGHTS THINKING ABOUT MY NEXT VICTIM. MAYBE SHE WILL BE THE BEAUTIFUL BLOND THAT BABYSITS NEAR THE LITTLE STORE AND WALKS DOWN THE DARK ALLEY EACH EVENING ABOUT SEVEN. OR MAYBE SHE WILL BE THE SHAPELY BLUE EYED BROWNETT THAT SAID NO WHEN I ASKED HER FOR A DATE IN HIGH SCHOOL. BUT MAYBE IT WILL NOT BE EITHER. BUT I SHALL CUT OFF HER FEMALE PARTS AND DEPOSIT THEM FOR THE WHOLE CITY TO SEE. SO DON'T MAKE IT TO EASY FOR ME. KEEP YOUR SISTERS, DAUGHTERS, AND WIVES OFF THE STREETS AND ALLEYS. MISS BATES WAS STUPID. SHE WENT TO THE SLAUGHTER LIKE A LAMB.SHE DID NOT PUT UP A STRUGGLE. BUT I DID. IT WAS A BALL. I FIRST PULLED THE MIDDLE WIRE FROM THE DISTRIBUTOR. THEN I WAITED FOR HER IN THE LIBRARY AND FOLLOWED HER OUT AFTER ABOUT TWO MINUTS. THE BATTERY MUST HAVE BEEN ABOUT DEAD BY THEN I THEN OFFERED TO HELP. SHE WAS THEN VERY WILLING TO TALK WITH ME. I TOLD HER THAT MY CAR WAS DOWN THE STREET AND THAT I WOULD GIVE HER A LIFT HOME. WHEN WE WERE AWAY FROM THE LIBRARY WALKING, I SAID IT WAS ABOUT TIME. SHE ASKED ME "ABOUT TIME FOR WHAT". I SAID IT WAS ABOUT TIME FOR HER TO DIE. I GRABBED HER AROUND THE NECK WITH MY HAND OVER HER MOUTH AND MY OTHER HAND WITH A SMALL KNIFE AT HER THROAT. SHE WENT VERY WILLINGLY. HER BREAST FELT VERY WARM AND FIRM UNDER MY HANDS, BUT ONLY ONE THING WAS ON MY MIND. MAKING HER PAY FOR THE BRUSH OFFS THAT SHE HAD GIVEN ME DURING THE YEARS PRIOR. SHE DIED HARD. SHE SQUIRMED AND SHOOK AS I CHOKED HER, AND HER LIPS TWICHED. SHE LET OUT A SCREAM ONCE AND I KICKED HER HEAD TO SHUT HER UP. I PLUNGED THE KNIFE INTO HER AND IT BROKE. I THEN FINISHED THE JOB BY CUTTING HER THROAT. I AM NOT SICK. I AM INSANE. BUT THAT WILL NOT STOP THE GAME. THIS LETTER SHOULD BE PUBLISHED FOR ALL TO READ IT. IT JUST MIGHT SAVE THAT GIRL IN THE ALLEY. BUT THAT'S UP TO YOU. IT WILL BE ON YOUR CONSCIENCE. NOT MINE. YES I DID MAKE THAT CALL TO YOU ALSO. IT WAS JUST A WARNING. BEWARE...I AM STALKING YOUR GIRLS NOW.

CC. CHIEF OF POLICE
ENTERPRISE

7½ L   8 1/16" W

Figure 6

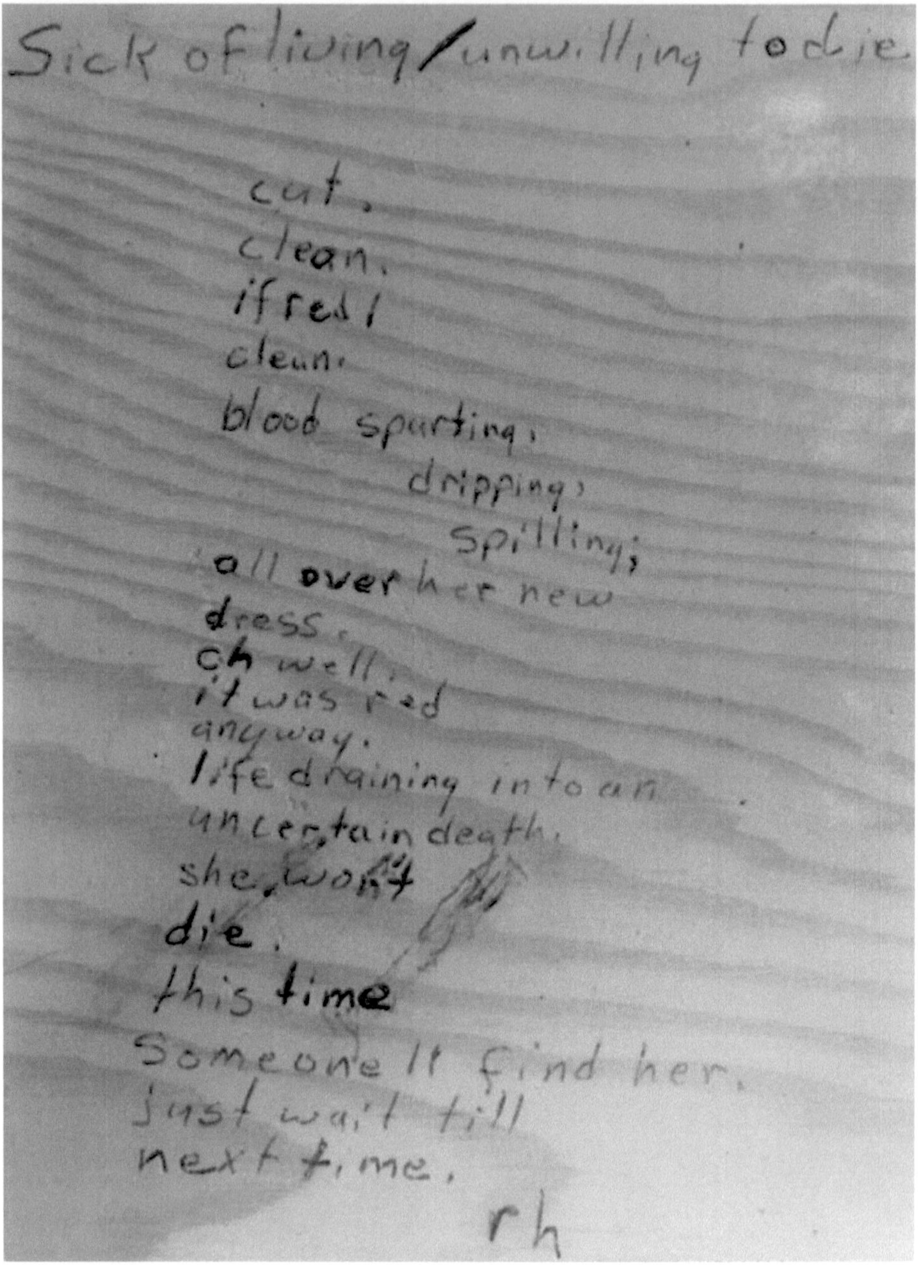

Sick of living/unwilling to die

cut.
clean.
if red!
clean.
blood spurting.
          dripping,
               spilling;
all over her new
dress.
oh well.
it was red
anyway.
life draining into an
uncertain death.
she won't
die.
this time
Someone'll find her.
just wait till
next time.

rh

Figure 7

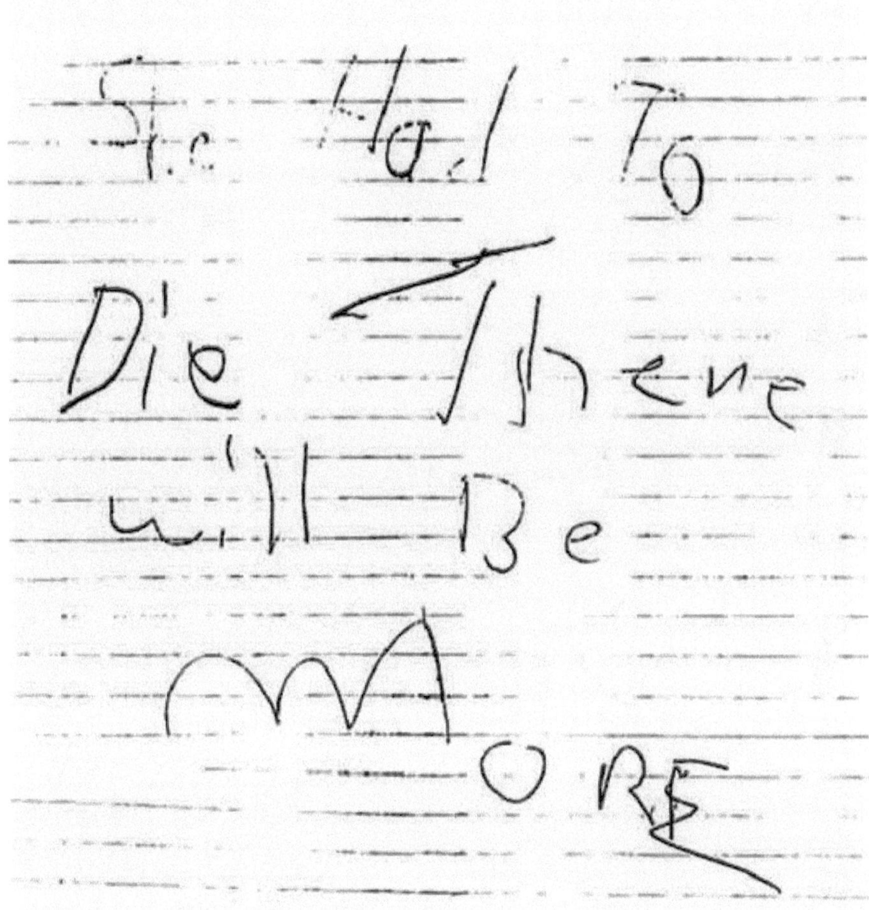

Figure 8

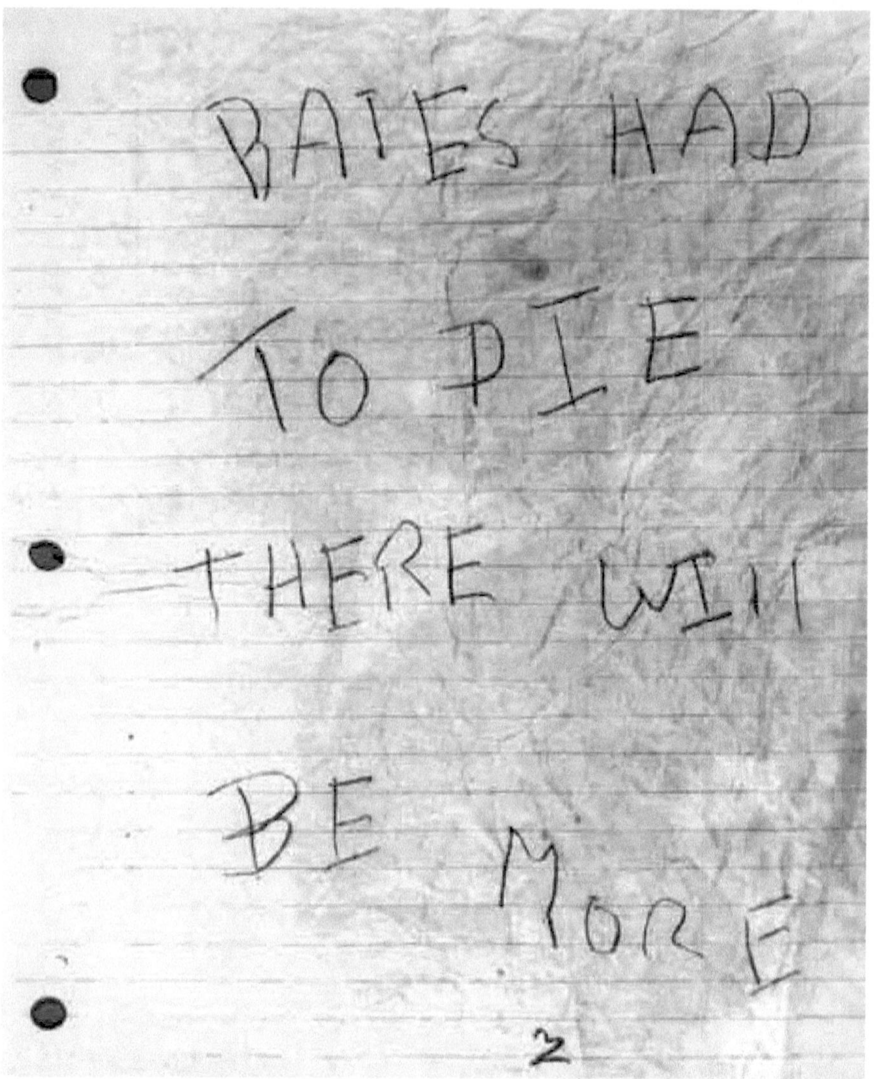

Figure 9

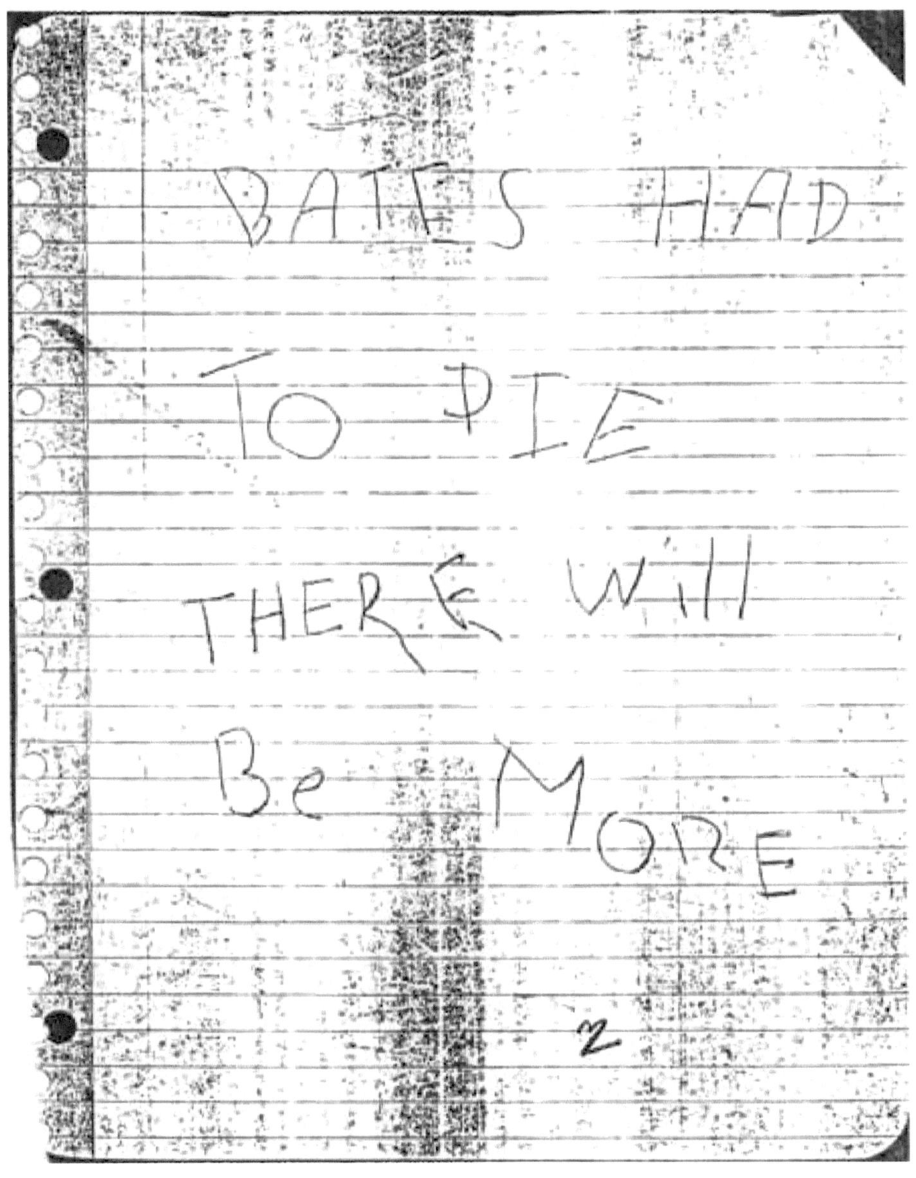

Figure 10

This is the Zodiac speaking
Like I have always said
I am crack proof. If the
Blue Meannies are evere
going to catch me, they had
best get off their fat asses
& do something. Because the
longer they fiddle & fart
around, the more slaves
I will collect for my after
life. I do have to give them
credit for stumbling across
my riverside activity, but
they are only finding the
easy ones, there are a hell
of a lot more down there.
The reason that I'm writing
to the Times is this, They
dont bury me on the back pages
like some of the others.
SFPD—0 ⊕—17+

Figure 11

Mailed November 29, 1966.

Mailed April 30, 1967.

Mailed April 30, 1967.

Mailed April 30, 1967.

Mailed March 13, 1971.

The L.A. Times
Los Angeles Calif
Please Rush to Editor
AIR Mail

AIR Mail

ENDNOTES G

[1] Kinkead, Thomas. Letter to Earl Randoll. October 20 1969, 2-3.
[2] "New Evidence in Zodiac Killings, A Link to Murder in Riverside," San Francisco Chronicle, November 16 1970, 1.
[3] "Zodiac Linked to Slaying of Riverside Coed," the Daily Report, November 16 1970, 1.
[4] "'Zodiac' is Linked to '66 Killing of Riverside Coed," the Fresno Bee, November 16 1970, 3-C.
[5] "Printing Link Could Lead to Capture of Zodiac Murderer," News Journal, November 19 1970, 24.
[6] "Definite link with Zodiac in Riverside coed's death," the Daily Review, November 17 1970, 3.
[7] "Riverside, California Population 2020," https://worldpopulationreview.com/us-cities/riverside-population/ (retrieved April 2020).
[8] "UNLOCKING A VERY COLD CASE," http://www.inlandempiremagazine.com/thisissue.html (retrieved June 2016).
[9] Jack Mathews. "Death on a dirt driveway, A life that ended too soon."
[10] Bates, Cheri. Letter to Joseph Bates. October 30 1966.
[11] California Department of Justice/Division of Law Enforcement/Bureau of Investigation, Zodiac Homicides, for Law Enforcement Use Only, 2.
[12] "RCC coed…," The Press-Enterprise, October 31 1966, A-3.
[13] Ibid.
[14] "Disabled Car Found Near Body," The Press-Enterprise, October 31 1966, 1.
[15] "UNLOCKING A VERY COLD CASE," http://www.inlandempiremagazine.com/thisissue.html (retrieved June 2016).
[16] Department of Justice," ANALYSIS OF ZODIAC HOMICIDES," 1971.
[17] "THROUGH HELL ON A BLUE PILL," Inside Detective, January 1969.
[18] Ibid.
[19] Ibid.
[20] "Police Seek More Clues in Riverside Coed Murder Case," The San Bernardino County Sun, November 2 1966, B-5.
[21] Department of Justice, Bureau of Criminal Investigation and Investigation Report, Case Number 1-15-311-F9-5861, 33.
[22] FBI report Re: DNA analysis, 1999, case nr: 95A-HQ-1282679.
[23] Autopsy report of Cheri Jo Bates, 31 October 1966, 1.
[24] Ibid, 4.
[25] Ibid, 3.
[26] "Police Seek More Clues in Riverside Coed Murder Case," The San Bernardino County Sun, November 2 1966, B-5.
[27] "Findings Point To White Male As Coed Slayer," The San Bernardino County Sun, November 9 1966, B-5.

[28] "THROUGH HELL ON A BLUE PILL," Inside Detective, January 1969, 6.
[29] Ibid.
[30] Ibid.
[31] Ibid.
[32] Ibid.
[33] Ibid.
[34] Ibid.
[35] Kinkead, Thomas. Letter to Earl Randoll. October 20 1969, 2.
[36] California Department of Justice/Division of Law Enforcement/Bureau of Investigation, Zodiac Homicides, for Law Enforcement Use Only, 8.
[37] Kinkead, Thomas. Letter to Earl Randoll. October 20 1969, 2.
[38] "THROUGH HELL ON A BLUE PILL," Inside Detective, January 1969.
[39] RPD Press Release, May 20 1982.
[40] Ibid.
[41] FBI report Re: DNA analysis, 1999/2000, case nr: 95A-HQ-1282679.
[42] "Confession letter structure part 1," http://www.zodiologists.com/confession_letter_structure_part1.html (retrieved July 2015).
[43] See, for example, KJV Isaiah 53:7.
[44] "Disabled Car Found Near Body," The Press-Enterprise, October 31 1966, 1.
[45] "Coed Stabbed to Death on Riverside College Campus," the Los Angeles Times, November 1 1966, 3.
[46] Freedom of Information and Privacy Acts, Subject: Zodiac Killer, File Number: 9-HQ-49911, Section 4 Federal Bureau of Investigation, 162.
[47] Department of Justice, Bureau of Criminal Investigation and Investigation Report, Case Number 1-15-311-F9-5861, 33.
[48] "RCC coed…," The Press-Enterprise, October 31 1966, A-3.
[49] "Coed Stabbed to Death on Riverside College Campus," the Los Angeles Times, November 1 1966, 3.
[50] "Butchered Coed's Body Discovered," Combined News Services, November 1 1966.
[51] "Police Seek More Clues in Riverside Coed Murder Case," The San Bernardino County Sun, November 2 1966, B-5.
[52] "QUIZZING GOES ON IN SLAYING OF COED," Press/Telegram, November 2 1966.
[53] "Disabled Car Found Near Body," The Press-Enterprise, October 31 1966, 1.
[54] "Coed Stabbed to Death on Riverside College Campus," the Los Angeles Times, November 1 1966, 3.
[55] Ibid.
[56] FBI report Re: DNA analysis, 1999, case nr: 95A-HQ-1282679.
[57] Autopsy report of Cheri Jo Bates, 31 October 1966, 8.
[58] "Police hunt killer of Riverside College coed," The Daily-Enterprise, November 1 1966, A-1.

[59] Ibid.
[60] Ibid.
[61] Kinkead, Thomas. Letter to Earl Randoll. October 20 1969, 2.
[62] "Letter Writer Admits Killing Riverside Coed," the San Bernardino County Sun, December 2 1966, B-4.
[63] Autopsy report of Cheri Jo Bates, 31 October 1966, 8.
[64] "Disabled Car Found Near Body," The Press-Enterprise, October 31 1966, 1.
[65] "Police hunt killer of Riverside College coed," The Daily-Enterprise, November 1 1966, A-1.
[66] "Letter Writer Admits Killing Riverside Coed," the San Bernardino County Sun, December 2 1966, B-4.
[67] "New Evidence in Zodiac Killings, A Link to Murder in Riverside" San Francisco Chronicle, November 16 1970, 1.
[68] "'Zodiac' Wrote Riverside Coed Death Messages," San Bernardino Press County Sun, November 17, 1970, B-5.
[69] Department of Justice, Bureau of Criminal Investigation and Investigation Report, Case Number 1-15-311-F9-5861, 35.
[70] Ibid.
[71] "New Evidence in Zodiac Killings, A Link to Murder in Riverside," San Francisco Chronicle, November 16 1970, 2.
[72] "Riverside Slaying in 1966: Zodiac Link is Definite," San Francisco Chronicle, November 17 1970.
[73] Ibid.
[74] Freedom of Information and Privacy Acts, Subject: Zodiac Killer, File Number: 9-HQ-49911, Section 5 Federal Bureau of Investigation, 50.
[75] Ibid, Section 4, 166.
[76] Ibid, 57.
[77] Ibid.
[78] "Riverside Slaying in 1966: Zodiac Link is Definite," San Francisco Chronicle, November 17 1970.
[79] Ibid.
[80] Ibid.
[81] "Closed Session in Riverside: Police Confer on Zodiac Killings," San Francisco Chronicle, November 19 1970.
[82] Ibid.
[83] Ibid.
[84] Ibid.
[85] "Detectives hope to find Zodiac's handwriting in City College records," the Press-Enterprise, November 24 1970.
[86] Ibid.
[87] Ibid.
[88] Ibid.
[89] Ibid.

[90] "Zodiac Writes Again—'17 Dead,'" San Francisco Chronicle, March 16 1971, 1.
[91] Ibid, back page.
[92] Keppel, Robert (2005). The Riverman: Ted Bundy and I Hunt for the Green River Killer (Paperback ed.). New York: Pocket Books. Updated after the arrest and confession of the Green River killer, Gary Ridgway.
[93] Ibid.
[94] Ibid.
[95] Ibid.

CHAPTER 8

POSSIBLE ZODIAC VICTIMS

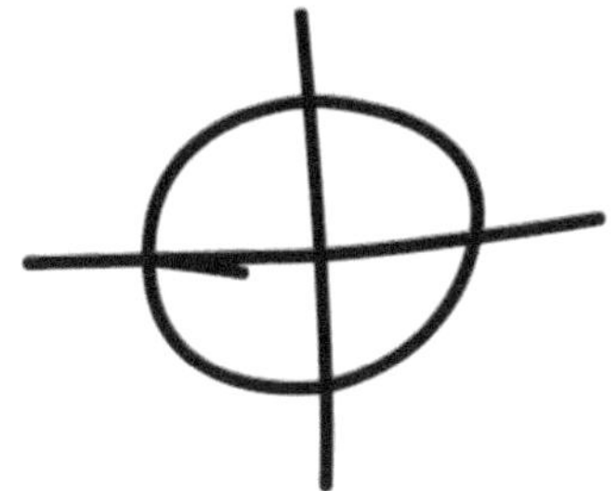

Monday, March 22, 1971

A mail carrier delivered a card to the Chronicle which was curiously addressed to the Chronicle, Times, and Examiner at the same time, while it was also specified that it should be delivered to Paul Avery. The correspondent, presumably the Zodiac, had included a superfluous "l" between the "r" and "y" in Avery. Zodiac had misspelled Avery in the same way on the envelope of the Halloween card. The handwriting was analyzed by Morrill who later expressed to the media that the handwriting attributes "conform and are consistent with all other Zodiac writings I have examined."[1] A four-cent postcard served as the foundation for the card, words had then been cut from newsprint and pasted onto the front and back, these additions included "Sought Victim 12," "Peek through the pines," "around in the snow," "Sierra Club," and "pass LAKE TAHOE areas." A drawing from an advertisement had been cut and pasted on the front as well.[2] Detectives "speculated"[3] that the card was a reference to Donna Lass who had disappeared in September of 1970 in South Lake Tahoe. Three decades later, South Lake Tahoe Sergeant Tom O'Conner said, "There are suspicions that Donna Lass was a victim of the Zodiac."[4] He then added, "But we haven't actually ever established that she was murdered. We haven't even found the body."[5] Lass, age 25, worked as a nurse at Sahara Tahoe Casino First Aid Station. She appears to have disappeared out of thin air. Just before 2 a.m. on Sunday, September 6, 1970, she made her last entry in a logbook at her work. Nothing seemed out of place until her disappearance. Her car was parked at her apartment on the Pioneer Trail Road. Her apartment was not disordered in any way, only the clothes she was wearing and her purse were missing.[6] At least one newspaper announced that she was last seen on September 7 accompanied by a young, blonde man near her home.[7] Police Chief Ray Lauritzen said of the disappearance, "From the beginning we have believed she was abducted and is dead."[8]

A thorough analysis of the card revealed that the picture on it was a building project established among pine trees by the Boise Cascade Corporation in Incline Village, roughly a 35 minutes' drive from Lass' apartment. Lauritzen sent detectives to search the snow-covered area. After "several hours of probing the area"[9] no clues had emerged. The chief said, "There's no point to a search at this time" and "It's unlikely that a victim would be uncovered before spring."[10] The search was called off. Lass was never found. The news media eagerly reported the arrival of the card and the new possible Zodiac victim: "'Elusive Zodiac Killer Claims New Victim,"[11] "Zodiac Killer says that he's struck again,"[12] "'Zodiac' Note Hints About 12th Victim."[13] Very little information is known about the disappearance of Lass and the above resume is based on secondary sources, none of the police reports about her disappearance have been made public. Even though the Zodiac's crimes and actions can rightfully be characterized as dynamic, the abduction and assumed killing of Lass do not seem to carry his fingerprint for the reason that her body was never found. She was probably buried somewhere, indicating that it was a different type of criminal operating; Zodiac had no qualms about leaving his victims in open locations where he knew they would be found soon after. If he had killed Lass, it is much more likely that he would have boasted about it and left the body in an open location. The card is not universally believed to be a real Zodiac communiqué, as the lack of handwriting ruled out an authoritative conclusion. However, we should note that the make-up of the card is similar in several ways to those received in the previous months:

1) In the top left corner, the circular part of the crosshair symbol had been punctured. Thirteen circular holes had been made in the October 5 card.
2) Same misspelling of Avery on the Halloween envelope.
3) Glue had been used in all three cards.
4) The handwriting was traced or overwritten several times just like on the envelope of the Halloween card.
5) The date at which the card was mailed suggests that the abduction of Kathleen Johns was commemorated.

Wednesday, April 7

The Zodiac Killer premiered in cinemas in California. Tom Hanson directed the 1 hour and 27-minute-long film. The manuscript had been based very loosely on the actual killings of the Zodiac. Despite it being an obvious very low-budget film, we would expect the Zodiac to send an explicit review due to his inability to stop writing about himself and his obsession with movies. He never did. Not even a veiled reference. Again, we see a manifestation of his unpredictable character.

Thursday, December 23

The first out of five *Dirty Harry* movies made its way into the cinema. It was immediately well received by critics, and it became a commercial success. Unlike *The Zodiac Killer*, which premiered a few months earlier, the producers had a $4 million budget to work with. The manuscript is noticeably inspired by the Zodiac's actions but with unique twists and turns. A maniac who calls himself Scorpio terrorizes San Francisco by killing people and sending taunting letters. Inspector Harry Callahan, known as Dirty Harry, is assigned to stop him. A cat and mouse game ensues. Mysteriously, Zodiac had nothing to say about *Dirty Harry*.

Friday, April 7, 1972

The San Francisco Chronicle reported that Isobel Watson, age 33, a legal secretary of San Francisco, in Marin County on Pine Hill Road was stabbed in a Zodiac-like knife attack. Det. Sgt. Narlow said, "I think it's a good chance it was him," and that the probability is "better than 50-50."[14] She exited a bus around 9 p.m., and as she was walking on Pine Hill Road a light-colored car came out of nowhere and almost hit her. The driver said he was sorry and offered to drive her home. She replied, "No."[15] He asked again, "Please let me drive you home."[16] She denied his services once again, and he unexpectedly changed character, hauled out a knife and cut/stabbed her in the neck and shoulders. Neighbors heard her screams, the lights went on, and the attacker rapidly got into his car and sped away. Watson described her deranged attacker as wearing heavy black-rimmed reading glasses. He was in his early 40s, about 5'9", and had neat brown hair. Narlow also said, "I've been chasing the S.O.B for two and a half years now, and Mrs. Watson's description seems to fit him to a T."[17]

Other Possible Zodiac Victims

In addition to the Watson case, which received little media coverage, the news media reported in 1972 that the Zodiac might have begun his killing career in 1963. Before we address those possible Zodiac killings, it has also been revealed that Zodiac is the prime candidate for a 1962 killing of a cab driver. In early 2020, several news stations reported having uncovered striking similarities between the slaying of Ray Davis and the Zodiac crimes. They speculated that he could have started his one-man epidemic of madness and murder already in 1962. When Zodiac was active, apparently no one had noticed the connection, and thus the killing of Ray Davis was largely forgotten. This went on until 2017 when an Oceanside historian and genealogist, Kristi Hawthorne, stumbled upon a newspaper article regarding the murder of Ray Davis while doing research on an unrelated subject. Being familiar with the main points of the Zodiac case, she noticed that the Zodiac's fingerprints were all over the case of Ray Davis, and she began searching for further information in the city's newspaper archive and elsewhere.

Monday, April 9, 1962

In 1962, Oceanside was a small city with a population of about 20,000 and had very low crime and murder rates. The city can be found around 466 miles southeast of the Presidio Heights crime scene. On the above-mentioned date, the dispatcher at the Oceanside Police Department received a cryptic one-way call: "I am going to pull something here in Oceanside, and you will never be able to figure it out."[18] The caller hung up, and the dispatcher probably assumed that it had been a crank caller wasting his time.

Tuesday, April 10, 1962

Raymond Davis, a 29-year-old cab driver, worked an evening shift for the Checker Cab Company. Ray, as his friends called him, was estranged from his wife, Marion Davis. She lived with her two children from a previous marriage in Pomona, around 77 miles from Oceanside, while Ray and his brother Jack had moved to Oceanside in January of 1962. Ray and Jack had moved from Owosso, Michigan, a city even smaller than Oceanside. They had rented a house at 525 South Tremont Street.

Ray had parked in the center of Oceanside at a taxi stand at the intersection of Mission Avenue and Tremont Street, the best place to get a fare late at night.[19] At 11:12 p.m., he briefly spoke to his dispatcher, Lowell Sikes, informing him that he was taking a fare to South Oceanside.[20] Two hours and thirty-five minutes later, at 1:45 a.m., Patrolman Terry L. Stephens discovered the body of Ray in the exclusive Saint Mao residential district. Ray was lying in a pool of his own blood in the alley behind 1926 South Pacific Street, the home of Oceanside's former Mayor Joe MacDonald. Right across the street was the home of Oceanside's current Mayor, Erwin Sklar.

Ray's cab, however, was not at the scene of his murder. At around 6:30 a.m., Sergeant John Quintero discovered the cab at the alley of the 400 block of South Pacific Street, about a mile and a half away from the dumpsite.[21] The engine was cold.[22] The evidence would later indicate that the killer had shot Ray from the backseat, and then dragged his body out of the right front door. The killer then got behind the wheel and drove the blood-soaked and stained cab, which had a bullet hole in the windshield, to the alley. The taxi meter showed $2.20. Adjusting for inflation, a fare worth $2.20 in 1962 would cost $18.86 in 2019. Police Chief William H. Wingard subsequently told the Oceanside Blade-Tribune that a tax meter check showed that the cab had not been driven anywhere else, except to the dumping site and then to the alley where he abandoned it.[23]

On the front seat, they found an open paperback novel, entitled "Dance With the Dead." A copy of Oceanside Daily Blade-Tribune, a flashlight, and cigarettes were also lying on the front seat.[24] If this book belonged to Ray or was left by the killer is not known at this time. A search through a digital copy of the book for keywords pertaining to the Zodiac case and the killing of Ray did not yield any noteworthy results. The police found Ray's wallet as well as money in his shirt pocket. The wallet was lying inside the cab on the floor in front of the right-hand seat in a pool of blood, indicating that robbery could be excluded as a motive.[25] Deputy Coroner Robert Creason told the Oceanside Blade-Tribune that seemingly the wallet had not been rifled.[26]

Ray's body was transported to the Seaside Mortuary at 802 South Pacific Street. L. H. Fairchild M.D. of the San Diego County Coroner's Office performed an autopsy on the body. Dr. Fairchild ascertained that Ray had died of "massive intrathoracic hemorrhage" due to a perforated wound through the right pulmonary vein of the heart as a result of a "bullet wound through the chest."[27] He noted that a contributing factor was a bullet wound through the brain.[28] The bullet had ruptured the right middle cerebral vein, near the Circle of Willis, which is a circle like structure consisting of several arteries, located at the base of the brain. Dr. Fairchild extracted two bullets from the body and handed them over to Detective Floyd R. Flowers. A forensic examination would later reveal that the murderer had pulled out a .22 caliber pistol loaded with long rifle ammunition while sitting on the backseat of the cab. He shot Ray twice and also fired a third bullet through the windshield, probably intending to hit Ray in the head. Police Chief Wingard later said that Ray had no enemies, and "There is an absence of any reason for the killing."[29]

Sunday, April 15, 1962

The phone rang again at the Oceanside Police Department. The caller said: "Do you remember me calling you last week and telling you that I was going to pull a real baffling crime? I killed the cab driver, and I am going to get me a bus driver next." The caller now had the full attention of the police, and they immediately issued a warning to all 25 bus drivers of the Oceanside Transportation System.

Tuesday, April 17, 1962

A woman from Oceanside called the dispatcher at the police station. She told the dispatcher that she had received a phone call from a man who had refused to identify himself, but told her: "Tonight is the night I'm going to kill that bus driver."[30] The man had also told her to relate this message to the police. At this point, the police had already implemented precautionary measures, and Marine Corps military police armed with shotguns rode with buses at night.

Analysis of Oceanside Phone Calls

1) "I am going to pull something here in Oceanside, and you will never be able to figure it out."

2) "Do you remember me calling you last week and telling you that I was going to pull a real baffling crime? I killed the cab driver, and I am going to get me a bus driver next."

3) "Tonight is the night I'm going to kill that bus driver."

The First Call

Although we only have 67 words to work with, we can learn a lot about the caller's psychology, intentions, and motivations by applying the principles of statement analysis to the three calls (also see Chapter 14). Statement analysis is a branch of linguistics that is aimed at detecting deception and extracting hidden information. A branch of statement analysis, called psycho-linguistic profiling, is focused on psychological characteristics which manifest themself from the analysis.

We will start with the initial phone call made to the Oceanside Police Department. First, we notice that the caller used "going to" rather than "I will;" there is a subtle difference between the two, although they can sometimes be used interchangeably. In this regard, the former is used to express future plans decided before the moment of speaking, while the latter is used to express future actions decided at the moment of speaking. Premeditation is indicated.

The words, "here in Oceanside," are not necessary for the sentence to make sense. Since unnecessary additions are important, it is indicated that location was important to the caller. This means that carrying out the murder in Oceanside was a priority to him. In retrospect we know that his vague allusion to crime, namely the word "something," meant the killing of Ray Davis. But at the time of the phone call this was not specified to any degree. We can therefore surmise that he had not decided upon what he would do, but he had clearly set his mind upon Oceanside. If we take this analysis one step further, we can deduce that Ray Davis was a victim of random violence, and, hence, he was not shot and killed as a result of a personal feud. Furthermore, the word, "here," indicates that the caller was present in Oceanside, physically and mentally during the call.

In the last part of the sentence, "you will never be able to figure it out," the *"it"* is a reference to the "something." Depending on the context, *figure out* can mean "to investigate or think something through in order to understand it."[31] The caller was telling us that he would do something, a murder we know in retrospect, which would bewilder the police.

The Second Call

Moving on to the next statement, the caller began the conversation by stating, "Do you remember me [...]." These four words are likely important pieces of the psychological puzzle, which must be solved to attain an understanding of the psychodynamics of Ray's killer. These words tell us that the killer wanted to be recognized, note the difference between "remember me" and, for example, "remember our conversation." The focus is on, "me," indicating we are dealing with a narcissistic, attention-seeking type of perpetrator. Before the dispatcher had the time to reply, he gave the game away and revealed the time and content of the conversation, virtual overkill, making sure that the dispatcher could not in any way have been mistaken.

The effect of adding the adjective "baffling," before "crime," puts his reprehensible act on a pedestal; he is underlining that it is not just any crime, but a "baffling crime." He is proud of his handiwork. The caller qualifies "baffling crime" with a "real," indicating that he was comparing his crime to others, generally considered to be baffling, presumably designated as such in newspapers at around the time of the killing. The adjective, "real," indicates that he did not *really* regard the other crimes as "baffling," but that his crime was something special: It was a "real baffling crime." He subconsciously categorized his murder above others, revealing great pride and a compulsive need to compare his deed to those of others; the caller had at some point in the past abandoned the thought of accomplishing goals, considered valuable and worthwhile by society, and decided to redeem his grandiose ambitions via murder and attain recognition by means of the notoriety emanating from the killing of Ray Davis. Obviously, one does not simply wake up and decide to use murder as a vehicle for attention; instead, the long and convoluted psychological and neurological processes started years earlier, conceivably initiated by an avalanche of perceived failures and defeats.

It is also significant that the caller demonstrated a need to draw a connection to the initial proclamation. In doing so, he established his credibility as the killer, and it was therefore a prioritization of the caller to not be dismissed by the police. Maybe the caller was used to being second-guessed.

Moving on with the analysis, the caller states, "I killed the cab driver," a cold and insensitive admission in which depersonalization is evident: The victim, Ray Davis, is reduced to his profession. The killer then said, "I am going to get *me* a bus driver next," which is revealing in how he perceived his victims. The words, "I am going to get me," are normally used in connection with possession, e.g. "I am going get me another dog." This indicates that the killer regarded his victims as possessions. The superfluous "me" underlines his self-centeredness. In the second call, he used a pronoun referring to himself a total of 13.5% of the total word count, a clear indication that the caller is self-centered.

We also need to consider if the caller intended to kill a bus driver, but good reason prevailed as the police acted upon the threat and took measures to protect all city busses. Initially, the caller was not specific about his crime, not even specifying that it would be a murder. In the second call, he changed his wording from "killed" to "going to get." In statement analysis a change in language indicates a change in reality. It therefore may be that the caller only intended to spread fear through the threat.

The Third Call

The third and last call only could have been made by the killer. We will in this analysis assume it was made by him. Rather than calling the police, he phoned a citizen and made the declaration, "Tonight is the night I'm going to kill that bus driver." If the caller had the intention of killing a bus driver, it is unlikely that he would have announced it in advance with such specificity – especially considering that his initial threat, which turned real, was entirely undefined. Lastly, he did not kill a bus driver; therefore, we can almost be certain that he was instead aiming for attention and widespread terrorism, exactly like the Zodiac did when he threatened to "wipe out a school bus some morning."

The Zodiac's Culpability

The psycho-linguistic profile of the caller is consistent in virtually all aspects with the exceedingly rare personality characteristics of the Zodiac (attention via murder, false threats, grandiosity, views victims as possessions or slaves, deliberately mysterious, etc.). Additionally, the wording, vocabulary, and ideas expressed during the calls are similar to the Zodiac's phraseology as seen below. As a whole, the evidence indicates that Zodiac most likely made the calls and killed Ray Davis.

Oceanside Slayer

"[Y]ou will never be able to figure it out."

Zodiac

"I hope you have fun trying to figgure out who I killed" (April 1970).
"The police shall never catch me, because I have been too clever for them" (November 1970).

Oceanside Slayer

"Do you remember me calling you last week and telling you that I was going to pull a real baffling crime?"

Zodiac

"I get awfully lonely when I am ignored, so lonely I could do my Thing!!!!!!" (November 1969).
"I shall no longer announce to anyone. when I comitt my murders" (November 1969).
"YES I DID MAKE THAT CALL TO YOU ALSO. IT WAS JUST A WARNING" (November 1966).

Oceanside Slayer

"I am going to pull something here in Oceanside."

Zodiac

"p.s. 2 cops pulled a goof abot 3 min after I left the cab" (November 1969).
"I will do something nasty" (January 1974).

Oceanside Slayer

"I killed the cab driver."

Zodiac

"I am the murderer of the taxi driver" (October 1969).
"I am the killer of the 2 teenagers" (July 1969).

Oceanside Slayer

"I am going to get me a bus driver next."

Zodiac

"School children make nice targets, I think I shall wipe out a school bus some morning" (October 1969).

"If you cops think Im going to take on a bus the way I stated I was, you deserve to have holes in your heads" (November 1969).
"Tell every one about the bus bomb with all the details" (April 1970).

Conclusions

At this time, experts are in the process of comparing the ballistics evidence from this case to that of other cases, including the .22 caliber bullets and casings used by the Zodiac at Lake Herman Road. However, it may be that different weapons were used or that the bullets are too damaged to make a definitive statement. Nevertheless, probability theory seems to dictate that the Zodiac most definitely is the prime candidate for the murder of Ray Davis. Probability theory is concerned with determining the likelihood of an event occurring in a random experiment. Consider the state of California in the relevant period. The average population of California from 1962 to 1969 was approximately 18.498 million.[32] Only a minuscule percentage of the population committed a murder. From 1962 to 1969 there were a total of 7,393 murders in California.[33] If we falsely assume that all of the murders were committed by different individuals, we conservatively get:

$$\frac{7{,}393 \text{ killers}}{18.498 \text{ millon people}} * 100\% \approx 0.04\%$$

Around 0.04% of the population would commit a murder between 1962 and 1969. This amounts to about 5 killers per 100,000 people in California. However, many of these killers were apprehended and were thereby not capable of committing both the Zodiac murders and the killing of Ray Davis. In 1965, US detectives had a 91% homicide clearance rate.[34] It follows:

$$7{,}393 \text{ killers} - (91\% * 7{,}393 \text{ killers}) = 665.37 \text{ killers on the loose}$$

This means that from 1962 to 1969, there was a theoretical maximum of 665.37 killers on the loose in California. Let us now realize that the vast majority of these killers were motivated by money or other personal reasons, like jealousy. The pool of suspects is further limited when we restrict the population to only include those killers who would announce their crimes to the police beforehand and would then take credit by making a call after the deed was done. Already at this point, it is exceedingly unlikely that the Zodiac is not responsible for killing Ray Davis, but the analysis continues. How many of these killers would target a cab driver in an exclusive neighborhood of a city? How many would use a .22 caliber pistol loaded with long rifle ammunition? The geography of the area allowed Ray's killer to dump his body in the ocean, just a short distance away from the dumpsite. Attention must have been vital for Ray Davis' killer as he chose an exclusive, upscale neighborhood, like Presidio Heights, not in any way accustomed to murders and crime. His phone calls similarly drew massive attention to the case. One of Zodiac's primary motivational forces was attention.

It is clear from this conservative calculation that there is a great likelihood that Zodiac killed Ray Davis.

While the media and investigators overlooked the killing of Ray Davis, they did report on possible Zodiac murders from 1963. An unknown assailant brought precut lengths of rope to a remote location on Gaviota Beach. He surprised a young couple and ordered the woman to tie the man. He then tied her hands. The couple attempted to escape, but was shot dead; his weapon had been loaded with Winchester-Western Super-X .22 long rifle cartridges. The secluded venue, ammunition, precut rope, and that he wanted the man to be secured first are all well-known Zodiac characteristics. Also, both killers felt an intrinsic bitterness toward couples. At a press conference, William Baker and John Carpender of the Santa Barbara County Sheriff's Department issued a statement about the recent developments:

> In June of 1963, a young teenage couple was found shot to death near an isolated stretch of beach, north of Santa Barbara. The victims, both Lompoc High School seniors, had been shot numerous times and their bodies placed in a small lean-to shack a short distance from the beach. An extensive investigation by Sheriff's Detectives failed to reach a successful solution to the killings. Although the case was never solved, no substantial leads could be developed. Over a year ago, Sheriff's Detectives began a thorough study of the case, examining and re-evaluating all aspects of the crime. A recent development has provided information that appears somewhat promising. Considerable evidence points to the murders of Linda EDWARDS and Robert DOMINGOS as being the work of the infamous ZODIAC. Although the anticipated response to this

> statement would be one of skepticism, let me say that we do not make this assertion frivolously. Many hundreds of hours, over the past several months, have been spent compiling information concerning the possibility that this man could have been responsible for the killings in 1963. Sheriff's Detectives have met with investigators from those areas where ZODIAC has, admittedly, been responsible for several murders. These agencies have conducted intensive investigations for the past several years in an effort to identify ZODIAC. After conferring with officers in these other jurisdictions, we have found that there appears to be a high degree of probability that this subject is responsible for the double murder in our County. Several significant similarities between our case and the others, as well as other evidence which I am not at liberty to disclose at this time, all tend to connect ZODIAC with this crime. In addition, we have information, to be investigated further, which may place him in the Santa Barbara area in 1963. All possibilities will be investigated thoroughly to confirm, or disprove, their validity. I would like to emphasize that we are not using the notoriety of ZODIAC to dispose of a difficult case, nor are we closing our minds to the possibility that he may not be responsible.[35]

Wednesday, June 5, 1963

At 2:36 p.m., George H. Domingos, reported his son, Robert, missing. The previous day it was 'Senior Ditch Day' at Lompoc High School. Instead of going with their classmates, Robert and his fiancée, Linda Faye Edwards, went to a remote spot on Gaviota Beach, located approximately 212 miles from the Ray Davis crime scene. The location is a five-hour drive from Vallejo and approximately 25 miles from Santa Barbara. The couple probably liked the privacy of the site since it was not their first visit.[36] George, accompanied by his nephew and cousin, decided to look for them. At around 9 p.m. they spotted a 1959 Pontiac parked under some eucalyptus trees, it was Robert's car. They were hesitant to go to the beach unaided and summoned Patrolman Paul

Shultz. Unlike the popular public beaches, it was difficult reaching the waterfront from their location. At the beach, they found a blanket belonging to the couple. Shultz walked alone to a lean-to shack that was concealed from view by trees and shrubbery. When he peered inside, he met with a repulsive sight: the bullet-riddled bodies of Robert and Linda. After the initial panic, the investigative procedures began. The investigation indicated that after the initial confrontation, the assailant ordered Linda to tie her fiancé with rope. He then proceeded to tie Linda's hands together. Robert, an active footballer, was able to free himself and "incapacitate"[37] the man long enough for them to escape briefly. He chased them. They ultimately fell to the ground as bullets struck their backs. He approached them and shot them several times hitting Robert in the back and Linda in the chest. In total, he shot Robert 11 times and Linda eight times. He had to recharge at least once. He then dragged Robert into the shack and placed him there, face down. Linda was put on top of him, face up. Although the autopsy ruled out "sexual activity,"[38] he ostensibly displayed some sexual curiosity when he cut Linda's bathing suit and exposed her breasts. He also placed a towel on Linda's face.

Detectives concluded that the killer must have been familiar with the shack since it was not visible from where the couple fell. Inside the shack, he left full and partially full 50-round boxes of the ammunition he had used along with several lengths of rope. Having placed the bodies and the evidence inside the shack, he attempted to light it on fire with matches he had brought along. A blanket covering the passage served as the ignition point. The evidence left at the scene and the failed attempt to cover his tracks indicated that the killer panicked and that he did not stay around for long before he fled the scene. Smoke from the fire would surely also have overwhelmed him with fear and paranoia.

Investigators put their focus on the ammunition boxes and determined that they had a lot number stamped on them. They did not have price stickers nor were there any evidence that these had been removed. The investigation showed that in the general area, the only retailer that sold this particular type and quantity without price stickers was at the Base Exchange at Vandenberg Air Force Base. A military connection was established.

It appeared that the assailant had used a rifle, which importantly had been loaded with the exact same type of ammunition used to kill Betty Lou Jensen and David Faraday in 1968.
The precut lengths of rope indicated a high degree of planning. The additional rope he discarded inside the shack, he may have intended to use to tie the ankles of the couple and possibly from that point on, hogtie them. The actual rope was generic 3/8" cotton. Not all of the knots were undone by the victims, and an analysis showed that he had used a particular knot more than once, and it was associated with "fishermen or other maritime use."[39]
When detectives combed through the site, they discovered discarded cigarette butts, but whether or not they belonged to the killer could not be established.
In the days before the brutal end of Robert and Linda, a shooter hidden from sight had operated in the same area as they were killed. On Saturday, June 1, 1963, James L. Summer, his son, and two friends were at the shack when someone fired two shots at them from the railroad tracks in the distance. The bullets "came close enough," and they could hear them "whistling through the air."[40] At daybreak, the next day, about a mile from the murder scene on Tajiguas Beach, a group of four girls and seven boys were camping when a rifleman fired shots at them. It sounded like a .22 rifle, the boys told the sheriff. In the midafternoon, south of Gaviota Beach, to the north and less than a mile from the murder scene, some youngsters were standing by parked cars and chatting when a sniper fired shots at them.[41] The conclusion must be that Robert and Linda's killer was searching for easy victims in the immediate days before he killed them. If bullets or casings were ever collected and compared is not known.

Detective Baker's Analysis

In the early 2000s, Detective Baker shared his conclusions regarding the Zodiac's connection with his decade's old unsolved crime case. He believes that the Zodiac intended to initiate his series of killings in 1963 with the murder of Domingos and Edwards, but because he lost "control at the scene"[42] he became frightened and his confidence was affected, and he "went into eclipse for a time."[43] When he returned in 1968, his "method of implementation" had changed but his "core motivation"[44] remained intact. The blitz attacks of December and July "partially restored"[45] his confidence. He then "consciously or subconsciously needed to atone for, or negate the stigma of, 1963."[46] He might well have intended it to be his last crime; however, the failure to kill Hartnell "prompted him to kill Stine"[47] as his final gesture. Baker concludes that the killing of Stine was an effort to

> establish, publicly, that he was capable of killing a man, thereby parrying real and potential critical jabs which suggested not only his ineptness when it came to killing men, but also brought into question his own manliness. It was, of course, an unintended footnote to the Stine killing that he blindsided the driver with a shot he didn't see coming, suggesting that Z hadn't the *huevos* to take on a man face to face, *mano a mano*.[48]

Baker is puzzled by the fact that Zodiac called the cops on September 20 since his hand printing on the door would have been sufficient to link him to the crime. It was "as though he not only put his actions in *Italics*, but *underscored* them as well, in ***bold*** type, and ***CAPS***."[49] In addition to "donning the hood, conversing with his victims, in daylight, he took extra steps to take immediate credit. That seems to point to [Lake Berryessa] as being some kind of *crescendo* to his murderous work, and representative of the significance that scenario held for him."[50] The hood and sunglasses might have served as a barrier between the victims and himself. It has "been theorized that [Zodiac] felt uncomfortable in any face-to-face interaction with the people he was about to kill, especially conversational exchanges with them."[51] Presumably, "he didn't want them to see his eyes, his expression, even perhaps the anxiety he was experiencing, which his eyes would have revealed/betrayed,"[52] Baker said. Baker sums up his analysis: The 1963 case "was a fiasco for the killer, and he was far from being proud of his deeds. There were no ensuing letters or phone calls taking credit for the crime. If, as I believe, [Zodiac] was responsible for the 1963 killings and [Lake Berryessa], and that [Lake Berryessa] was an intended means for [Zodiac] to redeem himself for the sloppy work 6 years before, then it makes sense that he would not have felt inclined to gloat in writing about his failed mission at Lake Berryessa."[53]

The Honeymoon Killings

In late December of 1968, San Diego Chief of Police, O. J. Roed, followed up with a letter to a conversation he had had with Thomas E. Joyce, Sheriff of Solana County. Four years earlier a couple had been killed under circumstances that paralleled the double murder of David Faraday and Betty Lou Jensen. In the letter, he provided a detailed summary of his case and asked for a casing so a ballistic comparison could be made.[§§§54]

In 1964, Johnny Ray, age 20, and Joyce Swindle, age 19, were brutally murdered. The couple was newlywed and relishing every minute of their honeymoon. Johnny told a friend that "he couldn't keep his wife away from the ocean, it fascinated her."[55] On Wednesday, February 5, on Ocean Beach in San Diego, they were enjoying the type of moment that could have served as a fictional scene in a romantic novel. They were only about 35 miles away from 1926 South Pacific Street in Oceanside where the body of Ray Davis was dumped.

Without a doubt, Joyce listened to the rhythmic and hypnotic lapping of sea waves and felt the crisp night breeze unsettling through her hair. Johnny had purchased a box of candy. No one could have predicted that a sniper was about to turn their romantic moment into a horror story. The moonless gloom concealed his presence as he hid on a crag overlooking the ocean. He had brought along a .22 Remington rifle, model 550-1. He took aim and gunned them down. He then moved closer and shot them both in the head, execution-style in a "kind of coup de grâce."[56] The crime took place in the timeframe 8:10-15 p.m.[57] They were found lying on a cement patio very close to the ocean. Joyce was dead. Johnny lived for a few more hours before he succumbed to his injuries in the hospital.

There were no witnesses to the double murder, but the subsequent investigation showed that an unrelated individual, John, had walked to the patio, the murder site, minutes before the killing. He had noticed a man standing on some rocks, around 40-50 feet

[§§§] Surely a mismatch due to the fact that two different weapons were used.

away. He did not see the Swindles. At approximately 8:16 p.m., another witness discerned that a man sprinted east on Del Monte Avenue, away from the crime scene.[58]

The police established that Joyce was probably struck first. The first or second bullet hit her left arm and continued into the chest area. The other one went through her spine causing instant paralysis. It was also indicated that at this point, Johnny turned toward the general direction of the shooter and started to bend over his beloved wife. Two bullets struck him during these moments. One went through his upper left arm and continued into his left thigh. The other one struck him 5 inches above the right eye. The sniper advanced to finish off both of his victims, first he shot Johnny in the left ear at point-blank, and then he fired his rifle at the back of Joyce's head. He had used a total of seven or eight shots, missing one or two. The killer took John's wallet.[****] Detectives perceived the robbery aspect with skepticism since the killer could not reasonably have assumed that a couple at their location would have any cash or values. Police Captain Ed De Bolt told journalists, "There is absolutely no indication of motive, unless the missing wallet indicates robbery," and "There is no triangle in the background of the two young people, nothing which would lead us to their killing."[59] Lieutenant William Schenck stated, "It's entirely possible they were killed by someone they never knew - someone whose only motive was excitement."[60] The news media and detectives almost immediately picked up the strong parallels to the killing of Robert and Linda. One headline read, "Killings Near Lompoc and San Diego Similar."[61] Roed told reporters that two detectives of Santa Barbara were "en route to San Diego with details of the Lompoc murders."[62]

A criminalist broke down the casings and bullet fragments from the two cases and discovered that two unique weapons had been used. Santa Barbara Sheriff, James Webster, declared, "the manner in which both couples were gunned down on the beach without apparent motive indicates that the same killer may have

[****] He may also have taken his watch.

committed both crimes, getting rid of his old rifle after the first crime."[63] James Webster could have continued his analysis of the parallels between the two cases. For example, both killers used a .22 rifle, possessed the rare psychological traits of a sniper, targeted couples, and administered a coup de grâce. It is highly unlikely that it is not the same man responsible for both of the crimes. In the future, perhaps DNA will establish that Zodiac is that individual. Until then we can appreciate several indications that support the hypothesis. Here are some of the strongest points:

1) At Lake Herman Road, the Zodiac used the same type of ammunition and caliber as the killer of Domingos and Edwards. The killer of Ray also used .22 long rifle ammunition.
2) At Lake Berryessa, he used an indistinguishable methodology to restrain the victims.
3) Zodiac targeted three couples.
4) Zodiac provided this list to Paul Avery: By fire, by gun, by knife, and by rope. The same paraphernalia was used in the Domingos and Edwards crime.
5) It has been observed that Zodiac identified himself with the psychological constituents of a sniper when he threatened to shoot children as they fled a school bus. It was implied in his statement that he would be positioned at a distance, like a sniper.
6) The persistent military connection is consistent with what we know about the Zodiac.
7) Ray Davis, David Faraday, Johnny Swindle, and Paul Stine were all shot in the head.
8) Zodiac told us, "There are a hell of a lot more down there." Maybe he was referring to Domingos, Edwards, the Swindles, and Ray Davis.

Monday, May 14, 1973

The Chronicle devoted a fairly large space in their newspaper to a portrait of Sherwood Morrill who had retired as the state's top examiner of questioned documents, a position he had held for many

years. He had now gone into private practice. Zodiac was still on his mind, "If he were standing beside me, say, in a bank, filling out a deposit slip, I'd know. I'd recognize that printing anywhere,"[64] he told Duffy Jennings, a reporter. He then described his job, "Basically, I identify handwriting, inks, typing, erasures, obliterations, alternations – even the paper itself." He added, "Handwriting is as individual as fingerprints. With sufficient samples of a person's handwriting – or in the Zodiac's case, printing – I can tell if he wrote the document in question."[65]
Although he had retired his work for the state, Morrill continued to assist investigators with Zodiac questioned printing.

Tuesday, January 29, 1974

The Zodiac successfully inserted himself into the awareness of millions of people by means of murder, terrorism, and enigmatic clues and twists. His reprehensible methods worked; he got attention, a lot of it. The news coverage and public interest probably reached a climax around the time he threatened to slay children in October 1969. Afterwards, the coverage peaked intermittently when new letters were received or discoveries were made. But as time went on, he slowly began to fade away as a result of his decision to cease communicating. After Zodiac had sent the L.A. Times letter and possibly the postcard in March 1971, he disappeared. He could have been back on the front pages on several occasions if he had written a letter, such as if he had taken credit for the Domingos and Edwards crime. Why would he not do that? What preoccupied him?
On January 29, 1974, he finally decided to return to the spotlight and front pages when he sent off a letter from San Mateo to the Chronicle.[66, 67] The SFPD took photocopies and forwarded them to the FBI for handwriting analysis. At this point, a handwriting expert for the SFPD – Morrill presumably – had concluded that it was a Zodiac letter.[68] The FBI expert could not perform an "unqualified determination" because he was only supplied with photocopies; however, it was "probably" prepared by Zodiac."[69]

The letter read:

I saw + think "The Exorcist"
was the best satirical comidy that I have ever seen.
Signed, yours truley:
He plunged him self into
the billowy wave
and an echo arose from
the sucides grave
titwillo titwillo
  titwillo
Ps. if I do not see this
note in your paper, I
will do something nasty,
which you know I'm capable of
doing.
      Me – 37
[Cryptic symbol] SFPD – 0

The envelope read:

San Fran. Chronicle
Please Rush To Editor

Observations

Why did the Zodiac return after almost three years to provide the editor of the Chronicle with a review of the Exorcist? The letter lacks the former standard opening, "This is the Zodiac speaking." It has been speculated that the first page has been withheld, but there is no mentioning of that in the police reports. Maybe this was Zodiac's way of saying goodbye by writing a final letter in which he implied that he was more evil and shocking than the most celebrated horror movie. His review blends in with the other evidence that he was glued to his TV during his spare time, particularly savoring movies with a theme related to violence. Yet, he mysteriously did not comment on movies related to his character.

It has been pointed out that Zodiac wrote "Signed, yours truely" and then added a comma, almost as if he would sign the letter with his name underneath.[70] Instead, he continued with a passage from his favorite opera, the Mikado. "Willow, tit-willow" is from Act II and is performed by The Lord High Executioner, Ko-Ko.[71] Zodiac quoted the second verse almost correctly, surprisingly without added distortions or perversions. Here are the original lyrics:

"Then he plunged himself into the billowy wave
And an echo arose from the suicide's grave
'Oh, willow, titwillow, titwillow'"[72]

Zodiac had in this instance quoted a verse about suicide, which invites the thought that he might have contemplated putting it all to an end. It is commonly said that before a person becomes a killer he or she wanted to kill themself. The third verse, which is not mentioned in the letter, is interesting as it refers to a "name." Maybe this is a hint that the cryptic symbol or code at the end of the letter contains his name. However, as of this writing, no one has even managed to set forth any persuasive arguments on how to interpret the symbol. The third verse reads:

"Now I feel just as sure as I'm sure that my name
Isn't Willow, titwillow, titwillow,
That 'twas blighted affection that made him exclaim
'Oh, willow, titwillow, titwillow!'
And if you remain callous and obdurate, I
Shall perish as he did, and you will know why,
Though I probably shall not exclaim as I die,
'Oh, willow, titwillow, titwillow!'"[73]

Zodiac ended the letter by putting his standard braggadocio to grotesque heights by indicating a body count of 37 victims. More important is that the SFPD crime lab lifted a palm print from the letter, characterized as a "writer's palm print."[74] It has never been matched to anyone.

In our analysis, we should consider Zodiac's widespread inclination to criticize the SFPD as well as his urge to claim a score higher than theirs. Other police stations, such as the Vallejo Police Department, could instead have been the subject of his anger but were not. Furthermore, he posted the majority of his communications in San Francisco indicating he spent more time there than in Vallejo, even though he showed familiarity with the city and its surroundings. Maybe he felt wrongfully treated by the SFPD in an unrelated matter, and he could not stop himself from bulling the police department. Retaliation was certainly a part of his psychological make-up. On the other hand, around the time the Zodiac posted his letters, a culture of opposition to the police had formed, and officers were often referred to as "pigs," an expression the Zodiac used more than once. The opposition to the police by certain groups led to several unprovoked ambush killings and attacks on police officers. Zodiac may have identified with one of these groups without having an actual personal issue with them.

Sunday, February 3

On this day, someone mailed a letter to the Chronicle with some additional information about the *Symbionese Liberation Army*, one of many left-wing extremist groups in the 1970s. The group committed numerous acts of violence, bombings, and bank robberies. The day after the letter was sent, the group kidnapped Patty Hearst, the granddaughter of a major newspaper publisher. This indicates that a member of the group authored the letter.[75] In any event, the Chronicle was suspicious and forwarded the letter to the SFPD. The FBI's handwriting expert was skeptical of this being a Zodiac letter due to the hand printing being inconsistent with the "hand printing characteristics contained in the Zodiac letters."[76] Ultimately, the expert could not determine if Zodiac wrote the letter. The reference to the Old Norse word "sla" and to the Symbionese Liberation Army coincides with the fact that one of the members of the group, Sara Jane Olson, had Norwegian-American parents. It is indicated that the Zodiac did not write the letter.[77]

The short letter read:

Dear Mr. Editor,
Did you know that the
initials SLAY (Symbionese
Liberation Army) spell "*sla,*"
an old Norse word
Meaning "kill."
a friend

The envelope read:

Editor
San Francisco Chronicle
San Francisco, California

Thursday, July 4

A card arrived at the Chronicle. It was postmarked on May 8 in Alameda County, which revealed that it had been delayed in the mail. The staff perceived the handwriting as similar to the Zodiac's, and the SFPD was called in. The FBI expert examined the hand printing and stated that it was not conclusively established that Zodiac had penned it because of "variations."[78] Similarities, however, indicated that it was "probably prepared"[79] by him.

The back of the card:

Editor
S F Chronicle
5th + Mission
San Fran

The message read:

Sirs—I would like to
express my
consternation concerning
your poor taste + lack of
sympathy for the public, as

evidenced by your running
of the ads for the movie
“Badlands,” featuring the
blurb: “In 1959 most people
were killing time. Kit + Holly
were killing people.” In
light of recent events, this
kind of murder-glorification
can only be deplorable at
best (not that glorification of
violence was ever justifiable)
why don’t you show some
concern for public sensibilities
+ cut the ad?

A Citizen

Wednesday, July 10

The Zodiac is “trying to slip letters and cards into the Chronicle without being detected. He’s not fooling anybody – no matter what his game is,”[80] said Inspector Dave Toschi in an article of the Chronicle. Toschi was referring to the so-called citizen card as well as one mailed on July 8 in San Rafael, Marin County.[††††] He also said, “There’s no doubt in my mind about either one. I took them to a documents expert and in less than five minutes he told me positively they were in fact written by the Zodiac.”[81] Questioned document examination is a complex discipline that comprises magnification and comparison of numerous aspects such as margins, baselines, strokes, pressure, speed, and so forth. The analyst, Morrill presumably, appears to have been biased or in a rush when making that conclusion. Five minutes or even 30 minutes would have been inadequate to conclude much about two communications that clearly deviated from the normal Zodiac

[††††] Only the citizen card and Red Phantom letter were mentioned in the article.

handwriting. The FBI expert stated that the July 8 letter "may have been prepared by someone other than the writer of the Zodiac letters."[82] None of the three questioned communications contained excess postage.

The July 8 letter read as follows:

Editor-
Put Marco back in the, hell-hole
from whence it came - he has
a serious psychological disorder –
always needs to feel superior. I
suggest you refer him to a shrink.
Meanwhile, cancel the Count Marco
column. Since the Count can
write anonymously, so can I -
the Red Phantom
(red with rage)

The envelope read:

R.P.
Editor
San Francisco Chronicle
San Francisco, California

Observations

Let us presuppose that Zodiac authored the two most recent communications. In the card, he advised the editor to take down an advertisement that supposedly indulged in "murder-glorification." The Zodiac is obviously one of the last persons in this world we would expect to make a statement like this. It makes little sense that he would pen a card pretending to be an empathetic person worried about the "sensibilities" of the public, unless it is not him, of course. Indeed, his motivation for writing the card is as complex and incomprehensible as the dark forces working within him. Badlands is a 1973 movie based loosely on a two-month killing rampage that ended in January 1958. A social outcast, Charles Starkweather, teamed up with his girlfriend, Caril Ann Fugate, age

14, and committed numerous murders including Fugate's family. Fugate, who has maintained her innocence saying that she was a hostage, was sentenced to life in prison but was released in 1976. Death always followed Charles Starkweather even in the minutes before his execution. Dr. Finkle, the prison physician, who should have pronounced him dead, suffered a fatal heart attack. The execution was carried on. Starkweather had no final words. He was only 20 years old.[83] In a final disturbing interview, the day before his end, he was asked, "If you could go back in time would you change anything?" He replied, "No, not really" and added, "I know I'm a monster." He also said, "If I could go back into time, I would kill as many more people as I could because I hate people. I know that they are gonna kill me in the electric chair. I don't really care because I'm gonna be famous for all time."[84] As opposed to being horrified by the advertisement, doubtless the Zodiac had quite a few things in common with Starkweather, and, of course, with the related character, Kit, in Badlands.

Despite the unusual content, the handwriting and certain distinct features in the citizen card indicate that Zodiac prepared it. For example, the tendency to use plus signs instead of the conjunctive "and" is a common Zodiac trait. The language of the citizen card is more comprehensive and articulate than any of the Zodiac letters, apart for the 1966 confession. These revelations suggest that Zodiac deliberately worsened his choice of words and grammar to throw off the police. The Exorcist letter could have signaled the end of his identification with the moniker "Zodiac," and he now felt like an ordinary citizen.

Count Marco, whose formal name was Marc H. Spinelli, was an anti-feministic columnist invariably despised by the female audience to the point where women would approach him on the street and slap his face. For 15 years he "gave outrageous advice to women."[85] It seems farfetched if not inconceivable that a seemingly moonstruck Zodiac, out of nowhere, adopted a feministic philosophy to the point where he would write a letter to the editor to demand that the Count's column be canceled. Maybe it was gratifying for him to communicate with the editor on some bizarre level, regardless of the topic in question. However, it is much more likely that the Red Phantom is not the Zodiac killer. After his brief reappearance in 1974, the Zodiac disappeared while being fully aware that it would almost require a miracle for

Inspector Toschi to knock on his door. Obvious copycat letters were still received, written by deranged people. One copycat letter in 1978 was initially believed to be a Zodiac letter after Morrill had authenticated it, but later it was conclusively deemed fake. Other cases became the top priority, and in 1976 Toschi was the only SFPD officer assigned to the case. In an interview, he admitted, "To be honest, I'm no closer now to solving the case."[86] Sadly he concluded, "It's been a paper case for me. My files are getting larger, but I doubt I'll get him unless he makes a mistake or strikes again. I don't know who or where he is."[87] Although the Zodiac disappeared in the 1970s, it is likely that he sent a final taunting card to the Chronicle in 1990, showing that he was still here and was not going anywhere. When it arrived it was not recognized for what it probably was, and it was stored for several years until discovered by coincidence in 2007.

Alive and Well in 1990

The exclamation, *Eureka*, is famously attributed to the Greek scientist, Archimedes; it means, *I have found (it)*. Supposedly he said *Eureka* when he sat down in his bathtub and recognized that the displacement of water must be equal to the volume of the item submerged. He then ran through the streets to tell everybody about his discovery.

In December 1990, someone felt the urge to post a card from *Eureka* to the editor of the Chronicle. When a staff member or editor opened the envelope, he found a *Secret Pal* card that read: "FROM YOUR SECRET PAL CAN'T GUESS WHO I AM YET? WELL LOOK INSIDE AND YOU'LL FIND OUT…" And continued with: "…THAT I'M GONNA KEEP YOU GUESSIN! HAPPY HOLLYDAYS ANYWAY." Whoever sent this card enjoyed his anonymity. At no place does the correspondent name himself; however, it is strikingly similar to the Halloween card sent to Avery 20 years earlier. Both were of the Secret Pal type and were taunting. The sender had enclosed a mysterious Xerox copy of a pair of keys and a cylinder-shaped object linked together by a chain. By carefully enlarging the Xerox, it has been discerned that both keys are engraved with "USPS," "DO NOT DUPLICATE," and a number – fueling speculation that the keys led to the Zodiac's identity in a PO-box.

The handwriting on the envelope has been observed to be eerily alike the Zodiac's in almost all aspects. In 2007 when the communiqué was uncovered, the Chronicle contacted a questioned document examiner, Lloyd Cunningham, who had once worked on the Zodiac case. He asserted to have remembered the Zodiac's handwriting attributes. He "pointed out several similarities between the writing on the envelope and the Zodiac's script."[88] He ultimately concluded that it was probably a forgery because the letters appeared to have been overwritten in a slow manner. He said, "The big problem you have here is, why would a person overwrite all of these letters?" He added, "The Zodiac never did that in any of his writings." "I could never conclude that this is the writing of the Zodiac." He then said, "It tends to lean the other way -- I have the impression that someone tried to imitate the Zodiac's handwriting."[89] Unfortunately, Lloyd's conclusion was based on a false statement since the Zodiac traced his writing several times, most notably on the envelope of the Halloween card. Besides, it would have been in line with logic to trace the letters because a single stroke with a pencil would not have been readable on the red colored envelope. Most, if not all, Zodiac copycat letters are easy to recognize because they have been constructed by mentally deranged persons. The essential constituents that make up a typical Zodiac forgery are that the copycat identifies himself as Zodiac, draws the crosshair symbol, or somehow else leaves no doubts that he is the Zodiac. We perceive none of these aspects in the card and envelope. The circumstances surrounding the card point only toward the Zodiac. If the Christmas card were a forgery, it would have been the most sophisticated hoax in the Zodiac case. Only the Zodiac would have the confidence to post the card without identification or obvious Zodiac references.

When the Zodiac was the hot topic, letters to the editor were scanned for his handwriting. The staff had not continued with this task until 1990, and as expected when the card arrived, it was immediately put away. Zodiac appears to have been lucky once again. First, the card was put away, and when it was finally recognized as a message from the Zodiac, it was categorized as a hoax based on false premises. Therefore, it appears that no forensic work was done on the envelope and the card, nor was the cryptic enclosing subjected to forensic analysis. The diabolical killer was lucky until the end. If the card had received some publicity in 1990,

Zodiac would perhaps have resumed his role as the most elusive and feared pen pal in California. Around the time that the Chronicle received the card, a killer, later identified as Heriberto Seda, committed numerous acts of violence and pretended to be the Zodiac killer. He did not fool anyone. Zodiac wanted to tell us that he was alive and well.

APPENDIX H

Figure 1

Suspected Zodiac card. Received March 22, 1971.

The San Francisco Chronicle; Paul Avery.

Figure 2

Police officer examining Ray Davis' cab for fingerprints.

Figure 3

Ray Davis' cab.

Figure 4

Linda Edwards and Robert Domingos.

Figure 5

The shack.

Figure 6

Johnny and Joyce Swindle.

Figure 7

Zodiac letter. Mailed January 29, 1974.

The San Francisco Chronicle.

Figure 8

Suspected Zodiac letter. Mailed February 3, 1974.

The San Francisco Chronicle.

Figure 9

Suspected Zodiac card. Mailed May 8, 1974.

The San Francisco Chronicle.

Figure 10

Suspected Zodiac letter. Mailed July 8, 1974.

The San Francisco Chronicle.

Figure 11

Envelope. Mailed December 1990.

The San Francisco Chronicle.

Figure 12

Suspected Zodiac card. Mailed December 1990.

The San Francisco Chronicle.

Figure 1

Sierra Club
around in the snow
Sought victim 12
"Peek through the pines,"
pass LAKE TAHOE areas

Zodiac
THIS SIDE OF CARD IS FOR ADDRESS
U.S. POSTAGE
The Times
S.F. Examiner
San Francisco Chronicle
att. Paul averly = Chronicle

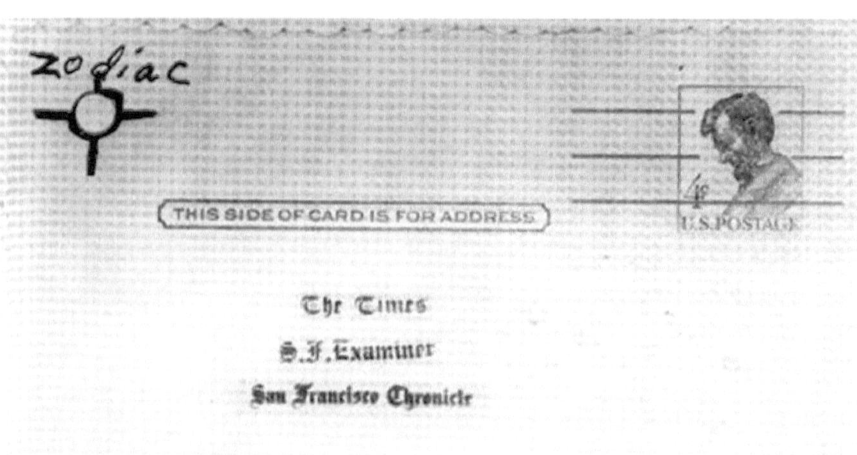

Figure 2

Figure 3

Figure 4

Figure 5

Figure 6

Figure 7

I saw + think "The Exorcist" was the best saterical comidy that I have ever seen.

Signed, yours truley :

He plunged him self into
the billowy wave
and an echo arose from
the sucides grave
tit willo tit willo
tit willo

Ps. if I do not see this note in your paper, I will do something nasty, which you know I'm capable of doing

Me - 37

SFPD - 0

Mailed January 29, 1974.

Figure 8

Dear Mr. Editor,

Did you know that the initials SLAY (Symbionese Liberation Army) spell "sla," an old Norse word meaning "kill".

a friend

Mailed February 3, 1974.

Editor
San Francisco Chronicle
San Francisco, California

Figure 9

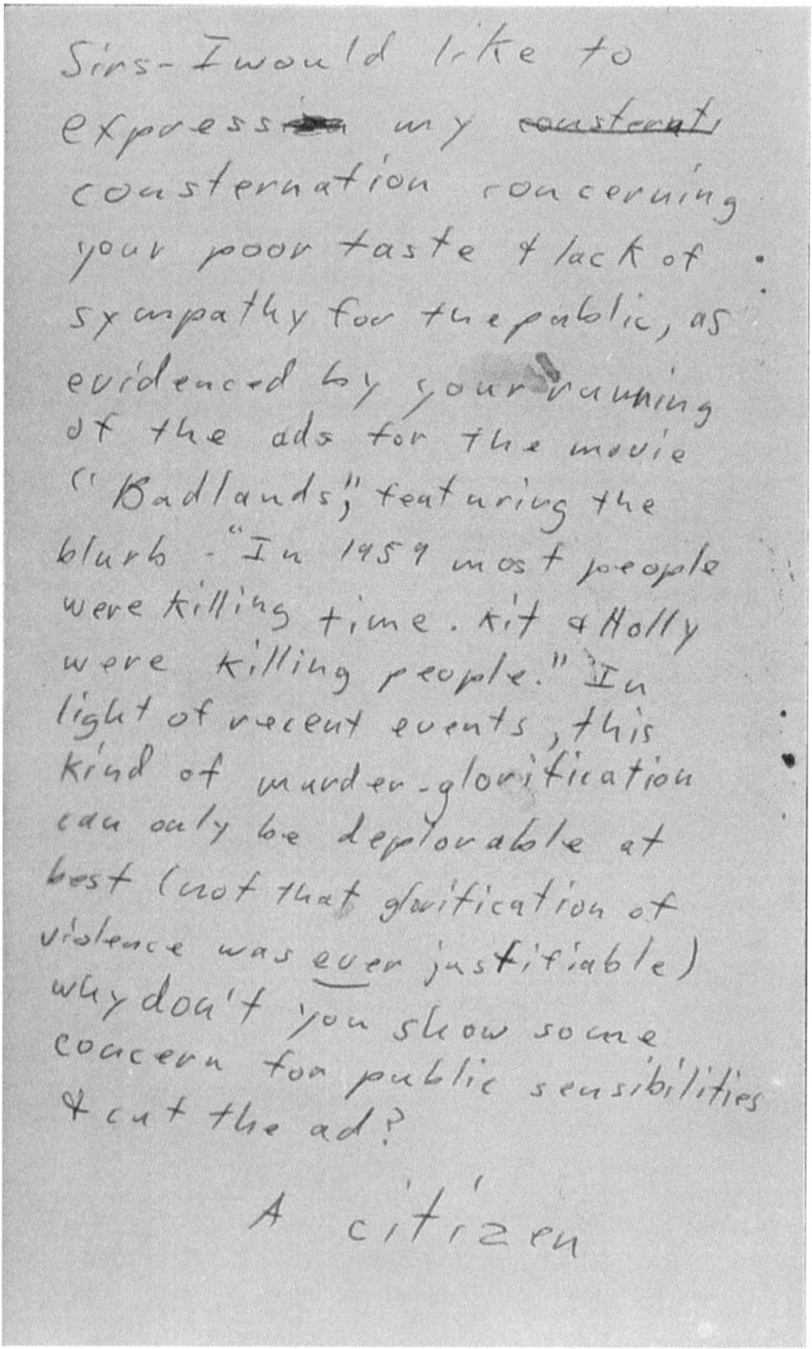

Sirs- I would like to express my ~~constant,~~ consternation concerning your poor taste & lack of sympathy for the public, as evidenced by your running of the ads for the movie "Badlands," featuring the blurb - "In 1959 most people were killing time. Kit & Holly were killing people." In light of recent events, this kind of murder-glorification can only be deplorable at best (not that glorification of violence was ever justifiable) why don't you show some concern for public sensibilities & cut the ad?

A citizen

Mailed May 8, 1974.

Figure 10

Editor—
Put Marco back in the hell-hole
from whence it came—he has
a serious psychological disorder—
always needs to feel superior. I
suggest you refer him to a shrink.
Meanwhile, cancel the Count Marco
column. Since the Count can
write anonymously, so can I—

the Red Phantom
(red with rage)

Mailed July 8, 1974.

Figure 11

Mailed December 1990.

Figure 12

...THAT I'M GONNA
KEEP YOU GUESSIN'!

HAPPY HOLIDAYS, ANYWAY

ENDNOTES H

[1] "Zodiac's New Message — A Hint of a Tahoe Body," San Francisco Chronicle, March 26 1971, 26.
[2] "'No Evidence Exists.' Deputies Discount Zodiac As Slayer of Two Here," Sacramento Union, March 1971.
[3] "'Zodiac' Note Hints About 12th Victim," Amarillo Globe-Times, March 26 1971, 1.
[4] "Long-Missing Woman May Be Victim of Zodiac Killer," http://articles.latimes.com/2000/sep/03/local/me-14718, (retrieved July 2015).
[5] Ibid.
[6] "Tahoe Girl May Be Victim of Zodiac," 1971.
[7] "Missing Tahoe Nurse Family Offers Reward," February 1971.
[8] "New Zodiac Note Says Victim In Tahoe Area Snow," the Times Standard, Eureka, 26 March 1971, 1.
[9] "Search called off for Zodiac victim in mountain area," the Bulletin, March 27 1971, 9.
[10] "'No Evidence Exists.' Deputies Discount Zodiac As Slayer of Two Here," Sacramento Union, March 1971.
[11] "Elusive Zodiac Killer Claims New Victim," the San Bernardino County Sun March 26, 1971, B5.
[12] "Zodiac Killer says that he's struck again," Boca Raton News, March 26 1971, 2.
[13] "'Zodiac' Note Hints About 12th Victim," Amarillo Globe-Times, March 26 1971, 1.
[14] "Zodiac-Like Knife Attack," San Francisco Chronicle, April 13, 1972.
[15] Ibid.
[16] Ibid.
[17] Ibid.
[18] "Marines Riding Shotgun On Buses," Valley Times North Hollywood, April 17, 1962, 1.
[19] "Oceanside Cabbie Slain," Oceanside Blade Tribune, April 11, 1962, 1.
[20] Ibid.
[21] "Oceanside Murder," https://drive.google.com/viewerng/viewer?url=https://interactive.cbs8.com/pdf/OceansideMurder1962.pdf (retrieved March 2020).
[22] "Oceanside Cabbie Slain," Oceanside Blade-Tribune, April 11, 1962, 1.
[23] "Police Seek Fresh Leads In Slaying Of Taxicab Driver," Oceanside Blade-Tribune, April 12, 1962.
[24] "Oceanside Cabbie Slain," Oceanside Blade-Tribune, April 11, 1962, 1.
[25] Ibid.
[26] Ibid.

[27] Office of the Coroner, Country of San Diego, California. File Number 38900. Raymond Davis. April 12, 1962. p. 3.
[28] Ibid.
[29] "Michigan Man Found Shot to Death in Alley," Ironwood Daily Globe Ironwood, April 13, 1962, 1.
[30] "New Threat to Murder Busman Told," Independent from Long Beach, April [18], 1962, 6.
[31] "figure out" https://www.vocabulary.com/dictionary/figure out (retrieved July 2020)
32 "California Crime Rates 1960 – 2018," www.disastercenter.com/crime/cacrime.htm (retrieved March 2020).
33 Ibid.
[34] "America's Declining Homicide Clearance Rates 1965-2018," www.murderdata.org/p/reported-homicide-clearance-rate-1980.html (retrieved March 2020).
[35] Santa Barbara County Sheriff's Department, Press Release, 1972.
[36] "Tom, what about the Santa Barbara cases...," http://www.zodiackiller.com/mba/opzv/72.html (retrieved August 2015).
[37] Ibid.
[38] Ibid.
[39] Ibid.
[40] "MURDER Suspect Object of Search," June 6, 1963, A4.
[41] "Questions regarding the crime scene," www.zodiackiller.fr.yuku.com/topic/2773/Questions-regarding-the-crime-scene?page=4 (retrieved August 2015).
[42] "Lake Berryessa: Unresolved Issues," www.zodiackiller.com/mba/csabh/813.html (retrieved August 2015).
[43] Ibid.
[44] Ibid.
[45] Ibid.
[46] Ibid.
[47] Ibid.
[48] "Mike Kelleher/This Is The Zodiac Speaking Part II," www.zodiackiller.com/mba/zm/598.html (retrieved August 2015).
[49] "One Size Fits All?" www.zodiackiller.com/mba/csabh/951.html (retrieved August 2015).
[50] Ibid.
[51] "Zodiac's Disguise" www.zodiackiller.com/mba/gzd/1334.html, (retrieved August 2015).
[52] Ibid.
[53] "Lake Berryessa: Behind the Hood," www.zodiackiller.com/mba/csabh/262.html (retrieved August 2015).
[54] Roed, O.J. Letter to Thomas Joyce. December 31, 1968.

[55] "Thrill Killer Sought In Calif. Murders," the Progress-Index February 10 1964, 8.
[56] Ibid.
[57] San Diego Police Department. Investigation and Activities Surrounding Murder Cases Al-3161 and AL-3162, 3.
[58] Ibid, 2.
[59] "Thrill Killer Sought In Calif. Murders," the Progress-Index February 10 1964, 8.
[60] Ibid.
[61] "Killings Near Lompoc and San Diego Similar," Independent Long Beach, 8 February 1964, B3.
[62] Ibid.
[63] "Honeymooner Killings Called Maniac's Work," Los Angeles Times, Saturday, February 8, 1964, 1.
[64] "He'd 'Recognize' Zodiac," San Francisco Chronicle, May 8 1973.
[65] Ibid.
[66] "Zodiac Mystery Letter – the First Since 1971," San Francisco Chronicle, January 31 1974, 1.
[67] "Cryptic letter: Zodiac ends long silence," the Daily Review, January 31 1974, 3.
[68] Freedom of Information and Privacy Acts, Subject: Zodiac Killer, File Number: 9-HQ-49911, Section 4 Federal Bureau of Investigation, 132.
[69] Ibid, 136.
[70] "THE MIKADO CODE?" https://www.zodiacciphers.com/zodiac-news/the-mikado-code (retrieved April 2020).
[71] "The Mikado," https://en.wikisource.org/wiki/The_Mikado (retrieved April 2020).
[72] Ibid.
[73] Ibid.
[74] "Zodiac Revisited," http://www.timesheraldonline.com/article/ZZ/20070222/NEWS/702229824 (retrieved June 2016).
[75] "SLA Letter," https://www.zodiacciphers.com/sla-letter.html (retrieved April 2020).
[76] Freedom of Information and Privacy Acts, Subject: Zodiac Killer, File Number: 9-HQ-49911, Section 4 Federal Bureau of Investigation, 149.
[77] "SLA Letter," https://www.zodiacciphers.com/sla-letter.html (retrieved April 2020).
[78] Freedom of Information and Privacy Acts, Subject: Zodiac Killer, File Number: 9-HQ-49911, Section 4 Federal Bureau of Investigation, 181.
[79] Ibid.
[80] "Zodiac's Letters to The Editor," San Francisco Chronicle, July 10 1974, 2.
[81] Ibid.

[82] Freedom of Information and Privacy Acts, Subject: Zodiac Killer, File Number: 9-HQ-49911, Section 4 Federal Bureau of Investigation, 181.
[83] "Calm To The End, No Final Words," the Miami News, June 25 1959, 1.
[84] "Charles Starkweather Last Interview," https://www.youtube.com/watch?v=lMPXdEAKji8 (retrieved July 2015).
[85] "OBITUARY -- Count Marco -- Outrageous S.F. Advice Columnist," http://www.sfgate.com/news/article/OBITUARY-Count-Marco-Outrageous-S-F-Advice-2961449.php (retrieved July 2015).
[86] "Lone Officer Continues Search for Zodiac," The Fort Scott Tribune, September 15, 1976, 1.
[87] Ibid.
[88] "Zodiac's written clues fascinate document expert," http://www.sfgate.com/news/article/Zodiac-s-written-clues-fascinate-document-expert-2644828.php (retrieved June 2016).
[89] Ibid.

CHAPTER 9

LINGUISTIC ANALYSIS

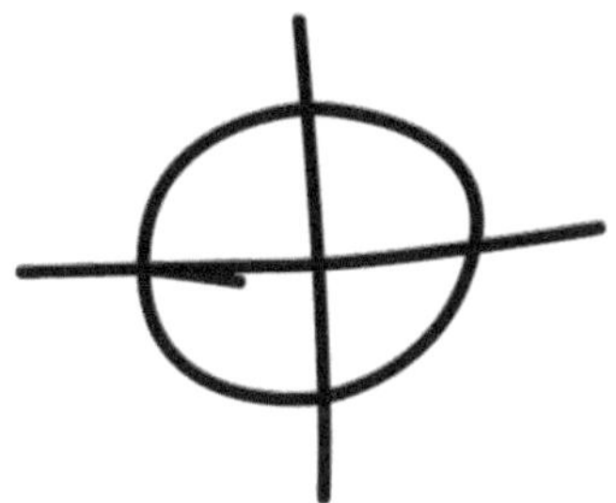

As we have seen, the Zodiac's words revealed, apart from their clear-cut meaning, many secondary aspects. In this chapter, we will dissect his communications to an even greater degree to see if his misspellings, grammar, and choice of words reveal any further information about him. The Zodiac misspelled words dozens of times but often inconsistently; for example, he wrote "controol" then two sentences later, he spelled it "control." Logic appears to dictate that it is unlikely that someone misspells a word only to write it correctly a few sentences later. This desultory pattern indicates that he was trying to confuse readers and analysts, but did so haphazardly as he did not proofread or keep track of which false leads he had offered, hence indicating a faulty working memory or great carelessness. It might blend in with the seeming spontaneous nature of his letters. In line with this line of reasoning, one police

report states that the Zodiac "misspells simple words apparently on purpose."[1] The same logic was echoed when Inspector Toschi said, "I think he's quite intelligent and better educated than someone who misspells as frequently as he does in his letters," and that, "he'll often misspell a word at the top of a letter, then spell it correctly at the bottom. It's his ego game."[2] Even Morrill did not believe the mistakes were genuine: "He is not an unintelligent man by a long shot. His paragraphing, his phrasing, his punctuation is very good. I am sure he has deliberately misspelled words in an attempt to lead us to believe that he is illiterate but in so doing he led us to the point that we believe just the opposite."[3]
Dyslexia is a multivariable learning disorder that is difficult to define, but may be defined as "a problem with language processing at the phoneme level."[4] It is generally characterized by problems with reading and spelling despite adequate intelligence and sufficient educational opportunities. Over the past years, scientists have "been able to identify the areas of the brain that are used for reading, and, very importantly, how the activation in these areas differs in typical readers and in dyslexic readers."[5] Hence, dyslexia is considered a neurological disorder. Although Dr. W. Pringle Morgan wrote the first description of dyslexia in 1896, hardly anything was known about it, except to researchers, when the Zodiac was in the spotlight. Poor grammar, spelling, etc. was certainly associated with a lack of education and other negative connotations. Howard E. Gardner, a professor of cognition and education at the Harvard Graduate School of Education, put it more bluntly in 2010: "Fifty years ago, students who were dyslexic were just considered stupid, and they could rarely have the opportunity to benefit from higher learning."[6] We will now analyze the Zodiac's language from the standpoint of dyslexia and see if the idiosyncrasies in his communications are consistent with what we know about dyslexia today. We will start with the inconsistent misspellings. *The Speech Language Dyslexia Clinic* states that "spelling the same word in different ways throughout a paper" is a common characteristic of dyslexia.[7] *Dyslexia Support Services and Educational Resources* states that a person suffering from dyslexia "often uses a number of different spellings for the same word in

one piece of writing."[8] Back then, Toschi used the inconsistent spellings as a rationale for believing that they were a ruse. Many researchers have concluded that the misspellings are a ruse because of the inconsistencies. With that in mind, it is striking that the Zodiac did not make *consistent* misspellings, indicating that he had special knowledge about this frequent characteristic or was genuinely dyslexic. However, it seems unlikely that he, for example, had access to the *International Journal of Disability Development and Education* that in 1966 published the article, "Prediction of Childhood Dyslexia" by John McLeod, which describes dyslexia as having many facets and much variability from patient to patient.[9]

Vowel Sounds

According to *Bright Solutions for Dyslexia, Inc.,* individuals with dyslexia have an "extreme difficulty with vowel sounds."[10] The Zodiac had a significant problem with vowel sounds, often confusing them, such as when he wrote "frunt" instead of "front;" and in these words similarly: "pencel," "backwords," "victoms," and "epasode."

Mirror writing

Letter reversals, pursuant to *Debunking the Myths about Dyslexia*, are "actually quite common. However, if this does not stop after two years of handwriting instruction, it becomes a red flag for dyslexia."[11] Letter reversals are seen in the two examples below. The Zodiac had a problem in differentiating between a *p* and a *b* (fig. 1).

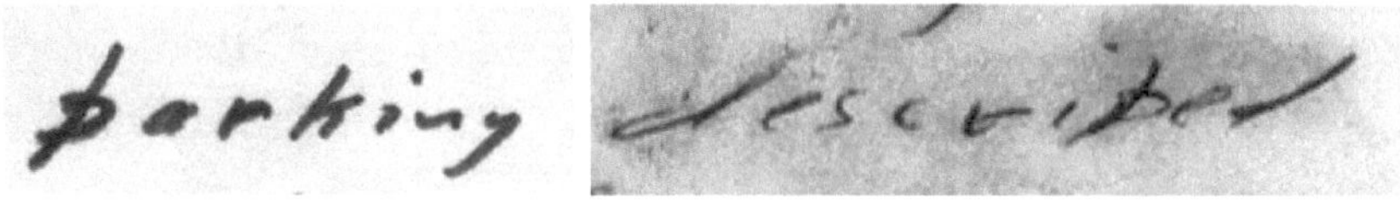

Figure 1

In the word, "ADDRESS," the letter "D" appears to have been added after Zodiac had realized that it should contain two of them. In the other example, he might have added an "i" after spelling it as *cypher* initially (fig. 2).

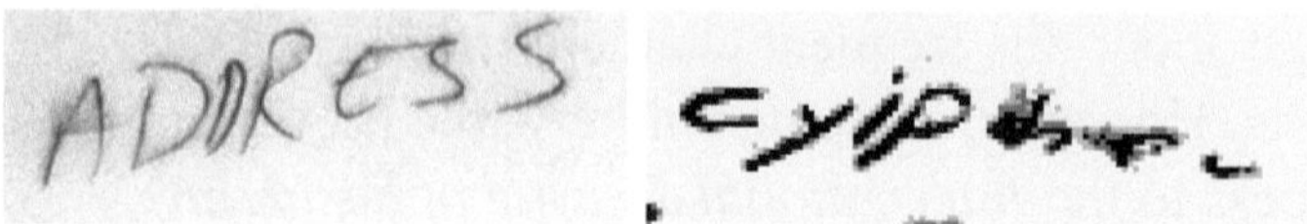

Figure 2

Suffix Problems

Dyslexia is characterized by "problems with grammar, such as learning prefixes or suffixes."[12] Frequently, the Zodiac did not leave out the silent *e* in non-finite-verbs with the suffix –ing, including "haveing," "useing," "uncompromiseing, and "shakeing." Incongruently, he followed the rule when he wrote "bouncing," needling," "irritating," and "stumbling." He added the suffix accurately to those that only required the addition e.g. walk → walk*ing*.

Inconsistent Handwriting

Closely related to dyslexia is dysgraphia, the two disorders "share symptoms and often occur together."[13] A sign may be irregular "sizes, shapes, or slant of letters" and inconsistent "spaces between words and letters."[14] The Zodiac's handwriting is consistent with these aspects of dysgraphia. In the example below, we see unusual inter-word separations (fig. 3).

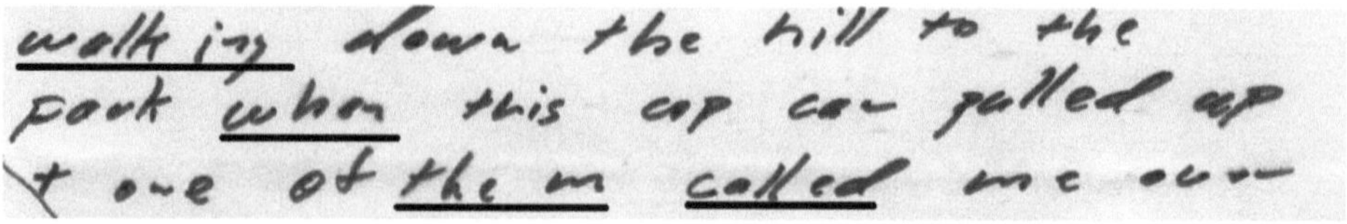

Figure 3

Disintegrated Handwriting

Several times, the Zodiac's handwriting appeared methodical and neat, but worsened as it progressed. It has been observed that the handwriting of dyslexics "may deteriorate readily under pressure"[15] (see Zodiac's July 26, 1970, letter).

Inconsistent Grammar

Zodiac's grammar was inconsistent in several instances. He demonstrated accurate use of "to" and "too," correct and incorrect use of semicolons, inconsistent capitalization and use of apostrophes. According to the *Davis Dyslexia Association* this inconsistency would be expected if Zodiac was dyslexic as the "most consistent thing about dyslexics is their inconsistency."[16] Underneath is a visual example of the inconsistency in the Zodiac's writing. He put the apostrophe in *don't* and *wouldn't* but not in "Im." He used a capital "K" in the middle of a sentence, and spelled *sure* phonetically (fig. 4). Individuals with dyslexia "often spell phonetically."[17] Ignorance of punctuation and misplaced capital letters are dyslexia symptoms according to *A to Z of Brain, Mind and Learning* (fig. 4).[18]

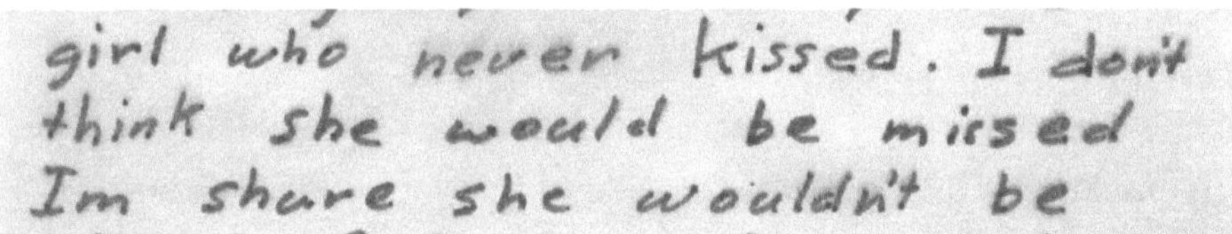

Figure 4

Compound words

A compound word is one that is composed of more than one word such as *nevertheless* or *nonetheless*. Whether words should be separated or not in a particular instance can be confusing even for people without dyslexia. The confusion will be even greater to someone not comfortable with the written language.

In the examples below, the Zodiac erroneously added a space between "my" and "self" and between "ant" and "hills" (fig. 5).

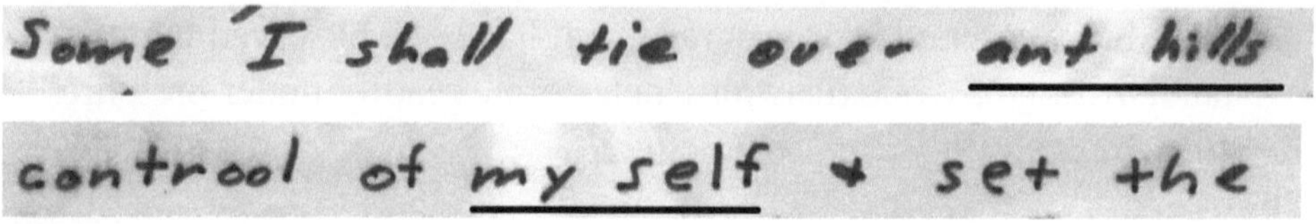

Figure 5

Double Letters

Double letters caused the Zodiac a great deal of trouble as evidenced by these misspellings: "coupple," "untill," "bussy," "dificult," and "butons." Problems with double letters are observed in the writing of dyslexics.

Sight Words

Sight words, commonly referred to as Dolch words, are high-frequency words such as do, because, why, and others. They "will cause a dyslexic problems because these words cannot be translated into visual pictures."[19] The Zodiac misspelled a number of these words.

Other Characteristics

Interestingly, the *Dyslexia Checklist: A Practical Reference for Parents and Teachers* states that individuals with dyslexia may show "special aptitude in visual-spatial thinking or three-dimensional awareness," and may have "strong technical and mechanical aptitude."[20] The *Checklist* also details that dyslexia is a risk factor for unemployment, underemployment, academic failure, mental problems, and altercations with the law.[21] It is perhaps surprising that, in some circumstances, dyslexics "excel at higher levels of math, such as algebra, geometry, and calculus."[22] Some of these qualities may arguably be attributed to the Zodiac. For example, he mentioned *radians*, a concept used in calculus. He had a good sense of his surroundings. His bomb drawings and other descriptions show his technical aptitude.

The Zodiac's Confession

In the confession, Zodiac spelled *victim* correctly, but as "victom" in other letters. In the confession and as the Zodiac, he misspelled *twitch*. Exactly how different the communications were can be objectively evaluated by means of statistics. Below is an overview showing the percentage of misspellings and average word length for all the major letters (fig. 6).[‡‡‡‡]

	April 20 1970	April 28 1970	June 26 1970	July 24 1970	July 26 1970	March 13 1971	January 29 1974
Avg. word length:	~3.6	~3.42	~3.61	~4.03	~4.08	~3.88	~4.29
Misspellings:	~4.98%	~4.4%	~2.8%	~6.7%	~6.3%	~2.8%	6.3%

	November 1966	31 July 1969, Chronicle	August 1969	October 1969	November 8 1969	November 9 1969	December 20 1969
Avg. word length:	~3.79	~3.77	~3.67	~3.99	~3.57	~3.74	~3.71
Misspellings:	~0.9%	~3.9%	~3.9%	~1.5%	~2.3%	~3.9%	~7.9%

Figure 6

After 1966, his letters had more misspellings, from 1.7 up to 8.8 times more, which may indicate that he deliberately added more when he entered the Zodiac persona. The average word length is very consistent, but reaches up to an average of ~4 letters per word when the communications are very short or contain quoted/paraphrased material.

‡‡‡‡ The numbers are actually approximations because word-counting software can be calibrated in more than one way.

The citizen letter, which the Zodiac may have authored, has an average word length of 4.62, while the number for the highly questionable Red Phantom letter is 4.51. This is higher than in any of the other letters. The citizen letter has two corrections, but other than that there are no misspellings in these. The overall question seems to be, did the Zodiac worsen his handwriting after 1966 in a manner consistent with a dyslexia diagnosis? Or did he improve his writing in the confession by consulting a dictionary or other material?
It is easy for a person with a good command of the written language to deliberately distort his language. However, it is much more difficult for someone uncomfortable with the written language to heighten his language artificially. By assuming that Zodiac lowered the quality of his writing, we have to conclude either that his knowledge about dyslexia was advanced or that he was lucky and random errors translated into what we know about dyslexia today. However, one possibility that accounts for most of the observations is that he suffered from a very mild version of dyslexia in his childhood, and as he grew up, he was able to overcome most of the symptoms. He then deliberately worsened these instinctual symptoms when he wanted to distort his language. Like in many other areas of the Zodiac case, it is difficult to reach a clear conclusion as the evidence points in several directions.

The Zodiac Might Have Been a Canadian

No one ever reported that Zodiac spoke with a distinguishable accent, but his choice of words and certain phrases point across the Atlantic Ocean to the British Isles or any other population in which British phrases are used. His frequent use of the modal verb *shall* instead of the more colloquial *will* is typical of British English.[23] Other aspects of his language also point away from the US. For example, he wrote, *Happy Christmas*, a British expression instead of the one typical of America, namely, *Merry Christmas*. The British are well known for their use of understatements in which the subject is deliberately downplayed. Zodiac used this figure of speech when he wrote that he was *mildly curious* about "how much money" had been offered for his arrest. In addition, the British may also be more prone to use words like "kiddies" and "nice" than Americans would. Zodiac also used phraseology associated with Britain at other times, although these instances are more ambiguous.

If Zodiac had wanted to convey the impression that he was British, he would in all probability have used a thick accent when he called the police, but he did not. It therefore seems likely that these characteristics were expressed unconsciously – perhaps his parents immigrated to the US from the United Kingdom, and they passed on common phrases and words, but his American peers influenced his accent. While this is possible, the most likely scenario when we take other evidence into consideration is that Zodiac was a Canadian who had relocated to the US. Canadian speakers are usually indistinguishable from American ones, but Canadian English is closer to British English, but spelling tends to be more flexible, combining both British and American rules, perhaps accounting for the fact that Zodiac never used typical British spellings like "colour." Furthermore, the art of understatements is considered a trait of Canadian humor.

On September 27, 1969, the Zodiac concocted a story about having escaped from the Deer Lodge prison, located over 1000 miles from the crime scene. If the Zodiac had been a lifelong Bay Area resident, he would almost certainly have picked a well-known prison in California, like the San Quentin State Prison or the California Medical Facility, to serve as the basis for the ruse. However, the Deer Lodge prison is located in the state of Montana which shares 14 Canadian border crossings with British Columbia, Alberta, and Saskatchewan provinces. It is also worth considering that the reason no one recognized the Zodiac's handwriting and physical description could be that his family resided far away from the Bay Area in Canada.

ENDNOTES I

[1] California Department of Justice/Division of Law Enforcement/Bureau of Investigation, Zodiac Homicides, for Law Enforcement Use Only, 6.
[2] "Lone Officer Continues Search for Zodiac," the Fort Scott Tribune, September 15 1976, 1B.
[3] David Fincher, Director, *Zodiac 2-Disc Director's Cut*, 2008.
[4] "Dyslexia and the Brain: What Does Current Research Tell Us?" http://www.readingrockets.org/article/dyslexia-and-brain-what-does-current-research-tell-us (retrieved April 2016).
[5] "Yalies with learning disabilities find support," www.yaleherald.com/news/yalies-with-learning-disabilities-find-support (retrieved April 2016).
[6] "Accommodate to Learn," www.thecrimson.com/article/2010/10/21/students-time-accommodations-mary/?page=2 (retrieved March 2016).
[7] "Dyslexia Signs & Symptoms," www.speech-language-dyslexia.com/signs.html (retrieved March 2016).
[8] "Signs and Symptoms of Dyslexia," http://dyslexiasupportservices.com.au/dyslexia/dyslexia_signs_symptoms.html (retrieved April 2016).
[9] "PREDICTION OF CHILDHOOD DYSLEXIA," http://www.tandfonline.com/doi/abs/10.1080/0156655660120303?journalCode=cijd18 (retrieved April 2016).
[10] "What is Dyslexia?" http://www.dys-add.com/dyslexia.html (retrieved April 2016).
[11] "Debunking the Myths about Dyslexia," http://dyslexiahelp.umich.edu/dyslexics/learn-about-dyslexia/what-is-dyslexia/debunking-common-myths-about-dyslexia (retrieved April 2016).
[12] "Signs and Symptoms of Dyslexia," http://www.dyslexiasupportservices.com.au/dyslexia/dyslexia_signs_symptoms.html (retrieved June 2016).
[13] "The Difference Between Dysgraphia and Dyslexia," https://www.understood.org/en/learning-attention-issues/child-learning-disabilities/dysgraphia/the-difference-between-dysgraphia-and-dyslexia (retrieved June 2016)
[14] "What is Dysgraphia?" https://dsf.net.au/what-is-dysgraphia/ (retrieved June 2016).
[15] "Dyslexia Supports," http://www2.ul.ie/web/WWW/Services/Student_Affairs/Student_Specialised_Supports/Disability_Support_Services/Information_for_Staff/Dyslexia_Supports (retrieved June 2016).
[16] "Test for Dyslexia: 37 Common Traits," http://www.dyslexia.com/library/symptoms.htm (retrieved April 2016).

[17] "Working Together: Computers and People with Learning Disabilities," http://www.washington.edu/doit/working-together-computers-and-people-learning-disabilities (retrieved April 2016).
[18] "Dyslexia Online," www.dyslexia.learninginfo.org (retrieved June 2016).
[19] "Dyslexia Australia," http://www.dyslexia-australia.com.au/solution.htm (retrieved June 2016).
[20] Sandra Rief, Judith Stern, Dyslexia Checklist: A Practical Reference for Parents and Teachers (Jossey-Bass 2010), 25.
[21] Ibid, 10.
[22] "What is Dyslexia?" http://www.dys-add.com/dyslexia.html (retrieved June 2016).
[23] "Shall and Will: Commonly Confused Words," http://grammar.about.com/od/alightersideofwriting/a/shallwillglossary.htm (retrieved June 2016).

CHAPTER 10

FUTURE INVESTIGATIVE STEPS

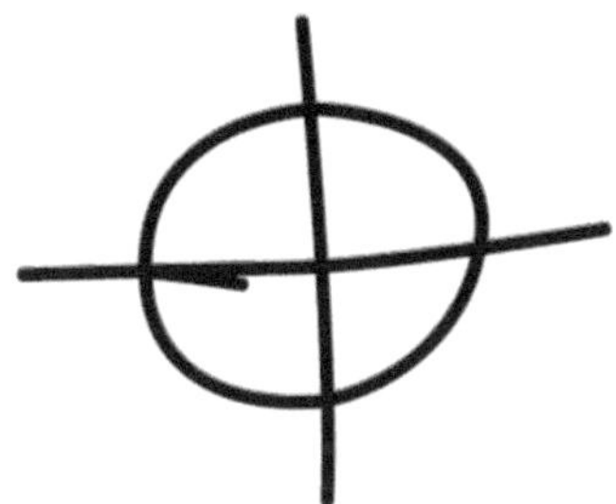

In October of 2002, it was reported that a partial DNA profile of the Zodiac had been extracted from one of his letters. In an interview, SFPD Inspector Kelly Carroll explained that the Zodiac "claimed to have disguised his appearance and to have disguised his fingerprints so that police couldn't find him. But one of the things that we did in examining the evidence is realize that in 1969 the idea of DNA was at best science fiction and so it was probable that Zodiac did not have any idea about disguising or hiding his DNA. And so we concluded that there was the possibility that we could recover biological material deposited by Zodiac when he licked the stamps and the envelopes that he used to send the letters."[1] At this time, the profile is "not enough"[2] to submit to DNA databases, but it can be used to eliminate or statistically implicate suspects.

In the 1970s and 1980s, the so-called Golden State Killer moved from town to town, terrorizing, killing, and raping his victims in a seemingly random pattern; thus, entrenching an element of fear and dread within a large percentage of California's population. The killer executed his crimes with accuracy and precision. He also relished close shaves with law enforcement authorities as it is documented that he would make phone calls to the police and his potential victims before and after committing the crimes. After countless rapes and murders, he suddenly vanished in 1986, fueling speculation that he was imprisoned or had died. With the advent of DNA technology in the mid-1980s, law enforcement began linking his crimes and checking his genetic material to known felons in state and federal databases. These databases would only furnish a result if the killer's genetic material was already registered or if one of his relatives had had their DNA collected and uploaded to the databases at some point. There was not a match. Instead, law enforcement officers uploaded his genetic material to GEDmatch, an open source database used by amateur genealogists. Surprisingly, they got a match among the almost one million distinct DNA profiles, but not for the killer's – they had found almost two dozen distant relatives of the killer, sharing the same great-great-great grandparents. Following the discovery, a complicated investigation began, and after constructing dozens of family trees and meticulously searching through public records, census reports, obituaries, and criminal databases they targeted Joseph James DeAngelo, a former police officer. Investigators put him under surveillance and picked up an item he had discarded. They extracted DNA from the item and then compared it to the killer's. It was a match. The killer had now been identified.
While previous DNA testing only yielded a partial profile of the Zodiac, which cannot be submitted to databases, it was reported in 2018 that investigators had sent off Zodiac letters and envelopes for testing using state of the art DNA extraction technology. If they can extract a full profile of the Zodiac, the plan is to follow the same steps as with the Golden State Killer. Perhaps the Zodiac is sitting in his retirement home, somewhere around San Francisco, following the DeAngelo case and hoping that the police will not find his DNA. And if they do, he is praying that none of his relatives have submitted their DNA to any of the public or state databases.

Given the age of the Zodiac case, it may very well be discovered one day that his partial DNA profile is consistent with person X's – but handwriting, fingerprints, and so forth are not available for comparison with what is believed to be Zodiac's. It might be that the probability of someone matching the profile is one in a hundred thousand individuals. What does this actually mean? One must be extremely careful with the probabilities inferred by DNA evidence; it can be deceiving. Let us take a general example. Assume suspect "X" commits a burglary in a region with exactly 10 million males. The forensic crew rapidly establishes that whoever committed the crime was alone. Despite the fact that the burglar wore surgical gloves and an intricate mask, he left a small amount of biological material when exiting through a window. A DNA profile is extracted, and it is established that it belongs to a male, and one in a hundred thousand individuals has matching DNA. Years later, Mr. Y applies for an advanced position in a government agency and agrees to supply a DNA sample. For whatever reason, his DNA is compared to the sample from the window. The result comes back: Mr. Y's DNA matches the DNA found at the crime scene. So, the question is: What is the probability that Mr. Y committed the crime? Almost zero!

Equating the probability of a match given innocence to the probability of innocence given a match is known as the *prosecutor's fallacy*. The population consists of 10 million males, meaning that the DNA profile could match 100 individuals. Only one of these individuals is guilty. Mr. Y is not any more likely to be guilty than the other 99 individuals (assuming none of the others can be excluded based on age and other factors).

Thus, the probability of him being innocent despite being a DNA match =

$$\frac{99}{100} * 100\ \% = 99\%$$

The prosecutor's fallacy is commonly made in the media and sometimes in court, occasionally resulting in a retrial (Sally Clark 2003). Now, if Mr. Y is proven to have been in the area of the crime scene at the right time there is a high likelihood that he is guilty. In the future, if a person happens to have a partial DNA match with the Zodiac, it is important to consult a textbook on conditional probability and make accurate calculations. DNA evidence can narrow down the list of suspects significantly and in conjunction with additional evidence might be enough to convict, but is usually in itself not enough to *throw away the key.* Moreover, in recent years, there has been a small surge in cold crime cases being solved due to DNA technology, confessions, and anonymous tips. Some of the cases have been extremely old, such as the 1957 kidnapping and murder of Maria Ridulph that was solved in 2012 when 73-year-old Jack McCullough was convicted and sentenced to life imprisonment. In 1971, taxi driver Ralph Smith was killed, but his family had to wait until 2014 when his murder was officially solved because of a confession. Eileen Ferro was only 21 years old when she was stabbed to death. Forty years went by until an arrest was made prompted by DNA evidence. As evidenced by these cases that remained cold for many years, it is entirely possible that one day the Zodiac's name will also be revealed. Since we know many details about the Zodiac and have evidence in different areas, he could be identified via a number of means. Some possible investigative strategies and considerations are listed in the following.

- A reexamination of the confirmed letters and rope from Lake Berryessa using the latest forensic technology could be of value. Technology is growing at an exponential rate, and perhaps within a few years we will be able to extract information from these items that will lead us closer to him. Yesterday's science fiction is tomorrow's reality. One of these developing methods is DNA phenotyping. Using only DNA, scientists can create an image of a person's face. Even if a complete DNA profile could be extracted from the items, a digital image of the Zodiac would probably not be of much value today, just like the wanted posters did not lead to his front door. However, other highly advanced investigative strategies are being developed as these words are being typed, and one of them might just shine light on the Zodiac's identity.
- In 1971, an unidentified man known as D.B. Cooper hijacked a plane. In midair, he jumped out with his ransom of $200,000 in cash and a parachute attached to his back and one to his front. He was never seen or heard from again. The flight staff characterized him as a business-executive type, dressed in a dark suit, and wearing a black

tie. He forgot the tie on board before he jumped into the darkness. Forty years later a team of scientists analyzed the tie and found rare metallic particles that suggest he worked as a manager in "an exotic metal fabrication facility that contained titanium, aluminum and other specialty metals."[3] Similarly, scientists might discover microscopic particles on Zodiac items that will become a point of investigation, such as on the rope and Paul Stine's shirt. His pocket and storage place could have transferred microscopic particles. The major issue is that the original investigators and experts could hardly have imagined the complexity of forensic science today, and much of the evidence has been handled without gloves or contaminated else how.

- The DNA evidence from Riverside should be compared with the partial profile believed to be the Zodiac's, and further analyses should be conducted, especially on the Timex watch (assuming it has not already been done). As previously mentioned, a hair was found underneath one of the stamps of a Zodiac envelope. If this hair can be compared to the hairs found in Cheri Jo Bates' hand, we will know with a degree of certainty if the Zodiac actually killed her (presumably this has already been done, and, therefore, the RPD stated that the Zodiac did not kill Cheri Jo Bates).
- The cigarette butts, which could have been left by the killer of Robert Domingos and Linda Edwards, might still hold some biological material that can point the finger at the Zodiac or away from him. The rope might also contain DNA or some unusual particles.
- Geographical profiling is an "investigative methodology that uses the locations of a connected series of crimes to determine the most probable area that an offender lives in."[4] A geo-profile was prepared in 2007 using the software, *Rigel*. The input included the Zodiac's five confirmed killings, but had it encompassed Cheri Jo Bates and/or the 1962, 1963, and 1964 killings it would have changed the outcome. Rigel indicated that "the most probable areas for the [Zodiac's] search base are: South-eastern Napa County, including American Canyon and north Vallejo; Eastern Solano County, including east and north Vallejo, Mare

Island, and Benicia; and Northern Contra Costa County, just south of Carquinez Strait, including Crockett."[5] This result is of course compatible with the Zodiac's own words that indicated a familiarity with Vallejo and the surrounding areas. On the other hand, it contrasts the strong evidence of his ties to San Francisco; almost all of his letters were postmarked in San Francisco, he was focused on SFPD rather than VPD, etc.

- After James Owen drove by the lovers' lane at an estimated 11:14 p.m. on December 20, 1968, Zodiac spent an additional two to three minutes shooting the victims and at the Rambler station wagon before leaving the area. He may have been ready to leave at 11:17 p.m. If he had traveled northwest along Lake Herman Road toward Vallejo, he would have encountered Stella Borges who reached the lovers' lane at 11:20 p.m. Thus, Zodiac drove southeast toward Benicia, which is specified in the geographical profile as one of the hotspot areas where he could have lived. The Zodiac had almost been exposed in the initial stages of the crime when Owen passed by. Immediately after the crime, the Zodiac may very well have been paranoid and started to ponder obsessively about what Owen had seen and what he did not see. When he left, he was undoubtedly high on adrenaline while feeling powerful. His murder-weapon was still in his car. No doubt, he was eager to dispose of it. In line with this reasoning, it seems reasonable that Zodiac went straight home. After killing Darlene Ferrin, he spent an unusual amount of time getting to the phone booth, 40 minutes in total. As argued on previous pages, he probably parked his car at his home, discarded the 9 mm pistol, changed his clothes, and drove in a different car to the phone booth; an organized killer like the Zodiac would have planned his escape route. With the murder-weapon still inside his car, he would not want to go directly into the city and possibly encounter police officers. Getting away from traffic would be the logical decision. If he simply turned left onto Lake Herman Road and continued to Benicia, took care of his business, and then proceeded to the phone booth at the corner of Tuolumne Street and Springs Road in Vallejo, it would have taken him about 40 minutes. Back then, there were only about 5000 residents in Benicia and not many of them fit the characteristics detailed on these pages. Nor did many of them have access to the cars associated with the case.

- Although highly unlikely, the possible solution to the 340 cipher could be the missing piece that investigators have been looking for. It is, however, infinitely more likely that it contains an angry, rambling message similar to the ones he wrote around the time the cipher was sent.
- Michael Mageau could see that Zodiac's car had California license plates and he might have seen the numbers and letters in a split second and forgotten about them. The same can be said about Bill Crow and his girlfriend. Forensic hypnosis could bring these memories to light. In the mid-seventies, three brothers, Richard and James Schoenfeld, and Frederick Woods kidnapped 26 kids and a bus driver. The driver managed to escape, and under hypnosis, he could recall the license plate of the van belonging to one of the kidnappers, and this ultimately solved the case.[6]

  It is a mantra in the field of hypnosis that our subconscious retains all memories; however, after more than 50 years, this route of investigation seems extremely unlikely to yield a usable result.

  As detailed in this book, we know a great deal about the Zodiac, enough to outline a detailed profile (see next chapter for a psychological profile). At this time, it is mostly of historical value.

Physical appearance

- Used glasses occasionally.
- Brown hair with reddish tint.
- Overweight.
- Size 10 ½ shoes.

Voice

- Monotonous, even, and consistent.

Location

- He spent most of his time in San Francisco. He was familiar with Vallejo, Riverside, and possibly Gaviota Beach at Santa Barbara, Ocean Beach at San Diego, and Oceanside. He may have been a Canadian who later moved to California.

Work

- Possibly a position in the military, engineering-type person.

Interests and capabilities

- A movie aficionado, particularly attracted to violent ones.
- Enjoyed opera.
- Cryptography.
- Proficient sewer.
- Probably spent a lot of time at a shooting range.
- Organized, detailed, good memory and spatial skills.
- Knowledge of electronics and able to construct devices.
- Knew bomb making.
- May have been mildly dyslexic.
- Familiar with biblical concepts and may have been raised as a Roman Catholic.

Possessions

- He had access to two and possibly three cars during the period December 1968 to September 1969. May also have had a 1947-52 Studebaker.
- Had a vinyl player and an LP of Groucho Marx's version of the Mikado.
- Large newspaper collection about the Zodiac.
- Trophies taken from Paul Stine.
- Several weapons.
- Claimed to have a basement, may have lived in a house.
- Used tools and other equipment to manufacture his homemade knife.
- Wing Walker military shoes and possibly shoes with a B. F. Goodrich Company heel.

- Wristwatch, presumably a Zodiac watch.

ENDNOTES J

[1] "Interview with Kelly Carroll," http://transcripts.cnn.com/TRANSCRIPTS/0210/27/sm.30.html (retrieved July 2015).
[2] "Partial DNA fingerprint clears only suspect in Zodiac killings," http://www.seattlepi.com/national/article/Partial-DNA-fingerprint-clears-only-suspect-in-1098479.php (retrieved July 2015).
[3] "Titanium Particles from Cooper's Tie," http://www.citizensleuths.com/titaniumparticles.html (retrieved August 2016).
[4] "Geographic profiling," https://www.ncjrs.gov/html/nij/mapping/ch6_1.html (retrieved August 2016)
[5] Dr. Kim Rossmo, Geographic Profile, Zodiac Serial Murders.
[6] "'I still sleep with a night light': Survivors of 1976 school bus kidnapping reveal their enduring fears - as their captor is freed," http://www.dailymail.co.uk/news/article-2202893/Chowchilla-bus-kidnap-Survivors-1976-bus-kidnapping-speak-enduring-memories-captor-freed.html (retrieved August 2016).

CHAPTER 11

PSYCHOLOGICAL PORTRAIT

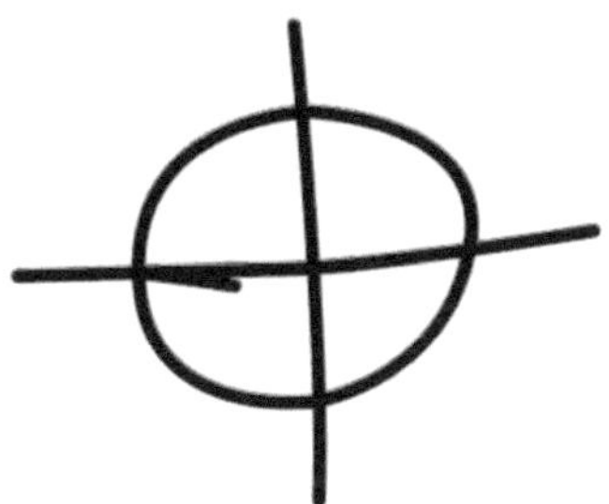

By definition, the Zodiac was a serial killer. Unlike the mass murderer who typically targets a great quantity in a single setting, the serial killer kills spasmodically. The intervals between murders are considered to be cooling periods - periods where the killer relives his past acts, plans and prepares for future crimes, and obsessively scrutinizes the news media for clues that the police might be pursuing. From the time Zodiac entered the scene in December 1968, the phases between his murders decreased dramatically, almost as if leading to a grand finale, a showdown between Inspector Toschi and Zodiac, guns drawn. In the end, his paranoia and anxiety were likely the pivotal factors which kept his murderous lust in control. Was he simply too afraid of being caught or did he fool us all, and Stine was simply the final element in a grandiose scheme based upon astrology?

Not all psychopaths are killers, but most serial killers are psychopaths. Psychopathy is a diagnosis that can only be ascertained with considerable effort. The psychopath does not regard their behavior and personality as aberrant, and therefore, they do not have a sincere wish for mental health assistance. Due to this fact, psychopaths are only studied indirectly such as when they are caught in a system from which they cannot escape. For example, when they are in prison and have something to gain by cooperating with mental health professionals, they are typically very willing to be interviewed; the personality traits of the psychopath are also studied indirectly when their victims are interviewed. It also follows that they are not motivated toward treatment, and it is generally agreed upon by mental health experts that there is no known treatment which can effectively alleviate the destructive symptoms of the psychopath.

There are three major systems or guidelines employed by professionals to diagnose psychopathy, although this term has been mostly abandoned. There is the American Diagnostic and Statistical Manual of Mental Disorders (DSM), the International Classification of Diseases (ICD), and the *Psychopathy Check List*. The core personality trait of the psychopath is their lack of conscience and scruples. They will have no regard for the rights and feelings of others. A distinct shallowness characterizes the emotions of the psychopath, and yet when the situation demands it, or if something is to gain, the psychopath finds it easy to show the appropriate emotional response. Interestingly, one study indicated that the psychopath is able to feel empathy, sympathy, and love to a certain extent, but is able to switch it off at will.[1]

It requires no lengthy discussion with multiple citations to demonstrate that Zodiac was a cold individual who never expressed any sympathy for his victims. His lack of empathy manifests itself repeatedly in his crimes and letters, such as when he terrorized thousands of parents and kids by threatening to kill schoolchildren. The Zodiac's focus was exclusively on his own needs, and he would implement his desires without regard for the wellbeing or sensibilities of his fellow man.

Pathological narcissism is a psychopathological condition that is a fundamental component of psychopathy. Psychopaths differ from narcissists who are capable of feeling shame and guilt; the psychopath is unscrupulous and destructive. Narcissism is characterized by pervasive self-centeredness. Distrust, status-seeking, paranoia, and extreme sensitivity to criticism are also essential components of their personality.[2] The sense of greatness experienced by the narcissist is either directly expressed and/or a permanent part of their fantasies. Specifically, they view themselves as special and talented to the point where they believe that regulations and laws do not apply to them; they will be preoccupied with concepts of power, success, and greatness. Expect the severe narcissist to indulge in grandiose exhibitionism: they will boast, exaggerate, distort, and invent stories of success. Alv A. Dahl, professor of psychiatry, wrote in his book about psychopaths that the narcissist "wants to be a known person," even "nationwide."[3] Jealousy and envy are also central characteristics, in particular when they perceive the success of others. They will downplay the value of others and criticize them to elevate themselves, perhaps even destroy the beauty in those who threaten their perceived superiority because of their innate jealousy. They anticipate special treatment because in their mind they are entitled to it. If mistreated, expect an aggressive response, or cold, cynical mistreatment of the person, especially while in front of others. The psychopath might plot revenge and kill in retaliation. In some instances of severe disappointment and failure, their rage can be directed inwards, resulting in suicidal ideations. The Zodiac is a prime example of a severe pathological narcissist, as well as a psychopath. He sent a death threat to Paul Avery as a response to his criticism, saying he would go on a killing rampage if his demands were not met, and he spent a great deal of time mocking and criticizing the police when they refused to dance to his tune. Zodiac's grandiosity and stratospheric arrogance is well documented in his communications, such as when he proclaimed that the investigators would never apprehend him because he had "been too clever for them." We should also note his grandiose disregard for human life. There are also obvious megalomaniac undertones to his favorite phrase, "This is the Zodiac speaking;" where he might as well have swapped "Zodiac" with "God," or "Master."

Although it might seem otherwise, the psychopath is difficult to spot. They wear the so-called *mask of sanity*, appearing normal, likeable, and charming, and their specialty is making a great first-

impression. They will then try to win your confidence and exploit your trust.
Bouts of emptiness and depression will appear if admiration, success, and respect are unmet because the severe narcissist is dependent upon external feedback. The Zodiac, himself, told us that he experienced loneliness due to being ignored by the media, and as a result he indicated that he felt like he wanted to kill someone. Stress is likely to exacerbate the destructive tendencies of the psychopath.
It is clear that his pathological narcissism played a major role in shaping and molding his actions and crime spree.
Using the established traits of psychopathy and narcissism, it is unveiled why he undertook specific actions despite their apparent irrationality, e.g. it is highly risky to provide the police with any information. Zodiac stepped into the public light due to his megalomania; his letters were a grandiose display, he probably picked the name "Zodiac" because he thought it would attract lots of attention, and his ciphers and bomb-diagrams were showcases of intelligence, designed to generate admiration and attract attention while terrorizing people. Using his own handwriting in his communications is also very likely to be related to his malignant disposition.
Several hypotheses have been formulated to explain why certain individuals develop narcissism. According to one school of thought, the development of the narcissist is arrested in early childhood. Other hypotheses explore the genetic and cultural link to narcissism. Zodiac's emotional development appears to have been halted in his childhood, as indicated by his infantile narcissistic outbursts, e.g. "Hey pig doesnt it rile you up to have your noze rubed in your booboos?"
It is essential for the narcissistic psychopath to be in control of everybody; they are domineering tyrants. Control and notoriety resonate with the core personality of the Zodiac. Invariably, he needed to govern his environment in both minor and major matters. Even deception, which the Zodiac used habitually, can be seen as a way of controlling one's environment by manipulating the reality of other people.
His insatiable obsession with fame and control even led him to demand that the public should wear his symbol. In his godlike

delusions, he then promised punishment when they had refused to obey his command.
Moreover, the psychopath lacks integrity; he will lie on impulse and is a master rationalizer. Zodiac lied to his victims and in his letters. When it was evident that he had left prints on Stine's cab despite cleaning it with a cloth, he superficially rationalized that he was leaving fake clues. He also lied about driving away slowly after killing Darlene Ferrin. This was a falsehood that showed us his grandiose nature because he lied to make himself look better by attempting to adjust the public perception of him. The story he fed to Bryan Hartnell and Cecelia Shepard was a concoction, and he lied many other times.
Psychopaths frequently need new impulses and get bored easily; they have a need for excitement.[4] This tendency may clarify why he chose to reemerge in 1974 and possibly in 1990, and it may even be the reason why he chose to disappear.
It is statistically established that most psychopaths lack the capability for realistic long-term planning. They have trouble keeping a job and staying in a relationship for an extended period, and they may move around a lot.[5] Contrary, there are quite a few indications that Zodiac did not have financial issues. We should also realize that the vast majority of psychopaths who are studied are those who are imprisoned, the so-called low-functioning psychopaths. Successful and socially acceptable psychopaths, which may include war-mongering politicians, business executives, snipers in the military, CIA torture specialists, executioners, and so forth, are almost never studied, and their behaviors might deviate significantly from the defeated and unsuccessful psychopaths who are caught and imprisoned.[6]
The social psychopath is often charming, smooth talking, and manipulative. Self-evidently, the Zodiac was manipulative and deceptive, but if he had a certain level of interpersonal charisma it was perhaps only hinted at while he conversed with Bryan Hartnell. Although the Zodiac was armed with a gun and knife, Bryan never felt that he was in any immediate danger. He was mostly worried about staying at the lake all night. Bryan's lack of horror may also have been related to the Zodiac's tranquil nature. He was calm and controlled until Bryan had resisted his demands too much. When Zodiac killed Stine, he had abandoned his usual deserted environment, and he now found himself in a populated area. Even

so, he coolly wiped off the interior and exterior of the cab before he nonchalantly walked away from the scene. By shooting a 9 mm pistol inside the cab, his ears must have been ringing, and he was likely smudged in blood. Although such an unusual state of tranquility could be expected from a full-blown psychopath, which the Zodiac undoubtedly was, it seems a distinct possibility that he had consumed Valium or some other psychotropic drug that induced an abnormal state of calmness. Valium was one of the most prescribed drugs in the world between 1968 and 1982.[7] Many studies have found that psychopaths have an increased risk of developing substance abuse.[8]

In the 1960s, the Zodiac would have been well aware of the emerging counterculture and especially left- and right-wing terrorist organizations, and the attention that resulted from bombings and other acts of violence carried out by these groups and organizations. He had probably read extensively about these groups, and obviously noticed that many of them had their own symbol and name. His inspiration to use a pseudonym, symbol, and threaten with widespread horror was undoubtedly derived from his fascination with these radical groups. He was quite likely jealous of them, and eventually he relieved the tension by entering the scene himself. The narcissistic aspect of him hungered for power to dominate the lives of others and to be recognized by everyone. His apparent obsession with attaining the same status and impact as the radical groups is perfectly exemplified in his attempts to get people in the Bay Area to use his symbol as a badge. He even mentioned Black Power and the peace symbol. The psychopathic aspect of the Zodiac wanted to destroy and kill, which he did. Just like the interior decoration and order of a house or apartment reveal information about its owner, the Zodiac's crimes provide us with an insight into his past and psyche. Zodiac revealed to us that he was a lonely and disturbed man who destroyed the beauty in others.

ENDNOTES K

[1] "Psychopathic criminals have empathy switch," https://www.bbc.com/news/science-environment-23431793 (retrieved April 2020).
[2] "Narcissistic Personality Disorder," https://www.helpguide.org/articles/mental-disorders/narcissistic-personality-disorder.htm (retrieved March 2020).
[3] Alv A. Dahl, Aud Dalsegg, Chamør og Tyran (Munksgaard 2002).
[4] Ibid.
[5] "13 signs you're dealing with a psychopath, according to experts," https://www.businessinsider.com/13-signs-youre-dealing-with-a-psychopath-according-to-experts-2018-2?r=US&IR=T (retrieved April 2020).
[6] "American Monster: Chris Kyle, the American Sniper," https://www.crimeandpower.com/2019/09/28/american-monster-chris-kyle-the-american-sniper/ (retrieved April 2020).
[7] "Valium: What is it used for and why are people buying it on the street?" https://metro.co.uk/2018/09/19/valium-what-is-it-used-for-and-why-are-people-buying-it-on-the-street-7956965/ (retrieved March 2020).
[8] "Antisocial Personality Disorder and Substance Abuse: Signs, Symptoms and Treatment" https://www.recovery.org/co-occurring-disorders/antipersonality/ (retrieved March 2020).

CHAPTER 12

HANDWRITING ANALYSIS

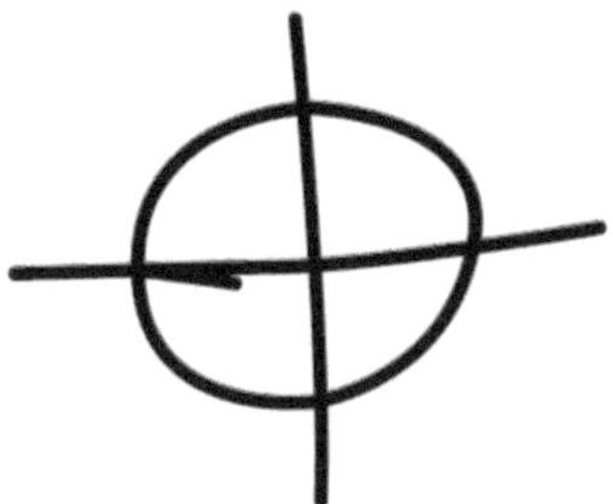

Handwriting analysis or graphology (not to be confused with questioned document examination) is the study of personality and related matters through handwriting. Graphologists see handwriting as a "medium through which the human psyche expresses itself."[1] Graphology is based on the principle that all actions are the product of a series of complex interactions within the brain, and it is therefore the brain that impels us to write.[2] The resulting lines, curves, loops, and dots on paper are consequently a manifestation of the inner self, regardless of the writing organ (left/right hand mouth/foot). By analyzing a long list of handwriting formations and their inter-relationship, a graphologist can determine a subject's personality and certain diseases affecting the nervous system.[3] Handwriting analysis can be categorized as a science based on indications such as the social sciences and medicine, which extrapolate general statements based on statistics, signs, and indications. However, graphology is not universally accepted as a tool for personality analysis. The reason is that studies designed to show if graphologists could predict personality and performance have produced mixed results. In addition, graphology might not be as attractive as other fields of study pertaining to psychology and human behavior due to its reputation as a pseudoscience. Thus, a search for "graphology" and "handwriting analysis" on pubmed.gov only yields 60 and 853 results respectively among a total of 30 million biomedical studies, even though, the first book about graphology was published in 1662.[4] For the reason that research pertaining to graphology is limited it suffers from a lack of standardization and systematization; different systems exist, but without consensus and integration. Dr. Pierre Etienne Cronje, a South African psychologist, explains the importance of these factors:

> Research in graphology has shown diverse results, ranging from negative to highly favourable. Many of the studies disregarding the value of graphology can be criticized on the grounds of their research methodology as well as the method used in handwriting analysis, namely the 'trait-method' whereby isolated graphological features are simplistically linked to personality as opposed to a more encompassing, holistic approach.[5]

On the other end of the spectrum, we find the so-called *Skeptic's Dictionary* that labels graphology as "pseudoscientific non-sense."[6] Another alleged skeptic wrote, "Graphology does not work. It provides no unique information or insight to graphologists. … Graphologists get their information from other sources, mostly the content of the writing (rather than the form of the writing). Graphology is no more legitimate than a psychic in a turban."[7] But is that really true? Most textbooks on graphology usually rely on older studies, but for the past two decades some interesting studies have been published. We will briefly mention some of them here. In a 2007 study, published in the *International Journal of Clinical Practice*, scientists evaluated if two graphologists could differentiate handwriting samples of subjects who had attempted to commit suicide from those of healthy subjects. The scientists concluded, "Graphological analysis is able to differentiate letters written by patients who attempt suicide from those written by healthy controls. This technique shows an acceptable degree of

accuracy and could therefore become an additional discharge or decision-making tool in Psychiatry or Internal Medicine."[8]
Rather than relying on human analysis, some scientists have turned to computer analysis of handwriting. In 2009, a study found that handwriting differs significantly when people write deceptive statements from when they are telling the truth.[9] The scientists concluded that their computerized handwriting evaluation system could become a valuable tool for detecting lies.
The paper also mentioned that their system has advantages over other lie detecting methods, since it is objective and non-intrusive.[10] The study can be found in the journal *Applied Cognitive Psychology*. A different study, which also used an automated system for handwriting analysis, noted in the discussion part that "Our results confirm that handwriting measures are sensitive to deceptive writing, and are aligned with previous results about handwriting and deception. They demonstrate that handwriting analysis could be applied to assist clinicians in detecting malingering."[11] The same methodology was also used in a 2018 study that was able to determine people's mood based on handwriting alone.[12] One of the scientists, Professor Sara Rosenblum, later commented, "The findings of the study may help therapists identify their patient's actual mood, something that naturally is very significant for the therapeutic process."[13] She also said, "No less importantly, we therapists can see whether our therapy is improving the patient's feelings, or at least involving the patient in a meaningful process, for better or for worse. In the future, we will try to examine whether we can also measure the level of the mood, i.e. how happy or sad someone is."[14]
The *Irish Journal of Psychological Medicine* published a case-study in 2012 that described a patient with numerous, severe mental issues that included incoherent speech, paranoid delusions, and auditory hallucinations. The patient was apparently also suffering from *graphomania*, an obsessive impulse to write. The scientists noted that his writing was unintelligible at the start of his admission, but as his psychosis resolved his handwriting changed and became more intelligible.[15] They ultimately concluded that the patient's handwriting "demonstrates clinical features of psychosis (e.g. clang associations) and graphological abnormalities associated with schizophrenia in the literature (rigidity in letter-formation,

mechanical expressions, and tendency toward over-use of straight lines)."[16]

A small study was undertaken in 2013 to examine possible intercorrelations between clinical findings of patients and graphological inferences. The study found "strong similarities" which confirmed "the value of graphology in psychological assessment."[17] It was concluded, "Graphology can thus be regarded a useful tool and viable option in psychological assessment and diagnosis."[18] Similarly, Dr. Gowda and coworkers conducted in 2015 a study to determine if there is a mutual relationship between clinical diagnosis and graphological analysis. The scientists reached the conclusion that "graphology may be a very effective projective tool for an assessment of a wide range of traits, especially in children to uncover undermined, and evolving traits that may play a very important role in accurate diagnosis."[19]

In 2016, a study, "Dysfluent Handwriting in Schizophrenic Outpatients,"[20] evaluated a set of 32 handwriting properties potentially related to schizophrenia. The scientists discovered that only 7 of the 32 handwriting properties were notably different in the handwriting of schizophrenic subjects from the healthy control group. They found that the differences were similar to characteristics found in the handwriting of patients diagnosed with depression, mania, bipolar disorder, increased distress, and increased anxiety. Using the properties they had zoomed in on, the scientists were not able to identify or diagnose schizophrenic disorder on the basis of handwriting. The findings of the study indicated that more research needed to be done before the various properties could be used to diagnose or differentiate schizophrenia from other disorders.

This study is similar to one from 2013 that found significant differences between a healthy control group and patients diagnosed with major depression and bipolar disorder. However, at this time it was not possible to distinguish depressed patients from bipolar ones, indicating that more research needs to be done in order to achieve greater specificity.[21] In 2019, a study examined if graphology could be useful in assessing major depression.[22] The scientists concluded, "Graphology has the potential to be a useful method for clinicians."[23] They, however, added that it "needs to honor the same scientific criteria demanded by psychology and psychiatry for their use by clinicians for diagnoses."[24] In the study they had "obtained substantially better results than previous studies regarding the psychometric properties and possible clinical utility of graphological methods. Therefore, we believe that by deepening the study of handwriting, it is possible to attain a satisfactory level of validity and reliability, as for many validated psychology tests."[25]

Graphologists have long maintained that intelligence and other aspects of cognition can be determined from an analysis of handwriting. In 2017, a group of scientists wanted to determine if handwriting could be used to detect mild cognitive impairment (MCI). The conclusion of their study read as follows: "Inclusion of quantitative handwriting analysis in psychological assessment may be a step forward towards a fast MCI diagnosis."[26]

BMC Pediatrics published a study in 2019 that set out to determine if graphological analysis could be an effective ADHD diagnostic tool for children.[27] The scientists concluded, "The handwriting of children with ADHD has specific characteristics. Graphology may serve as a clinically useful tool in the diagnosis of ADHD."[28]

In regard to neurodegenerative diseases, like amyotrophic lateral sclerosis and Parkinson's disease, several studies have investigated if an early diagnosis is possible using handwriting analysis. Neurodegenerative diseases obviously entail radical physiological as well as personality and behavioral changes. Until now, diagnosing one of these diseases has been an issue as an expert physician can usually only identify the symptoms after the disease has progressed considerably. In 2013, it was reported that "handwriting assessment can be used for early detection of Parkinson's disease" as studies had found "distinct differences between the handwriting of patients with Parkinson's disease and that of healthy people."[29] One study initiated by Professor Rosenblum was able to make a diagnosis of Parkinson's with 97.5% accuracy while 100% of the healthy control group was positively identified via handwriting analysis.[30] Professor Rosenblum later stated, "Identifying the handwriting changes could lead to an early diagnosis of the illness and neurological intervention at a critical moment."[31] The professor concludes, "This study is a breakthrough toward an objective diagnosis of the disease."[32]

Contrary to the aforementioned alleged skeptics there are numerous, well-done, peer-reviewed studies that show beyond a reasonable doubt that handwriting does reveal significant information about personality, health, and veracity. In the remainder of this chapter, the Zodiac's handwriting is analyzed.

Handwriting Analysis of the Zodiac

The Zodiac's handwriting is strictly confined to printing, and it contains no indications that he had been instructed in a more advanced penmanship such as the *Palmer Method*, which, by 1928, was the most prevalent in the USA. The inter-word spacing and the spacing between the imaginary baselines are often larger than average, and the capitals are of a modest size without any ornamentation (fig. 1). These are clear indications that Zodiac preferred to keep other people at a distance and needed plenty of elbow room. It is also indicated that he found it difficult to trust others. The line-spacing also gives us clues about the degree to which the Zodiac was organized, and how much interaction he needed with his environment.[33] In this instance, it is clear that the Zodiac was organized and would function best with minimal interaction. Skills in regard to organization and planning are also indicated by the margins in the Zodiac's handwriting. The margins are generally balanced. Sometimes, Zodiac added a hyphen when a word was too long and had to be continued on the next line; this is a good indication of planning skills.

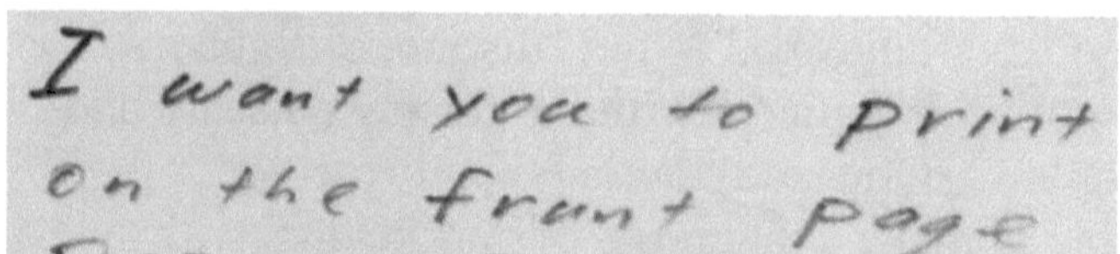

Figure 1. Wide inter-word and line spacing.

Building meaningful and deep relationships would likely have been difficult as well (no connections between letters, few lower loops in the lowercase letter "y").[34, 35] As we shall see, he was likely a man with very strong appetites, emotions, and opinions but if you were to meet him, his demeanor would probably be unremarkable. Furthermore, it should be noted that the spacing between words, although generally wide, is often irregular. Irregular word spacing indicates an unpredictable or impulsive individual, but also hints at simultaneous conflicting feelings toward social interaction.[36] These implications are further strengthened by the inter-letter spacing that wavers in a seemingly random pattern between cramped, normal, and wide (fig. 2). These irregular patterns are also indicative of alternating confidence, distrust, and are frequently found in the handwriting of emotional people.

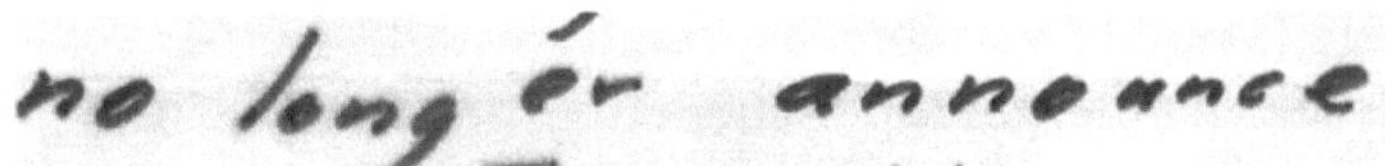

Figure 2. Erratic inter-letter spacing.

The handwriting indicates that the Zodiac was a loner with a limited social life, a lone-wolf. It will be shown later in this profile that he likely was a conceited individual who looked down on others; arrogance also serves as a barrier for social interaction. Paradoxically, his handwriting also indicates that he felt lonely and perhaps jealous when perceiving the intimacy of others (large spaces between words, strong rightward slant). He would likely also experience bouts of anxiety and panic attacks. The major handwriting characteristics signaling anxiety include irregular ink flow, squeezed letters, erratic spacing, and irregular slant (uneven inclination of letters).

While deception can be detected within a statement, indications of deception will also appear in the handwriting of those who use it to the extent that it becomes ingrained in their personality. In the following, we will examine the Zodiac's handwriting for communication related traits, including deception.

Oval shapes provide us with some information. In the Zodiac's handwriting, most of the ovals, for example, the letter "o," are fully closed at the top. In combination with characteristics discussed earlier, the implication is that Zodiac was secretive, closed, probably distrustful, yet he was longing for communication.[37]

Moving on, the lowercase letter "q" almost always has the shape of the number "8." Figure-eight structures signify fluidity, meaning "ease of mental processes [or] the smooth change from one phase of thought to another.[38]

They are frequently found in the writing of individuals who can easily express themselves verbally or in writing (fig. 3).[39]

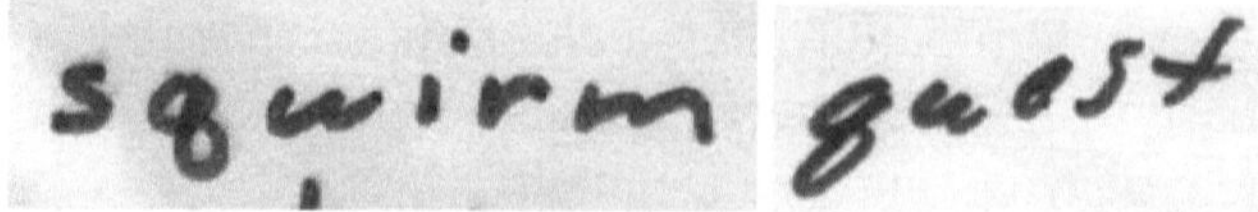

Figure 3. Figure-eight structures.

The size of letters is highly variable, especially within words. Occasionally a pattern emerges when the letters grow larger in succession. In a jumbled handwriting like this one, this pattern signifies that Zodiac would resort to crude measures to win an argument, and especially that he wanted the last word (fig. 4).

Figure 4. Notice "oos" and "uss" which increase in size.

A similar pattern is sometimes seen when the second hump or final section of the letters "m" and "n" is larger than the first (fig. 5).[40] These are associated with a fear of being ridiculed. It is a sign of excessive public self-consciousness. The previously discussed characteristics related to anxiety confirm that it very likely is a part of his emotional makeup. Self-consciousness is excessive self-awareness in public situations. Self-conscious persons often feel as if others are talking negatively about them behind their backs.

Figure 5. In these two examples, the second hump of the letter "m" is larger than the first.

In regard to dishonesty, numerous handwriting properties associated with such behavior are found in his letters and cards. For example, many letters are unrecognizable or ambiguous. In addition to other characteristics in the handwriting, the significance and meaning of these handwriting structures (as well as others) depend on the form standard of the handwriting. The form standard or level is a measure of a variety of properties to determine the "harmony" and "rhythm" of the handwriting. The Zodiac's arrhythmic handwriting scores low on these parameters. The form standard is important when determining the positive or negative connotations of a particular formation. For example, a small handwriting may signal intelligence, concentration, and an ability to think in great detail if the form level is high. On the other hand, if the form level is low, the small handwriting is more likely to be associated with low confidence, shyness, and a too great focus on minor details.

Some of the other signs of deception that we find in the Zodiac's handwriting include abnormal fragmentations and letters filled with ink.[41] The latter is considered a strong indication of pathological lying (fig. 6).

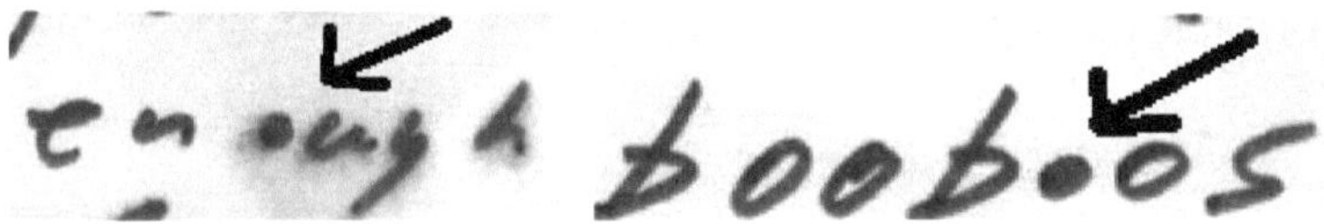

Figure 6. Ink filled letters.

Having covered some of the characteristics associated with dishonesty, we will now consider some external aspects that may indicate how this particular type of behavior may be expressed. It is likely significant that several characteristics (discussed later) indicate that he had an unhealthy need for recognition and attention. Based on these aspects, we would therefore expect the Zodiac to be inclined to exaggerate or simply lie about his achievements. If we put the generous spacing between baselines and the general roundness of the writing into the equation, it is indicated that he was calculating by nature and concealing of his motivations.

One of the most unusual aspects of the handwriting is the slant. It changes between vertical, extremely rightward, and erratic, even within a single word or sentence (fig. 7). In some of his letters, the slant is initially vertical, but further down the page the characteristic, rightward pattern reemerges. We might be observing an inner struggle to control himself and his emotions. These alternations foreshadow that the Zodiac was emotionally unpredictable, impulsive, and that inner tranquility would occur on only rare occasions.[42] He might have been rambling about a particular subject yet be distant and withdrawn at other times; he was more emotional and intuitive than logical. It is also reasonable to conjecture that he possessed a low level of self-understanding.

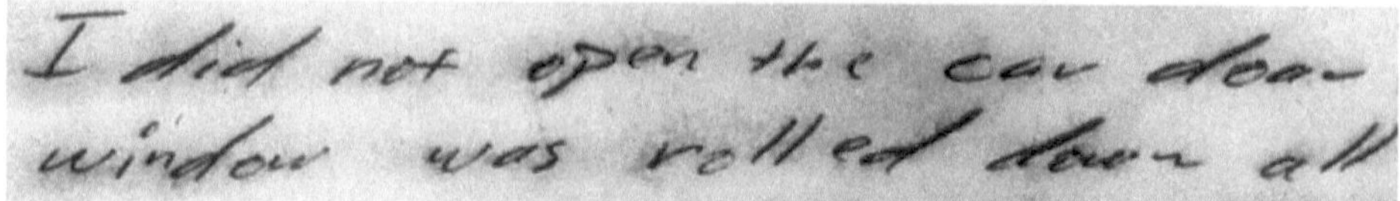

Figure 7. Erratic slant.

Figure 8 is an extreme example of how the tilt or slant of the letters suddenly collapses to the right to the point where the letters are nearly horizontal. It signals that he may lose his temper violently and explosively. He may initially be calm and collected, but without warning he will be carried away. This is the handwriting of a highly emotional person.

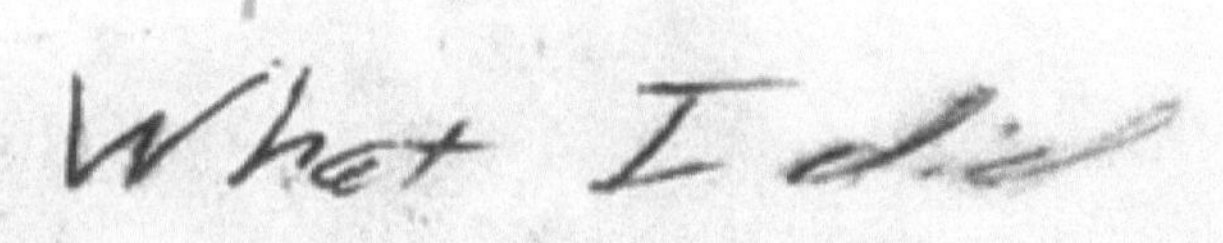

Figure 8. Extreme slant pattern.

The baselines are the imaginary lines underneath sentences. The direction of these provides us with information about the writer's outlook on life, emotional stability, and reliability. If we examine the baselines in the Zodiac's handwriting, it is clear that a variety of patterns exists. The lines are mostly irregular, but sometimes even, and occasionally sharply to slightly falling (fig. 9). Generally, it is likely that Zodiac was moody and struggling on a day-to-day basis. It is also implied that he had not reached a high level of emotional maturity.[43] The falling lines suggest depression, a lack of energy, and emptiness. Occasionally letters jut up, but only to descend sharply back to the baseline, forming a concave pattern within a word (fig. 10). Convex patterns also appear. The concave patterns signal transient bouts of euphoria quickly followed by melancholy; bipolar tendencies. Punctuations throughout his letters are made with extra pressure (fig. 11). Forceful punctuation points to anger, tension, and a low frustration threshold. In summary, Zodiac was likely an unbalanced individual with tendencies toward anger and acting out.

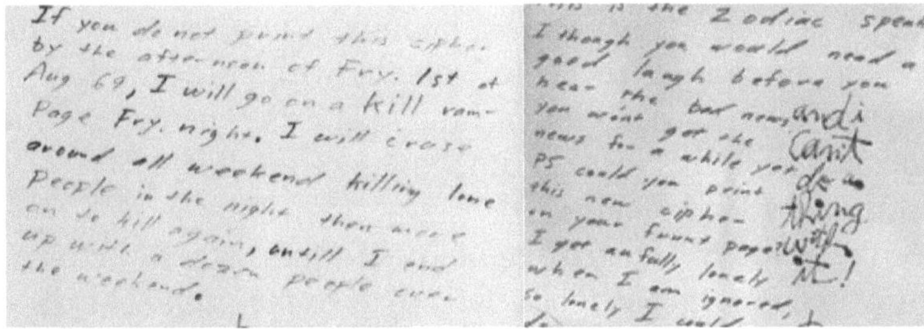
Figure 9. Irregular while at the same time descending baselines.

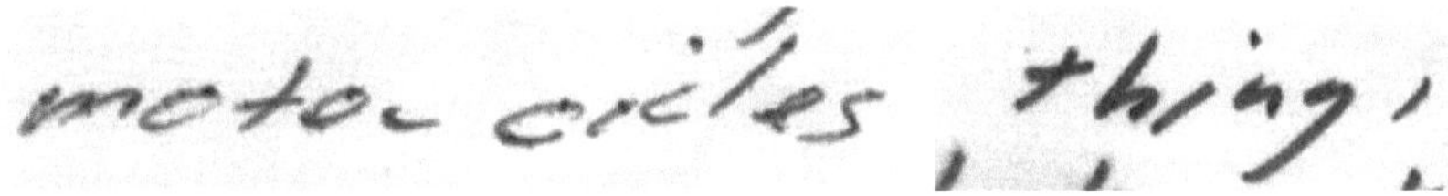
Figure 10. Convex/concave patterns

Figure 11. A heavy punctuation mark.

The personal pronoun "I" (PPI) is an essential letter to analyze as it is directly related to the writer's ego and sense of self-worth. It also shows the importance the writer places on him-/herself in relation to other people. The PPI in the Zodiac's handwriting is frequently oversized. These ones mirror an unrealistic and grandiose self-image and point toward exaggerated pride and a grandiose code of conduct (fig. 12).[44] One graphologist noted that oversized PPIs signify a writer who "wishes to be noticed as an exceptional being."[45] The PPIs also indicate that Zodiac would, most of the time, consider his needs more important than that of others.

Figure 12. An example of an oversized PPI.

The upper extension of the lowercase letter "d" relates information to the graphologist about the writer's level of pride. The upper extension is frequently out of proportion to other letters (fig. 13). There is a high degree of likelihood that the Zodiac was a vain individual. These “d” stems also imply a desire for acknowledgment and approval. Overall, the Zodiac’s writing has a vertical emphasis. Vertical expansion, namely tall upper extensions such as in the lowercase letter “l,” reflects the writer’s desire for prestige and stature; the writer is reaching upwards. The upper zone is also associated with the abstract, imagination, intellectual pursuits, spirituality, and idealism.

The slant of the letter “d” does often not conform to other letters. The pattern which emerges is that it falls over to the right. This is known as a *manic “d”* (fig. 14). It indicates that the Zodiac was extremely sensitive to criticism, and that he may have reacted impulsively, losing mental and emotional control, if he felt that his pride had been insulted.[46]

The size of the letter “Z” in “Zodiac” is directly related to how he perceived himself. In the example below, the “Z” is emphasized beyond the norm (fig. 15).[47] It points toward arrogance, boastfulness, narcissism, and especially that he wanted to be noticed. In some instances, the “Z” is relatively small. The lack of consistency provides further evidence of his unstable and fragile disposition.

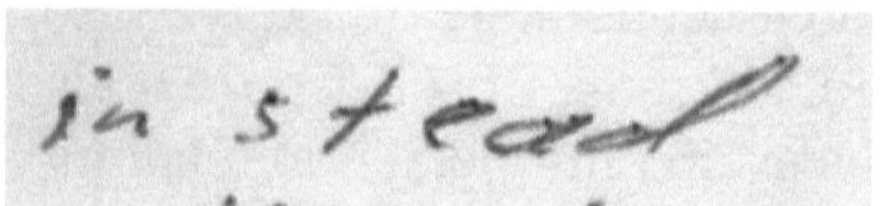

Figure 13. The stem of the letter “d” is out of proportion to other letters.

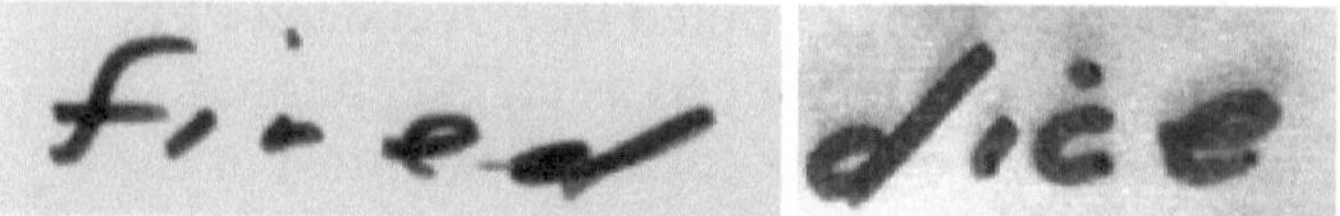

Figure 14. Notice how the letter “d” collapses to the far right.

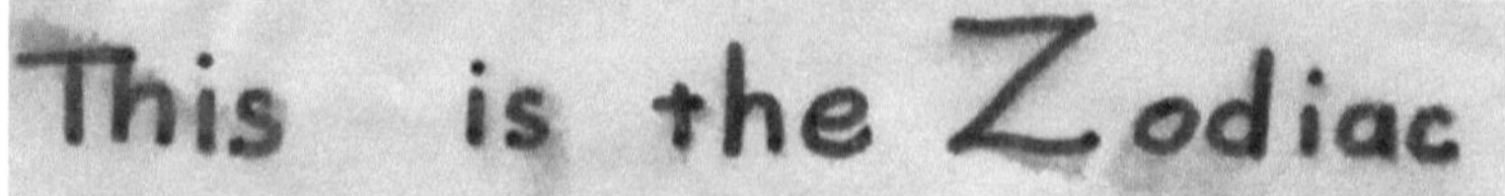

Figure 15. The “Z” in “Zodiac” takes on a grandiose appearance.

The middle zone consists of single zone letters like “a,” “o,” “n,” and “m.” The part of a bizonal letter, like a “d,” “y,” and “g,” that remains in the same domain as single zone letters are also part of the middle zone (fig. 16). In some handwriting fonts, the letter "f" intersects all three zones. If we observe how the Zodiac executed the middle zone letters, it is apparent that they sometimes are distorted, unintelligible, or objectively unusual when compared to standard copybook writing (fig. 17). Furthermore, when we inspect the t-bar of the lowercase letter "t," it frequently slopes downward, but then at its center point it ascends upward, forming a concave crossbar (fig. 18). These crossbars are more than often placed low on the stem. The combination of distorted middle zone letters and these crossbars indicates the previously mentioned vanity and megalomania are due to overcompensation for feelings of inferiority and inadequacy. The concave t-bars also indicate emotional shallowness and general superficiality.[48] Unusual and even aberrant thinking are also indicated by the middle zone letters. The lower extension of the lowercase letter "g" does not form a "hook" or loop, except on rare occasions. When we do see a loop, they are always incomplete, meaning they do not reach the baseline. The lower extension is related to the physical as well as the sexual realm. Previously, we cited some findings of graphologist, William F. Baker. He concluded based on the absence of lower loops that the Zodiac might have been impotent.

UPPER ZONE
MIDDLE ZONE analysis
LOWER ZONE

Figure 16. The three zones of handwriting.

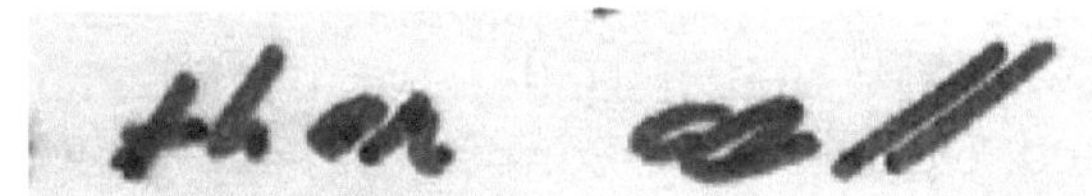

Figure 17. Distorted middle zone letters.

think the the

Figure 18. Concave t-bars.

Another characteristic that is found in numerous samples of his writing is what graphologists call the *defiant k* or *rebellious k.* This is simply a capital "K" appearing at a place where it should have been a lowercase one (fig. 19). In a handwriting of a high form standard, the defiant "K" indicates a writer who rebels, does not follow conventions, or somehow else defies the status quo. Successful entrepreneurs frequently have this particular characteristic in their handwriting. In a handwriting that contains many disturbances, like the Zodiac's, it points toward opposition of authority and of rules and regulations. Less frequently, we see other capital letters, like an "A" appearing in the middle of a sentence (fig. 20). All things considered, this is another indication of his unpredictability. How may this express itself in terms of behavior? For example, he might suddenly "blow up" on somebody.

Figure 19. The so-called defiant k.

Figure 20. A capital "A" in the middle of a sentence.

The Zodiac penned his communications with various writing speeds. The ones that are written quickly appear spontaneous and natural; they give the appearance of having been written by someone who is busy and in a hurry, e.g. the letter to the Los Angeles Times in March 1971. The Melvin Belli letter, on the other hand, is meticulously crafted. Doctors are notorious for having supposedly unintelligible handwriting due to their busy lifestyle. Maybe the Zodiac was a very busy individual himself due to his profession or otherwise. Fast writing is associated with fast thinking, learning, and impatience. The Zodiac's handwriting contains some strokes, lines, and structures associated with shallowness and superficiality, e.g. concave t-bars and when the lowercase letter "m" lacks depth, i.e. the stroke in the middle of the letter does not reach the baseline. Hence, this is very likely the writing of a shallow thinker. On the other hand, the handwriting of very keen and able individuals sometimes display characteristics associated with superficiality. They are accustomed to only skim the surface of a subject as they do not need more than a superficial glance to gain an understanding.

This graphological analysis of the Zodiac's handwriting primarily addresses the dominant features, rather than focusing on less prominent and frequent handwriting characteristics. The pen pressure is one important and dominant aspect of the Zodiac's handwriting. In virtually all of his letters, the pressure pattern is of a low quality. There are many ink-filled ovals and the writing is recurrently smudged and smeared (fig. 21). The ink pattern of the Zodiac's handwriting is strongly indicative of preoccupation with sensual gratification rather than intellectual pursuit. In handwritings of a low form standard it points toward brutality, roughness, and crudeness.[49] Substance abuse is likely when the entire handwriting is considered. The smeared and smudged handwriting also implies that he was a man with a big appetite for material goods, food, and related matters.

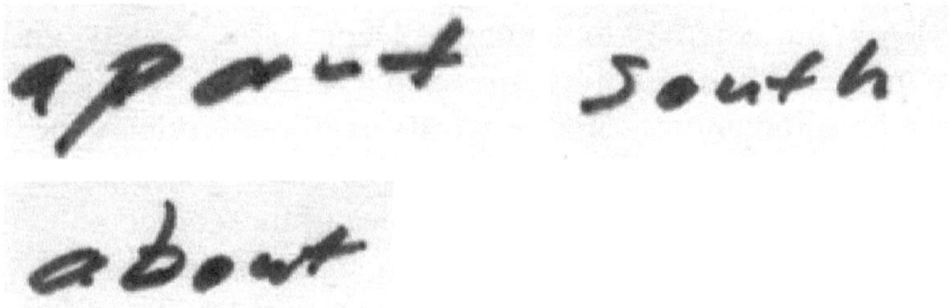

Figure 21. Low quality pressure pattern.

As previously shown, the handwriting paints a picture of the Zodiac as a megalomaniac with unrealistic ambitions and desires for prestige and acknowledgement. When we take a closer look at the lowercase letter "t," the horizontal bar is frequently placed low on the stem. There are instances where the bar is parallel to the baseline. The cross-bars relate information about the writer's confidence in achieving goals. The low and concave crossbars in the Zodiac's handwriting are usually found in the writings of people with severe feelings of inadequacy and lack of confidence in their ability to achieve valuable goals. It is very likely that the Zodiac feared failure and would consequently set low goals for himself. His unrealistic and warped self-image covered for his low self-esteem. He would most likely have avoided situations that he felt could result in failure and, to him, humiliation. The slant, baselines, and other aspects covered in this analysis all point to someone who would be easily distracted and would find great difficulty in maintaining his direction.

Individual Observations

Handwriting gives us an insight into the writer's personality. However, temporary circumstances, such as illness and optimism, present at the time of the writing or even within a specific word or sentence, may be detected via magnification or careful observation of the handwriting. For example, a teenager madly in love might embellish or enlarge the name of the person he or she is in love with. Certain individual letters are analyzed in the following.

December 1966

Whoever wrote the message on the desk, discovered in Riverside in 1966, was likely burdened by melancholy. Depression, anxiety, and tension are indicated by the falling lines and overwritten words. The concave baseline underneath the word, "spilling," reflects the writer's euphoria and sudden decent into sadness and melancholia. Concave structures are found in many samples of the Zodiac's handwriting. The ink pattern is smudged and smeared like the Zodiac's, but we must consider the writing instrument and surface in this instance as it was written on a wooden desk.

April 30, 1967

An obvious example of disguised handwriting similar to the ones penned by David Berkowitz or the Son of Sam as he called himself. Berkowitz targeted couples in the 1970s with his .44 revolver and wrote disturbing letters, just like the Zodiac, to investigators and the press.
Although the writing is contrived, it is clear that it is oversized, and the Zodiac did not confine the writing to the pre-written lines of the papers, but instead wrote all over them. These handwriting properties are interpreted as someone who is hungry for attention

and will cross boundaries to get it. Lower- and uppercase letters are used randomly; the baselines are extremely erratic. This is the writing of a highly unbalanced person who is desperate for attention.

July 1969

Depression and negativity are signified by several elements in the handwriting, most notably by the descending baselines. The pressure pattern in the Chronicle letter appears to be extremely erratic; his pen could have been running out of ink. It also appears that he used a different pen to write the Examiner letter.

August 1969

Interestingly, we do not perceive the same depressive pattern just a few days later in his letter to the Examiner. Perchance the attention he attained had an anti-depressive effect. This and the other three letters appear to have been written hastily, indicating impatience.

September 1969

The writing on the car door is remarkably similar to the writing in his letters, notwithstanding that he had just stabbed two people a few minutes prior. We can conclude that extreme violence did not affect him much; he was not quivering or feeling overly distressed while writing the message.

October 1969

This letter is different from all others in several regards. From the perspective of a graphologist, this letter is extremely disturbing. His arrogance, vanity, and sense of self-importance had reached an astronomical level (the stem of the letter "d" is longer than previously). Something had made him feel completely superior since August.

There are many signs of tension hinting that he was deteriorating mentally and possibly physically. Upon magnification of the handwriting, it can be observed that there are unusual distortions in the pressure pattern not seen in any of the other Zodiac letters. In addition, small ink spots or dots appear at random places all over the writing. These dots are usually associated with pain or injury. The location of the ink spots indicates where the writer might be feeling the pain; for example, if the ink spots are found in the upper zone it indicates a head injury. No distinct pattern is discernable. The ink spots do not appear to be the result of a faulty pen as they then would be more likely to only be visible at the beginning or end of a particular stroke. One other interpretation of these unusual ink spots is that the Zodiac was heavily drugged while writing the letter.[50]

November 1969 (JESTERS By Forget Me Not Cards)

The Zodiac's scrawl on the card is marked by disassociated words and baselines that drop down at an acute angle. The word "Thing" is overwritten and underlined several times which bespeak his rage and temper tantrum while writing the letter. The Zodiac was clearly depressed, extremely angry, and tense while writing the message. It is also likely that he was intensely stressed by feelings of abandonment.

November 1969 (Bus-Bomb letter)

This letter was mailed the next day, and it is different from the card in some respects. For one, the disassociation and depressive tendencies are not as pronounced. The mere act of writing to the press had perhaps an alleviating effect on his unstable mood. Nevertheless, the handwriting is extremely disturbing. It is likely that he was under the influence of some narcotic while writing it. Perhaps, he self-medicated with narcotics and prescription medicine, like Valium, when he felt depressed.

December 1969

The Melvin Belli letter is a controversial letter due to the content. A superficial glance at the printing might easily tempt someone to reach the conclusion that a hand different than Zodiac's wrote it. However, undoubtedly the same maniac who prepared the previous letters also penned this one. He showed the same attention to detail when he drew the symbols and letters of his ciphers. The spontaneity and speed that characterized the first Zodiac letters are missing. The impression is that of ulterior motives and deliberation. Or, perhaps, the Zodiac wrote this letter with great affection due to respect for the recipient. The former is the most likely.

April 1970 (April 20 letter and April 28 card)

The so-called "My name is" letter is unremarkable in the sense that it deviates little from what has been received up to this point. The meticulous printing on the *Jolly Roger* greeting card is more stable and organized. However, near the end of the card, a somewhat more erratic pattern emerges.

June 1970

The vertical slant is indicative of emotional control and neutrality, coolness. Apart from in the Belli letter and the Jolly Roger greeting card, the slant had been extremely erratic up to this point. It is possible that Zodiac began trying to control himself from December, which is the first instance of vertical slant in a large sample of his handwriting.
A few times, the writing is on the verge of returning to the characteristic, rightward, erratic slant, but he kept going back to the vertical pattern. It seems as if the Zodiac was trying to control himself and his emotions during this period.

July 26 1970

Although the start of the letter is ordered and meticulous, the slant becomes extremely rightward and there are numerous disturbances in the middle zone letters and in the pressure pattern. The size of the PPI fluctuates to a high degree. The lower-case letter "l" is much taller than what we usually see. His imagination and emotions were running wild. It seems likely that he was under the influence of narcotics, medication, and/or alcohol while writing the letter. Pages 3-5 were clearly written at a different time and under different circumstances, except for the note about radians on the last page, which has the same constituents as the printing on the first two pages.

March 1971

The Los Angeles Times letter is very similar to some of his letters from 1969, particularly his initial three letters from July. The sharply falling baselines echo his sadness and feelings of hopelessness. Note that he does not capitalize the first letter in "riverside." When someone fails to capitalize a name, it is indicative of aversion.

January 29, 1974

There is little out of the ordinary to note about the Zodiac's 1974 Exorcist letter. The handwriting is similar to the scrawl we find in his other letters and cards, except that the dots of the letter "i" are circular in contrast to the points he typically made; some of them are ink-filled. The circular dots may be a sign of attention seeking; they are frequently found in the writing of teenagers and creative people. The ink-filled ones suggest preoccupation with thoughts of a destructive nature. The letter "o" in "tit willo" is unusually small. Exactly how this should be understood is not clear.

Discussion

It remains a possibility that alcohol, drugs, and possibly dyslexia contributed to some of the distortions covered in the analysis. For example, the erratic letter and word spacing could have been a result of him trying to figure out the spelling and grammar. Alcohol and drugs affect handwriting. It is possible that without a chemical influence, the Zodiac's handwriting would appear more balanced. Other unknown factors could have affected the handwriting, too. Nevertheless, the graphological analysis mirrors the psychological portrait of the Zodiac to a high degree.

ENDNOTES L

[1] "The Viability of Graphology in Psycho-educational Assessment." Pierre Etienne Cronje. University of South Africa, 2009, 4.
[2] Ibid, 18.
[3] Ibid.
[4] "Handprints of the Mind: Decoding Personality Traits and Handwritings," https://www.ncbi.nlm.nih.gov/pmc/articles/PMC4676206/ (retrieved April 2020).
[5] "The Viability of Graphology in Psycho-educational Assessment." Pierre Etienne Cronje. University of South Africa, 2009, v.
[6] "graphology (graphoanalysis)," www.skepdic.com/graphol.html (retrieved April 2020).
[7] "Graphology," https://theness.com/neurologicablog/index.php/graphology/ (retrieved April 2020).
[8] Mouly S *et al*. "Graphology for the diagnosis of suicide attempts: a blind proof of principle controlled study" (International Journal of Clinical Practice 2007).
[9] "Comparing the handwriting behaviours of true and false writing with computerized handwriting measures," https://onlinelibrary.wiley.com/doi/full/10.1002/acp.1621 (retrieved April 2020).
[10] "Can handwriting analysis be used to detect lies?" http://healthland.time.com/2009/08/28/can-handwriting-analysis-be-used-to-detect-lies/ (retrieved March 2017).
[11] "Detection of Deception Via Handwriting Behaviors Using a Computerized Tool: Toward an Evaluation of Malingering," https://www.researchgate.net/publication/272015458_Detection_of_Deception_Via_Handwriting_Behaviors_Using_a_Computerized_Tool_Toward_an_Evaluation_of_Malingering (retrieved April 2020).
[12] "Mood Impact on Automaticity of Performance: Handwriting as Exemplar," https://www.researchgate.net/publication/322356820_Mood_Impact_on_Automaticity_of_Performance_Handwriting_as_Exemplar (retrieved April 2020).
[13] "Israeli Study Shows How Our Handwriting Can Reveal Our Moods," www.nocamels.com/2018/10/mood-handwriting-haifa-israel (retrieved April 2020).
[14] Ibid.
[15] "Graphology and psychiatric diagnosis: Is the writing on the wall?" https://www.cambridge.org/core/journals/irish-journal-of-psychological-medicine/article/graphology-and-psychiatric-diagnosis-is-the-writing-on-the-wall/9A886DC121D14E1978AC8099F2A98943 (retrieved April 2020).
[16] Ibid.
[17] "Graphology in Psychological Assessment: A Diagnosis in Writing," www.hrpub.org/download/20131201/UJP3-19401051.pdf (retrieved April 2020).
[18] Ibid.

[19] "Handprints of the Mind: Decoding Personality Traits and Handwritings," https://www.ncbi.nlm.nih.gov/pmc/articles/PMC4676206/ (retrieved April 2020)
[20] "Dysfluent Handwriting in Schizophrenic Outpatients," https://pubmed.ncbi.nlm.nih.gov/27166334/?from_term=handwriting+analysis&from_page=2&from_pos=5 (retrieved April 2020).
[21] "Little evidence for the graphical markers of depression," https://www.ncbi.nlm.nih.gov/pubmed/24422358 (retrieved April 2020).
[22] "Is Graphology Useful in Assessing Major Depression?" https://www.researchgate.net/publication/322748522_Is_Graphology_Useful_in_Assessing_Major_Depression (retrieved April 2020).
[23] Ibid.
[24] Ibid.
[25] Ibid.
[26] "Spatial and Dynamical Handwriting Analysis in Mild Cognitive Impairment," https://pubmed.ncbi.nlm.nih.gov/28126631/?from_term=handwriting+analysis&from_pos=3 (retrieved April 2020).
[27] "Handwriting in children with Attention Deficient Hyperactive Disorder: role of graphology," https://bmcpediatr.biomedcentral.com/articles/10.1186/s12887-019-1854-3 (retrieved April 2020).
[28] Ibid.
[29] "Handwriting assessment can be used for early detection of Parkinson's disease," https://www.jpost.com/health-and-science/handwriting-assessment-can-be-used-for-early-detection-of-parkinsons-disease-325798 (retrieved April 2020).
[30] "Handwriting as an objective tool for Parkinson's disease diagnosis," https://link.springer.com/article/10.1007/s00415-013-6996-x (retrieved April 2020).
[31] "Handwriting assessment can be used for early detection of Parkinson's disease," https://www.jpost.com/health-and-science/handwriting-assessment-can-be-used-for-early-detection-of-parkinsons-disease-325798 (retrieved April 2020).
[32] Ibid.
[33] "The Viability of Graphology in Psycho-educational Assessment." Pierre Etienne Cronje. University of South Africa, 2009, 27.
[34] Marie Bernard, Sexual Deviations as Seen in Handwriting (Whitston 1990).
[35] "The Viability of Graphology in Psycho-educational Assessment." Pierre Etienne Cronje. University of South Africa, 2009, 44.
[36] Malford Wilcox Thewlis, Handwriting and the Emotions (American Graphological Society 1954).
[37] Basic Traits of Graphoanalysis (International Graphoanalysis Society 1968), 66.
[38] Ibid, 31.

[39] "What Your Handwriting Says About Your Personality," www.americanprofile.com/articles/what-your-handwriting-says-about-your-personality (retrieved April 2015).
[40] Basic Traits of Graphoanalysis Vol. 2 (International Graphoanalysis Society 1970), 71.
[41] "The Viability of Graphology in Psycho-educational Assessment." Pierre Etienne Cronje. University of South Africa, 2009, 60.
[42] Ibid, 41.
[43] Marie Bernard, Sexual Deviations as Seen in Handwriting (Whitston 1990).
[44] "The Viability of Graphology in Psycho-educational Assessment." Pierre Etienne Cronje. University of South Africa, 2009, 55.
[45] "Ego Symbol 'I': A Graphologist's look at the letter I," www.copperarea.com/pages/ego-symbol-i-a-graphologists-look-at-the-letter-i/ (retrieved May 2020).
[46] Malford Wilcox Thewlis, Handwriting and the Emotions (American Graphological Society 1954).
[47] Jane Green, You and Your Private I: Personality and the Written Self Image (Llewellyn Publications 1983).
[48] Basic Traits of Graphoanalysis Vol. 2 (International Graphoanalysis Society 1970).
[49] 47
[50] "The Viability of Graphology in Psycho-educational Assessment." Pierre Etienne Cronje. University of South Africa, 2009, 131.

CHAPTER 13

THE ZODIAC KILLER IN VIEW OF DEINDIVIDUATION THEORY

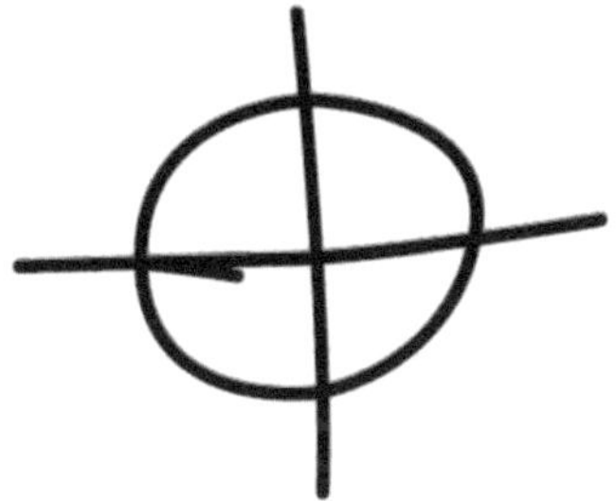

Introduction

As we have seen in this book, the Zodiac killer began his official crime career at the end of December 1968 when he gunned down David Arthur Faraday and Betty Lou Jensen just outside Vallejo, California. The double murder was quick and there was no evidence of intimate interaction between the killer and his victims. On July 4, 1969, the Zodiac committed his third murder when he sprayed Michael Mageau and Darlene Ferrin with bullets. Mageau lived to recant the horrific ordeal, and from his statements, it is clear that the attack was swift, lacking of any intimate interaction, and no mask or uniform was worn by the Zodiac. At the end of that July, the Zodiac began writing letters to the print media. In

September 1969, he struck again and attacked another couple, this time at Lake Berryessa, the largest lake in Napa County. Investigators would later establish that the Zodiac had deviated from his established pattern and was in this incident dressed in a ceremonial/executioner's costume while his eyes were hidden by sunglasses. To add onto that, he had a lengthy conversation with the couple, tied them up, and brutally stabbed both of them with a knife. This attack was significantly different, more intimate and physical than his previous crimes. The Zodiac continued sending letters and cards to the media, but he then stopped abruptly. When he returned in 1974, he no longer went by the name Zodiac but rather as "citizen" as was seen in his last communiqué which was in the form of a card. The card was different from his previous letters in almost all of its aspects, save for his handwriting. For the most part, his letters and cards had been filled with hate, anger, taunts, threats, and descriptions of some of his killings. The card from the citizen scolded the editor of the Chronicle for indulging in "murder-glorification" by running an advertisement for the movie Badlands. Zodiac also made the point that "glorification of violence" was never justifiable.

No solid theories have been proposed which explain (1) his use of a costume, and (2) his transition from a cold-blooded killer to a concerned citizen who is outraged by an advertisement for fictional violence. By means of deindividuation theory, it is argued that the physical and close interaction at Lake Berryessa was only possible for him due to the anonymity element of the superfluous garment and sunglasses, and that, due to a transition of mental and/or emotional forces as well as a transition related to self-awareness, he no longer regarded himself as a murderer. Herein, the Zodiac had become a citizen.

Deindividuation Theory

In the literature of social psychology, an emerging theory pertaining to anonymity and antisocial behavior began developing in the 1950s. Social psychologists wanted to understand the dynamics of aggression, especially in the context of groups. Decades later, we now have numerous studies which show that, under some circumstances, a person may lose their sense of being a distinct individual, which can lead to reduced self-evaluation due to a lack of self-awareness. What happens is that anonymity reduces responsibility and transgressions of general social norms can more smoothly take place. It has been "long demonstrated that individuals who believe their identity is hidden are less inclined to act in an altruistic manner and are more inclined to engage in anti-social behavior."[1] The anonymity process may be facilitated or exacerbated by the introduction of certain cosmetic additions such as uniforms, masks, and body paint. The use of military uniforms can result in an identification with a particular role (e.g. government mercenary), and the moral boundaries and restraints that otherwise characterized the individual, gradually disappear. If such additions are worn at all times, much of their effect disappears; hence, many military forces have manufactured a variety of uniforms for special occasions, such as combat. Deindividuation is especially associated with antisocial behavior committed by groups, e.g. during a riot, but also in individuals such as a rapist wearing a mask.

The well-known Milgram experiment was replicated by Dr. Phillip Zimbardo in 1969, but he changed the setup to test if deindividuation increased aggression. Originally, Dr. Stanley Milgram conducted a series of experiments in the 1960s to see if ordinary people would obey even the most abhorrent of orders. It was discovered that the vast majority of subjects were willing to administer lethal electric shocks to a defenseless person (a confederate of Milgram). The experiment has been replicated many times across the globe, always achieving very similar results. The last time the study was replicated was in 2015. The scientists observed that a staggering 90% inflicted the highest dosage of voltage (the lethal level). The lead author of the study, Dr. Thomasz Grzyb, concluded: "Half a century after Milgram's original research into obedience to authority, a striking majority of subjects are still willing to electrocute a helpless individual."[2] In Zimbardo's version of the study, the test subjects who were ordered to administer electric shocks were "either individuated with a name tag or deindividuated by wearing a hood. The deindividuated participants gave more shocks, supporting the idea of deindividuation."[3]

In a 1973 cross-culture study it was discovered that warriors who wore face paint or garments to conceal their appearance were much more likely to kill, torture, and mutilate captives.[4] Three years later, in 1976, a Halloween study comprising 1,300 trick-or-treating children yielded a very interesting result. The children were given an opportunity to steal candy and money under various conditions. It was observed that under conditions of anonymity and in the presence of a group, significantly more stealing took place.[5]
In 1981, Malmuth and Check questioned male university students about, "how likely they personally would be to rape if they could be assured of not being caught. On the average, about 35% indicated some likelihood of raping."[6] In a 2003 study of 500 violent attacks in Northern Ireland, 203 were carried out by attackers who had used a disguise. The author of the study concluded that "significant positive relationships existed between the use of disguises and several measures of aggression. Disguised offenders inflicted more serious physical injuries, attacked more people at the scene, engaged in more acts of vandalism, and were more likely to threaten victims after the attacks."[7]

The Zodiac's Costume

It is important to note that the use of the concealing elements went hand in hand with an amplified degree of violence and interaction with the victims, Bryan Hartnell and Cecilia Shepard.[8] It is reasonable to conclude that the Zodiac felt less confident in his ability to mete out an intimate killing as his other confirmed murders and attacks were swift. The costume and sunglasses would have served as a barrier between him and the victims; his self-awareness and evaluation would likely have decreased allowing him to introduce a darker and more elevated level of violence. Anonymity and deindividuation could have liberated the Zodiac from his inhibitions, and he would have felt a loss of humane responsibility, allowing him to be free to act out a violent fantasy. When the Zodiac approached the victims, he told them an elaborate story about being an escaped convict who needed their car and money. He got both of the victims tied up and then savagely stabbed both of them repeatedly. Eventually, he did not take any items, and an investigation showed that he had concocted the story he fed to the victims. If Zodiac subconsciously needed to deindividuate himself, the spurious story and executioner's type costume would have allowed him to identify with a particular role, very much like a soldier dressed in combat gear. The Zodiac would have transitioned from his regular self to a cold blooded killer on a mission, resulting in him becoming an objectified tool, hence lowering or blurring his sense of responsibility.

In several of his ensuing letters, he quoted and alluded to the famous opera, *the Mikado*, and in particular he appeared to identify with the role of Ko-Ko, the Lord High Executioner. On July 26, 1970, the Zodiac devoted nearly five pages of a letter to the opera as he described in lurid details how he would kill people in line with the work of the Lord High Executioner. If the Zodiac assumed the role of an executioner, it would also have been a more feasible task for him to dehumanize his victims.

The Citizen

In August 1969, a letter arrived at the San Francisco Examiner. It began as follows, "This is the Zodiac speaking." This was the first time that the killer had uniquely identified himself. In his initial three letters, he referred to himself as a "murderer" and a "killer." The use of the name "Zodiac" could have been a component of his deindividuation process as it would have allowed him to focus and identify with the skills, capabilities, and temperaments of his imagined character, Zodiac, hence resulting in a loss of self-identity as well as an ability to block out possible feelings of guilt. When he resumed writing in 1974, he first sent an unsigned letter in January containing a reference to suicide. In May, he sent the card that was signed with "citizen." Taken at face value, his allusion to suicide is significant inasmuch as suicide is related to high self-awareness.[9] As previously mentioned, deindividuation is characterized by anonymity and consequently reduced self-awareness; the individual becomes distant from the real self. It is therefore indicated that the Zodiac went through a transition from perceiving himself as a murderer to a citizen who was outraged by violence. It should be mentioned that Zodiac's individuation process or transition may have started as early as October 1969 as he committed his last confirmed murder in that month and ostensibly never killed again. Furthermore, professor of psychology, Dr. David van Nuys, has observed a dichotomy between the Zodiac's initial letters from 1969 and those received in 1970, leading him to theorize that the Zodiac had lost control along this continuum. The Zodiac's suicide reference, which was actually an inexact quotation from the Mikado, "might be a literal killing of his body, or it might signal the death of his 'High Executioner' sub-personality,"[10] Dr. Nuys theorized. He suspected that "he may have been institutionalized, or in therapy, or on some medication that was helping to bring his violent behavior under control."[11]

Conclusion

In view of the change in how the Zodiac killed swiftly using guns to the more intimate knife attack complete with a costume, it is quite possible that deindividuation came into play along with other psychological processes.

The apparent loss of his Zodiac identity may have been the result of increased self-awareness. On the other hand, the citizen card could have been a form of manipulation or an attempt to get into the spotlight indirectly. It is even possible that the card could have been falsely attributed to the Zodiac as questioned document examination can produce false positives.

ENDNOTES M

[1] Silke, A. "Deindividuation, anonymity, and violence: Findings from Northern Ireland." The Journal of Social Psychology.
[2] "Conducting the Milgram Experiment in Poland, Psychologists Show People Still Obey," www.spsp.org/news-center/press-releases/milgram-poland-obey (retrieved May 2020).
[3] "Revise Psychology: Deindividuation," https://revisepsychology.wordpress.com/2012/05/15/ 2-deindividuation (retrieved June 2018).
[4] Watson, R. I. "Investigation into deindividuation using a cross-cultural survey technique." Journal of Personality and Social Psychology (1973).
[5] Diener, E., Fraser, S. C., Beaman, A. L., & Kelem, R. T. "Effects of deindividuation variables on stealing among Halloween trick-or-treaters." Journal of Personality and Social Psychology (1976).
[6] Malamuth, N. M. "Rape proclivity among males." Journal of Social Issues (1976). http://dx.doi.org/10.1111/j.1540-4560.1981.tb01075.x. (retrieved June 2018).
[7] Silke, A. "Deindividuation, anonymity, and violence: Findings from Northern Ireland." The Journal of Social Psychology.
[8] Department of Justice, Bureau of Criminal Investigation and Investigation Report, Case Number 1-15-311-F9-5861, 19.
[9] Selimbegovic, L., Chatard, A. "The mirror effect: Self-awareness alone increases suicide thought accessibility." Consciousness and Cognition (2013).
[10] Kelleher, Van Nuys, "This is the Zodiac Speaking: Into the Mind of a Serial Killer" (Praeger Publishers 2002), 186.
[11] Ibid.

CHAPTER 14

STATEMENT ANALYSIS

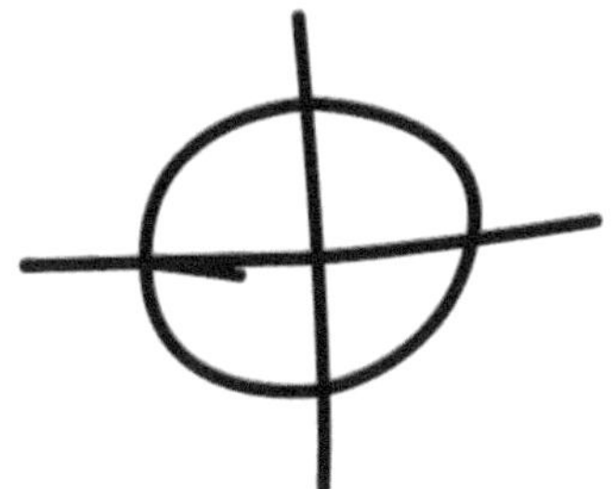

Introduction

Statement analysis® is a linguistic method that has emerged as a powerful technique to detect deception and extract veiled information. The foundation of statement analysis is the concept that people mean exactly what they say or write. A statement analyst will scrutinize, deconstruct and examine sentences word for word according to each respective definition as well as pay heed to omissions and grammar among other objective aspects. A statement reflects the subject's beliefs and view of reality. A statement can be truthful, but may not reflect actual reality. This can be defined as "that which exists objectively and in fact."[1] Statement analysis had not formally been invented when Zodiac actively taunted the editor of the San Francisco Chronicle, but it would have been of assistance to the Zodiac task force as an analyst could have taken a deep look at his statements and threats.

The Zodiac case attracts a wide audience which is partly due to a variety of intriguing and unanswered questions related to the evidence of the case, the Zodiac's motivations, his actual victim count, and persisting theories related to his identity. In this chapter, statements from Zodiac and police officers who worked on the case are subjected to analysis in an effort to cast light on several debated issues. Some statements are given an in-depth look while others are given relatively brief examinations.

The Evidence

In his lengthy November 1969 letter, the Zodiac made a number of important statements regarding evidence that had been compiled against him. Journalist Paul Avery had described the evidence in an article published on October 18, 1969, titled, "Zodiac Portrait of a Killer."[2]

Zodiac's Disguise

"1 I look like the description passed out only when I do my thing, the rest of the time I look entirle different. I shall not tell you what my descise consists of when I kill [.]"

Analysis

Contrary to general belief, Zodiac did not deny that the composite drawing looked like him. He specifically stated the description which was very simple and did not specify facial structures: white male adult, 35-45 years old, about 5'8", heavily built, short brown hair, and possibly with a reddish shade. Zodiac likely wanted the reader to infer that he meant the composite drawing, but in statement analysis, we do not make such assumptions. We cannot believe that he perceived himself as different from the drawing as he did not state it. Zodiac goes on to write, "only when I do my thing." He conveys that the description is only valid when he does "his thing," a vague and unspecified term. Most likely, he wanted the reader to assume that "his thing" is synonymous with "killing," but at the end of the paragraph he uses the word "kill," indicating that he was trying to deceive the reader. Zodiac did not write that he disguised himself during the Stine crime which was the basis for the composite drawing and description. It follows that we have no reason to believe he did.

The shortest sentence is the best and any extra words provide us with additional information. Zodiac wanted us to believe that "the rest of the time I look entirle different." First, the sentence is unnecessary as it could have been ended after "thing." There is an obvious need to persuade the reader by emphasizing that he does not look like the description. Frequently, when a deceptive person issues a denial, it will be followed by an additional denial because the initial one is weak. Second, the word "entirely" means "wholly or fully; completely"[3] according to www.dictionary.com. The use of the word is disingenuous. For example, he certainly did not disguise that he was a white male adult; hence, he did not look "entirle" different "the rest of the time." He is exaggerating his position.

The missing period after "kill" indicates conflict. Although, the Zodiac stopped his sentence, the missing period suggests that he may have had more information he purposely withheld. The sentence falls short of affirming that he wore a disguise during the Stine crime. Furthermore, the disguise could consist of nothing perhaps that is the reason why he refrained from specifying its components. There is no reason to assume that he wore a disguise.

Fingerprints

"2 As of yet I have left no fingerprints behind me contrary to what the police say in my killings I wear transparent finger tip guards. All it is is 2 coats of airplane cement coated on my finger tips – quite unnoticible + very efective."

Analysis

First, the paragraph is disjointed and confusing. An assertion containing these properties is weak. By writing "as of yet," Zodiac conveys that until this point in time, but not necessarily from this point on, he has "left no fingerprints." This can be seen as an attempt to portray honesty and openness. People who speak the truth rarely have a need to assert their integrity, but liars often do.

Zodiac did not deny that he left fingerprints on Stine's cab. The police had stated they were confident that these prints had been left by the killer. His assertion is actually in the positive, "*I have left*." We can compare his statement to Richard Beasley's, the Craigslist killer, claim of innocence and notice the similarities. Beasley said, "I state here today officially and for the record: I have killed nobody, and that's a fact."[4] Like Beasley, Zodiac expressed himself in general terms which facilitate lying. People who tell direct lies are in the absolute minority.

Zodiac's claim is also weakened by the need to explain why he "left no fingerprints." The initial part of the sentence was not strong enough and he went on to try to persuade the reader into thinking why he could not have left prints. We must note, however, that a subordinating conjunction e.g. "because" or a semicolon is missing between "say" and "in." Zodiac could not linguistically establish the very concise rationale between leaving "no prints" and wearing fingertip guards.

The first part of the sentence, "I have left," is in the present perfect tense which can be used to indicate a link between the present and the past. The present perfect tense is used when the time of the action in question is not specified. Zodiac then switches to the present tense when writing "in my killings I wear." By switching to the present tense, he avoids writing that he actually wore the guards during the Stine crime. The present tense is sometimes used when stating a universal truth. This means the Zodiac may have attempted to give the appearance that he always wore these guards, even though, we know he did not wear guards during the murder of Cecelia Shepard on September 27, 1969, at Lake Berryessa.

Zodiac then proceeds to explain the mechanics of the transparent fingertip guards. The introductory part, "all it is," is unnecessary and is used to underline the simplicity of the guards. He has a need to persuade. He continues by making an *em dash* separating the description of the guards from "quite unnoticible + very efective." The Zodiac demonstrates a persistent need to persuade the reader about his fingerprint claim. Here, he forwards the notion that the guards are simple (all it is) and very effective and quite unnoticeable. If we look closely, the Zodiac did not state that the guards are effective against leaving fingerprints, he probably wanted us to make this assumption. Regardless, in the context of fingerprint protection equipment, it is redundant to speak of the

degree of effectiveness as the gear either protects or does not. On a related note, since Zodiac limits his focus to fingerprints it is likely that he did not know that most of one's hands can leave an identifying print.
The need to qualify "unnoticeable" weakens the assertion because exactly what "quite unnoticeable" corresponds to in the Zodiac's personal dictionary we cannot tell. When a person deceives, he or she will commonly use qualifiers as the word or sentence does not have the strength to stand alone. In conclusion, Zodiac's statement about fingerprints is deceptive.

Killing Tools

" 3 my killing tools have been boughten through the mail order outfits before the ban went into efect. except one + it was bought out of the state."

Analysis

Deceptive people often want the recipient to make various assumptions. For example, rather than answering a specific question, such as "Did you kill Mr. X?" A guilty person will often speak in general terms, like, "I *would* never do that," or "I am not a murderer," or "I'm innocent," or change the accusation: "I didn't *hurt* Mr. X," etc. In statement analysis, these are weak denials. In the above sentence, the Zodiac wants us to make the connection between killing tools and the firearms he had used to kill and injure his victims. He claims possession of these tools by using the pronoun "my," which is not capitalized, but he then switches to passive language and does not state that *he* bought the tools using the specified methods. Passive language is used to conceal identities. Based upon the passive language, we have to question who actually obtained the firearms and whether he is truthful. While passive language is acceptable in scholarly articles and some other places, like this book, it is sometimes used as a masking agent, e.g. "the gun went off." Here the passive language conceals the shooter's identity and even gender. Complicating matters, however, is that pathological liars, like the Zodiac, sometimes use passive language even when telling the truth; concealing becomes ingrained in their language due to habitual lying.

A period is not needed after “efect” which is misspelled, and “except” is not capitalized. These are indications that the information is not coming from episodic memory. Episodic memory is “person’s unique memory of a specific event, so it will be different from someone else’s recollection of the same experience.”[5]

The Fouke-Zodiac Incident

Introduction

The next part of this analysis will pay special heed to the Fouke-Zodiac incident in an attempt to answer the long debated issue: Did Officers Donald Fouke and Eric Zelms stop and question the Zodiac after the murder of Paul Stine or did they simply drive by him?
As described in detail in Chapter 4, after exiting Stine’s cab, which was parked adjacent to 3898 Washington Street, San Francisco, Zodiac walked north on Cherry Street and then proceeded down Jackson Street. The Zodiac, in his November letter, claimed that a police car with two officers questioned him. He gave them a ruse and the officers drove away while he disappeared. On the other hand, Fouke explained in an interdepartmental memorandum that when they had responded to the Stine crime, they had received an erroneous description of the suspect. When Fouke and Zelms went down Jackson Street, they saw a man walking in an easterly direction, but he “was not stopped” as they were looking for a black man. There is no doubt that the individual was the Zodiac. We will now take a closer look at the issue by first analyzing the account offered by the Zodiac.

Zodiac’s Claim: I Spoke to the Police

“p.s. 2 cops pulled a goof abot 3 min after I left the cab. I was walking down the hill to the park when this cop car pulled up + one of them called me over + asked if I saw any one acting supicisous or strange in the last 5 to 10 min + I said yes there was this man who was runnig by waveing a gun + the cops peeled rubber + went around the corner as I directed them + I dissapeared into the park a block + a half away never to be seen again."

Analysis

What we first notice is that the Zodiac wrote "abot 3 min." The number three is known as a "liar's number."[6] Statistically, it is often used in fictitious settings (The Three Little Pigs, The Story of Three Wonderful Beggars, The Three Enchanted Princes, etc.) or if the subject is unsure of which number to use.[7] Whenever it is used, we pay close attention. The word "about," which is misspelled, is not an exact measurement of time indicating that Zodiac was unsure of the actual number of minutes. Inclusion of the word "left" to link two places together (from cab to location of interaction with the officers) is most of the time found in statements that are related to time pressure. Research has shown that "70% of the time, the word 'left' is used because the person was pressed for time."[8]

An analyst can sometimes infer a subject's priorities by noting where information is mentioned in a statement. In this statement, it appears that the Zodiac's priority is that the police officers "pulled a goof," that is, they made a mistake. His second priority is that it happened in close proximity to leaving the cab. Similarly, in these words, "any one acting supicisous or strange," the priority is on suspicious rather than strange behavior. If this had been a concoction, the priority might not have followed this logical sequence.

Unlike in some of the previous statements, he does not use passive language inappropriately. This shows personal commitment to the statement.

If a statement revolves around an incident, it will contain a before-, during- and after-segment. The last segment, which describes what happened after the incident, is frequently very short or missing in deceptive statements as the deceiver's attention is directed toward delivering the incident, and fabricating an ending is not important. The three segments in this instance are consistent with a truthful statement. As a general rule for a truthful statement, before ≈ after ≈ 25%, and the during segment ≈ 50% of the word count.

Zodiac writes "this cop car," but "a cop car" would have been appropriate. The determiner "this" indicates closeness and specificity. Why would the Zodiac want to associate himself with the car? He similarly indicates closeness and specificity when writing "this man."

He goes on to state that the police car "pulled up" which means it stopped. He states that one of them asked him to approach the police car, but he does not write that he actually walked to the car, and thus we should not believe that he did.

Verbs can either be in soft tone (e.g. said) or strong tone (e.g. demanded). Whether or not these verbs are used consistently and appropriately, can be a sign of truthfulness or deception. The paragraph contains "asked" and "said" which are both soft tone verbs. The phrasal verb, "called over," is also soft tone language as opposed to being told to come over to the police car. If the incident took place as described, the soft tone language is justified considering that the Zodiac would not have been considered a suspect. The consistency indicates it is a truthful statement.

The Zodiac uses the "+" sign as a synonym for "and" throughout the sentence and without any exceptions in the letter that it was a part of. In authenticated Zodiac letters, he rarely uses "and." The adherence to his internal dictionary is an indication of veracity as a change in language indicates a change in reality.

The "as" in "went around the corner as I directed them" is important because the Zodiac felt the need to explain why the officers went around the corner indicating a need to persuade us that he "directed them." The need to explain is a slight indication of deception.

For the most part, Zodiac uses first person singular and simple past tense in the paragraph, except in a couple of instances, such as when he writes, "I was walking." Here he uses past continuous tense which is formed by was/were plus present participle and is used "to show that an ongoing past action was happening at a specific moment of interruption."[9] The Zodiac's use is appropriate as the interruption is the police car that came by. Zodiac uses "saw" as opposed to "had seen," which is correct as the use of simple past indicates that "the action that takes place is over and done with."[10] "Had seen" would have been appropriate if the action had happened "at an unspecified time before now or one where the action extends to the present."[11]

The sentence, "I said yes there was this man who was runnig by waveing a gun" is accurate grammatically as the use of past progressive tense, which is formed by subject plus was/were plus present participle, can be used to indicate "events that lasted for a duration of time in the past."[12] The use of the present tense "acting" after "saw" is appropriate since it also follows the past progressive tense. An inappropriate slip into present tense suggests that a sentence or a part of it is not retrieved from episodic memory; thus, based on the verb tenses and the other aspects that have been mentioned, the statement appears truthful, except that he probably did not direct the officers.

Denial by SFPD Captain Lee

In the article, "Another Grim Message: 'I've killed Seven' The Zodiac Claims," Paul Avery quotes Martin Lee, the Captain of San Francisco Police Department. Lee addressed the Zodiac's claim that he had talked to the officers. He said: "[I]t is preposterous that he was stopped and questioned by the officers. That just didn't happen."

Analysis

The word preposterous means "contrary to nature, reason, or common sense."[13] It does not mean "not true" which would have constituted a good denial. When Captain Lee stated that "it is preposterous that he was stopped and questioned by the officers," it suggests that he was convinced that Zodiac "was stopped and questioned." The sentence is not a denial, but a positive affirmation. If he had added "to believe" after preposterous it would have been a denial. Captain Lee then says, "[t]hat just didn't happen." The use of "that" instead of "it" indicates that he is distancing himself from his statement or the event.

The word "just" is commonly used to minimize events or actions undertaken. It is an indication that more things transpired than what Captain Lee stated. It is a weak and possibly deceptive denial. Here are two examples that show how the word "just" can be used to deceive. The Golden State killer told a female victim that "I just want your money."[14] It was a lie and he subsequently raped her. Serial killer Richard Ramirez was once asked, "Who are you?" He replied, "Just a guy. Just a guy."[15]

Donald Fouke's Interdepartmental Memorandum

Donald Fouke also had the chance to describe what transpired after they had received a broadcast about the murder of Paul Stine. Fouke typed:

"I respectfully wish to report the following, that while responding to the area of Cherry and Washington Streets a suspect fitting the description of the Zodiac killer was observed by officer Fouke walking in an easterly direction on Jackson street and then turn north on Maple street. This subject was not stopped as the description received from communications was that of a negro male. When the right description was broadcast reporting officer informed communications that a possible suspect had been seen going north on Maple Street into the Presidio, The area of Julius Kahn playground and a search was started which had negative results.

The suspect that was observed by officer Fouke was a WMA 35-45 Yrs about 5'10", 180-200 lbs. Medium heavy build – Barrel chested – Medium complexion – Light-colored hair possibly greying in rear (May have been lighting that caused this effect.) Crew cut – Wearing glasses – Dressed in dark blue waist length zipper type jacket (Navy or royal blue) Elastic cuffs and waist band zipped part way up. Brown wool pants pleeted type baggy in rear (Rust brown) May have been wearing low cut shoes.

Subject at no time appeared to be in a hurry walking with a shuffling lope, Slightly bent forward head down. The subjects general appearance to classifiy him as a group would be that he might be of Welsh ancestry.

My partner that night was officer E. Zelms # 1348 of Richmond station. I do not know if he observed this subject or not."

Analysis

Fouke began his statement by affirming that he wished "to report the following," so it may be that there are matters he did not want to report.

There are no synonyms in statement analysis and sometimes parts of a personal dictionary show up in a statement. However, it must be kept in mind that some people will purposely change their language so they do not sound redundant. Law enforcement is one of those groups of people that might do this. In this statement, it can be seen that when Fouke initially noticed the man, he was a "suspect" which is interesting terminology as he did not fit the description of being a black man. If he did not fit the description, he would not be a suspect. It may be that when Fouke got a good look at him and realized the man was not black, the man was no longer a suspect and became a "subject." When the corrected description was sent out, he realized the man he saw may have been the perpetrator. This might have caused him to go back to calling him a "suspect." Those changes would be justified. The problem is, he should now constantly refer to him as a "suspect" since toward the end of his statement he calls him a "subject" three times.

Moving on, Fouke writes that he observed the subject walking on Jackson Street "and then" he went north on Maple Street. "Then" can mean "immediately" or "soon thereafter." In lieu of immediately providing a description of the Zodiac, Fouke goes on to state that the "subject was not stopped as the description received from communications was that of a [N]egro male." Fouke does not state that he did not stop the subject; the passivity of the sentence (removal of "I", "we," "reporting officer," or "Officer Fouke") may indicate deception as passive language conceals identity and limits commitment. Although many police officers fill out their reports in passive language for objectivity, much like scientists and scholars, Fouke switches between first and third person throughout the statement, an indication of deception.

If we consider that order of information indicates priority, it is apparent that Fouke considered it more important to state that Zodiac was not stopped rather than providing a description of him, which he does afterward. Negatives are important in statement analysis especially if they are issued when it is expected that the subject should tell us what happened. Fouke told us what did not transpire between him and the Zodiac. This negative indicates that the topic is important and sensitive to Fouke as an infinite number of things did not happen, but only a finite number of things took place. Fouke also provides a reason as to why he did not stop the subject (he did not fit the broadcast description). Why would he do that? It establishes a rationale or alibi and makes the scenario proposed by Fouke more likely. This is a strong indication of deception.

We must also pay close attention to the exact wording of Fouke's denial: "The subject was not stopped." The statement does not preclude that the subject stopped on his own accord. Fouke is stating that someone (he has removed himself from the sentence) did not stop the subject. This is probably literally true as the subject might have stopped by himself if the police car pulled up. We cannot believe that Fouke did not stop and speak with the Zodiac as his exact words mean something else. Lying through misrepresentation is common.

Chronologically, Fouke states that he observed the subject walking on Jackson Street and then made a turn onto Maple Street. Hereafter, Fouke breaks off from the chronological order and states what did not happen. Rather than describing what happened, Fouke writes, "*when* the right description." The word "when" spans time and thus the essential seconds and minutes between observing the subject to receiving the broadcast were intentionally left out. This is compelling evidence of deception.

The memorandum contains an important contradiction in Fouke's last assertion that he does "not know if [Zelms] observed" the subject. Incongruously, Fouke had at this point already affirmed that he had "informed communications" about the "possible suspect." Fouke and Zelms were driving together that night. Note that Zelms accompanied Fouke in the police car during the encounter with the man, while Fouke informed communications, and while they searched for the man. It is inconceivable that they did not discuss everything related to the issue in great detail. Fouke and Zelms had had an encounter with the culprit of a brutal murder, they had him in a vulnerable position, and through misfortune they had let him walk away. Unquestionably, as soon as they had "received the right description" it would have produced a psychological and biological response mimicking that of stress and trauma characterized by increased heart rate, pupil dilation, heightened senses, and increased strength and performance due to a carefully orchestrated sequence of hormones being released. They likely feared getting fired or reprimanded or that it would result in a major scandal. The situation is incompatible with the apathy of Fouke's statement. Inconsistencies and misplaced emotions are commonly found in deceptive statements.

Likewise it is highly suspect and inconsistent with the content of the memorandum that Fouke first made the report over a month

after the encounter. His report characterizes the man as a "suspect" and describes how a search had been initiated after he had contacted the police central. Thereby, he knew the significance of the ordeal, yet waited until November 1969.
The description of the subject is exceedingly detailed, specifying his possible ancestry, clothes, and hair color. Although police officers are trained observers, the description by Fouke is overly detailed. Fouke even went as far as describing that the subject's hair might have been greying in the rear. Exactly how he was able to perceive this feature as well as the turn from Jackson Street to Maple Street he did not explain.
In conclusion, the account offered by Fouke is unreliable and deceptive. The topic is very important and sensitive to him.

Denials by Donald Fouke

Years later, Fouke made additional comments about the event in question and made several denials.[16] We have selected three statements for analysis:

1) "We never stopped the man. We never talked to him. That is an emphatic statement by me. I wouldn't make the denial."
2) "We did not stop the Zodiac. We didn't stop anyone. I wish Eric Zelms were alive today to tell you so."
3) Question: "Can you guess how fast you were driving on the street when you saw him?"
Fouke: "Well, until I saw him, probably about 35 or 40 miles an hour on a 25-mile-an-hour street. Slowed down as we passed him. I don't know, we are still rolling. Saw that it is a white male, step on the gas. Five, ten, fifteen seconds tops from first spotting him till passing him."

Analysis

The word "never" means "not ever," but not "no." "Never" is also not time-specific and thus its usage facilitates deception. It is frequently used in deceptive statements. Fouke states "we never stopped" or "talked to him." His use of "we" limits responsibility as it has less impact than putting himself into the statement via the personal pronoun "I." Fouke goes on to state, "[t]hat is an emphatic statement by me." Fouke's repeated denials indicate that they are weak and need support. We must, on the other hand, also consider that he may have believed that many doubted him so he had to reiterate his denials. There is a contrast to be noted here since "that" is used when we distance ourselves from a topic or subject. Thus, Fouke states that it is a statement by him "expressed or performed with emphasis,"[17] which is the definition of "emphatic," yet he is distancing himself from this emphasis via the word "that." The sentence, "I wouldn't make the denial," falls short of saying that he would not make the denial if it had happened. It is a contradictory statement because he made a denial de facto yet says he would not make "the denial."

We must pay attention to the vocabulary of Donald Fouke. In the first statement, he issued a weak denial in addressing whether or not they stopped and talked to "the man." In the second statement, his proclamation that "[w]e did not stop the Zodiac" is a better denial. We should recall that a change in language indicates a change in reality. In this context, the subject was first a "man" and only later Fouke discovered that the "man" was the "Zodiac." Fouke can truthfully say that "we" did not stop the Zodiac, but his statement that "we never" stopped and talked to "the man" is unreliable. Fouke continues by using the general term "anyone." His repetitions indicate a need to persuade the listener.

If the event transpired, surely Fouke would wish that Eric Zelms would support his denial. Fouke does not say that Zelms would tell the truth that they did not stop and talk to him.

In statement number three, Fouke goes beyond answering the question. It is significant that he first says that they passed him, after which he states, "I don't know, we are still rolling." Therefore, after they had passed him, Fouke is unsure of whether or not they stopped. It is either the car rolls or it is stopped. There is no in-between. Fouke also switches inappropriately to the present tense, "we are," which indicates that the statement may not have been retrieved from episodic memory.

If we look closely at the sentence, Fouke used the unnecessary word "still." Words that are not essential for a sentence are very important. In this context, "still," means that the police car was rolling "up to and including the present."[18] Usage of this word in this context would only be logical if they did stop as the word "still" implies a comparison between stopping and not stopping. It is very powerful linguistic evidence that they did stop. Specifically, Fouke states that they passed him and then he "[doesn't] know" if they were still rolling. Furthermore, there is present tense and a missing pronoun in the next sentence: "Saw that it is a white male, step on the gas." It suggests that more things may have transpired between seeing it was a "white male" and the conclusion, "step on the gas."

In conclusion, Fouke's denials are deceptive. If we extrapolate a scenario from the linguistic evidence, what emerges is that they initially passed him, they stopped, and at this time Fouke may have observed his hair in the rear. After they had talked to him (Zodiac may not have walked to the police car as indicated by his statement), it would have been easy due to their vantage point to see which way he walked after their conversation. The Zodiac did probably not direct the officers as indicated by the analysis.

The Bus Bomb

In a letter from October 1969, the Zodiac threatened to kill schoolchildren. When the threat was published, it sparked massive panic in San Francisco and elsewhere. The public demanded safety initiatives and consequently officers started to board school buses with loaded shotguns or they tailed buses in police cars.

Zodiac wrote:

"School children make nice targets, I think I shall wipe out a school bus some morning. Just shoot out the frunt tire + then pick off the kiddies as they come bouncing out."

Analysis

Zodiac's threat directed toward schoolchildren is a weak one. He writes "I think," which means to "form or have in the mind," that he "shall," which means "will have to" wipe out a school bus. The composition of "think" and "shall" is weak. In addition, "some morning" is unspecific which further weakens the threat. Zodiac leaves himself out of the last sentence. The use of the word "just" suggests that he is trying to persuade us into believing how easy it would be to accomplish the act. Thus, Zodiac might not have had intentions of targeting schoolchildren in the specified manner.

Did the Zodiac Murder Cheri Jo Bates?

In the 1970s, the police embraced the notion that the Zodiac had killed Cheri Jo Bates in Riverside, California, and the connection was widely reported. In March 1971, Zodiac, in a letter to the Los Angeles Times, made a statement about Riverside. He wrote:

"I do have to give them credit for stumbling across my riverside activity, but they are only finding the easy ones, there are a hell of a lot more down there."

Analysis

Contrary to popular perception, the statement is not about Cheri Jo Bates or victims, but about unspecified "activity." Pronouns are instinctive and show ownership. Via the pronoun "my," Zodiac takes possession of "riverside activity." Given his choice of words, there is no reason to believe he killed Bates or that activity signifies murder (as it would be an interpretation). Instead, Zodiac tells us he was involved in some kind of unspecified activity in Riverside. Zodiac then writes, "but," which negates or minimizes what came before it, "they are only finding the easy ones." It is very likely that Zodiac wanted the reader to make a deceptive inference between "activity" and murder. His inability to state explicitly that he had killed in Riverside is an indication that he did not kill Bates. Lying via misrepresentation is a common form of deception.

In Zodiac's confession letter of 1966, he wrote: "I AM STALKING YOUR GIRLS NOW." The word, "NOW," is not necessary and is therefore important. In statement analysis, we believe what people tell us, and we have to be "talked out of" believing in a particular assertion. The word "NOW," means from now on, and *not before this time*. Although, the Zodiac spends a great deal of the confession letter trying to persuade readers that he is a killer and will kill again, he concludes the letter by stating that he is "stalking" rather than "killing" "your girls now." Believe him.

Conclusions

This analysis has concluded the following:

1. Zodiac's statements about the evidence (description, disguise, and fingerprints) are characterized by deceptive language. His statement related to acquiring his weapons by mail order may or may not be true. The sentence about acquiring one out of state is likely deceptive.

2. The language employed by the Zodiac to describe his encounter with Officers Fouke and Zelms is consistent with language coming from episodic memory, except the part about directing the officers.

3. The statement from Captain Lee indicates that he believed the officers stopped and talked to the Zodiac, and that he attempted to downplay the incident.

4. Donald Fouke's denials are deceptive.

5. The analysis indicates that Zodiac did not plan to follow through on his threat toward schoolchildren.

6. Zodiac's statement about Riverside is deceptive.

ENDNOTES N

® Statement Analysis is a registered trademark of Mark McClish.
[1] "Reality," https://www.thefreedictionary.com/reality (retrieved June 2019).
[2] "Zodiac Portrait of a Killer," San Francisco Chronicle, October 18, 1969.
[3] "Entirely," https://www.dictionary.com/browse/entirely (retrieved June 2019).
[4] "Daughter of serial killer who hunted victims in woods speaks out," https://truecrimedaily.com/2016/04/14/daughter-of-one-of-ohios-most-ruthless-killers-speaks-out/ (retrieved June 2019).
[5] "Episodic Memory: Definition and Examples," https://www.livescience.com/43682-episodic-memory.html (retrieved June 2019).
[6] "The Use of the Number Three," www.statementanalysis.com/research/three/ (retrieved June 2019).
[7] Ibid.
[8] "Understanding the Word, 'Left' In Analysis," www.statement-analysis.blogspot.com/2014/03/understanding-word-left-in-analysis.html (retrieved June 2019).
[9] "Past Continuous," https://www.englishpage.com/verbpage/pastcontinuous.html (retrieved June 2019).
[10] "Seen vs. Saw: What's the Difference?" https://writingexplained.org/seen-vs-saw-difference (retrieved June 2019).
[11] Ibid.
[12] "What is the Past Progressive Tense? Definition, Examples of English Tenses," https://writingexplained.org/grammar-dictionary/past-progressive-tense (retrieved June 2019).
[13] "Preposterous," https://www.dictionary.com/browse/preposterous (retrieved June 2019).
[14] "Golden State Killer: hope for unsolved serial murder case as ex-cop arrested," https://www.theguardian.com/us-news/2018/apr/25/golden-state-serial-killer-california-arrest-east-area-rapist (retrieved June 2019).
[15] "A Conversation with Richard Ramirez–The Night Stalker–Reported by Mike Watkiss," https://www.youtube.com/watch?v=MC5huwZoPZA (retrieved June 2019).
[16] David Fincher, Director, Zodiac 2-Disc Director's Cut, 2008.
[17] "Emphatic," https://www.thefreedictionary.com/emphatic (retrieved June 2019).
[18] "Still," https://www.encyclopedia.com/science-and-technology/technology/technology-terms-and-concepts/still (retrieved June 2019).

CHAPTER 15

EPILOGUE

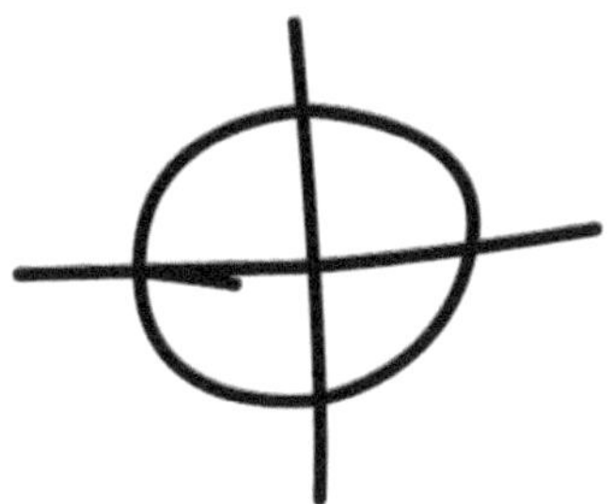

When the Zodiac first entered the public stage, his actions were shocking, intriguing, and largely incomprehensible. Even though, more than 50 years have passed, the Zodiac still remains a mystery, and the case is still relevant and important: His letters and actions provide us with a rare view into the mind of a serial killer on the loose. The case is obviously also important for the reason that justice has not been served. We are able to study the Zodiac through multiple letters in addition to phone calls and his crimes. Not surprisingly, all of his correspondences were without real substance and were designed to taunt and terrorize the public. However, we could hardly have expected him to blab about the putative mental and physical beatings of his childhood, and discuss what ultimately pushed him into the abyss to become a murderer. Was he always a killer by heart, or simply a product of his upbringing and social circumstances? Like Andrew Kehoe, one the most notorious bombers in US history, put it, "Criminals are made, not born."[§§§§] Perhaps something else can explain in human terms his zeal for blood and terror. Given the rambling nature of his letters and occasional inconsistent logic, it is reasonable to assume that he would have been unable to even remotely account for his actions.

The Zodiac seemed to have an innate hatred for couples, attacking at least three and possibly as many as five of them. In this light, it seems very likely that he was deeply envious and frustrated with his own love life. However, his motivation was multi-layered and evolving; for example, he probably killed Stine to prove that he could kill a man, which is something that he had failed to do in two of his attacks. Notoriety and publicity were also key motivational forces since they were sufficient to gratify him after killing Stine. If we examine the timeline, it is apparent that he wrote few letters when he was active killing people, and penned many when he was bragging and taking false credit for killings he had not committed. It is intriguing why the Zodiac mysteriously decided to cease communicating from March 1971 to January 1974. He was a criminal, and he could have been locked up for some unrelated crime; however, given the quality and strength of the evidence gathered from the crime scenes and letters, it seems somewhat unlikely that he would not have been identified shortly after his arrest. However, we should keep in mind that the Automated Fingerprint Identification System did not exist back then, as well as other advanced technologies.

On the face of it, it seems somewhat unlikely that he was busy with relationship related matters due to his twisted psychology. However, some serial killers, including some who arguably share psychological characteristics with the Zodiac, were married during their crime sprees, such as Dennis Rader, the BTK killer.

Even if the Zodiac was busy with wife and kids, he could surely have found time to write a letter, or so it would seem. It is more

[§§§§] "Bath school disaster" https://www.britannica.com/event/Bath-school-disaster-1927 (May 2020).

reasonable that he *could* not write a letter because he was in an asylum, or in a position that he found to be too revealing if he went to the nearest mailbox and posted a letter. Considering his argued military background, we should consider that he was stationed in a different country or state – or he was in Canada, spending time with family. His family would most likely have known about his frequent trips to the Bay Area, and it would have aroused suspicions if the Zodiac suddenly started writing letters from this area.

In 1972, the media advocated his involvement in the knife attack on Watson and the brutal slaying of Domingos and Edwards. The Zodiac was never mentioned as a suspect in the killing of Ray Davis, but the evidence strongly suggests that he killed him and made the phone calls. Why did he not pick up his favorite felt tip pen and take credit in a letter to the editor of the San Francisco Chronicle? It would have served his interests on several levels. For example, had he verified his culpability, it would undoubtedly have resulted in front-page coverage, and it would have perplexed everyone to a great extent. So why did he not do it?

As documented in the preceding chapters, the Zodiac was an evolving and varying serial killer in his implementation and tactics, yet he was consistently a terrorist, someone who uses violence or threats to promulgate fear in the public's collective peace of mind. It was not enough for him to snatch lives. He wanted everyone to feel and experience the fear. In the confession, he displayed his love for chaos in the population, this time directed at females. Later, he switched focus. He was undoubtedly delighted to see that fear spread in the public, and it may have been sufficient to assuage his murderous impulses. We may even speculate that his murders were aimed at raising fear and anxiety levels in the population to such a degree that he would be on everyone's lips and therefore be remembered. Having achieved his purpose, he no longer felt an imminent impulse to kill.

There existed a paradoxical combination of fear intermixed with fearlessness within the Zodiac's mind. He was taking risks in the minutes and hours prior to his crimes. This behavior may have translated itself into actions in his private life; he was perhaps an irresponsible driver or engaged in some other reckless type of activity. Nonetheless, he appears to have afraid of getting caught to the extent that he pretended to be a prime candidate for a mental institution. If he is ever identified (still alive), he will conceivably continue on that note or adopt a similar defense.

One possibility that has not been discussed in the book is if the Zodiac murders could have been perpetrated by more than one individual. This notion lacks hard evidence and there are strong indications of the opposite that a so-called lone wolf was behind all the madness. Zodiac referred to himself singularly, the physical descriptions of him were generally consistent, and the handwriting belonged to the same person.

The final death toll is a matter that will probably never be known with certainty. However, we do know conclusively that he killed five and critically wounded two, but he may have killed as many as 11 people, starting in 1962.

Today, the Zodiac case is old and cold. The police reports are dusty, and many of the original investigators have passed away. Even so, we should never forget that the Zodiac's victims were real and the families and friends are still searching for answers and justice. If he is alive today, the Zodiac would be an old man carrying around a dark secret. Perhaps his luck is finally running out, and he will soon return to the front page of his favorite newspaper, the Chronicle, arrested and in handcuffs. We are waiting for that day to come.

Sources

The following is a list of the major sources that served as the basis for this book. The total length of the reports might vary depending on where they are retrieved. All of them can be accessed via the Internet. If additional reports are released in the future, a few of the crimes could be expanded upon. The reports that are still being withheld, detail forensic work and investigative steps undertaken by law enforcement. There is likely nothing groundbreaking hidden in the unpublished reports, after all over 2200 pages have been released so far. There could be additional Zodiac letters hidden in some dusty police locker, but there are no indications of this. Hence, only scattered details could be added to the chapters of this book. The longest chapter of this story that which describes the life and making of the Zodiac, has not been written. This we have to wait for.

Roed, O.J. Letter to Thomas Joyce. December 31, 1968.

San Diego Police Department. Investigation and Activities Surrounding Murder Cases Al-3161 and AL-3162.

Office of the Coroner, Country of San Diego, California. File Number 38900. Raymond Davis. April 12, 1962. 4 pages.

Solano County Sheriff's Office Report, Vallejo, Case Number V25564. 76 pages .

Death Certificate: Betty Lou Jensen, County of Solano, File No. 101652. 1 pages.

Death Certificate: David Arthur Faraday, County of Solano, File No. 101653. 1 pages.

Office of the Coroner of Solano County. Autopsy Report, Betty Lou Jensen. 1 page.

Office of the Coroner of Solano County. Autopsy Report, David Arthur Faraday. 1 page.

Department of Justice, Bureau of Criminal Identification and Investigation, Case Number 37-F-2795, Report by David Q. Burd. 3 pages.

Crime Report, Vallejo Police Department, Case Number 243146. 97 pages.

Office of the Coroner of Solano County. Autopsy Report, Darlene Ferrin. 3 pages.

Department of Justice, Bureau of Criminal Investigation and Investigation Report, Case Number 1-15-311-F9-5861. 35 pages.

California Department of Justice/Division of Law Enforcement/Bureau of Investigation, Zodiac Homicides. For Law Enforcement Use Only. 10 pages.

Report by Det./Sgt. Hal Snook, Napa County Sheriff's Department Supplement Crime Report, Case Number 105907. 4 pages.

Napa Sheriff's Office. Dialogue Between an Unknown Assailant and Bryan Hartnell. 2 pages.

Interview of Bryan Calvin Hartnell by Det./Sgt. John Robertson at Queen of the Valley Hospital. Sunday, September 28, 1969 (Transcribed from tape recording by M. Feurle). 13 pages.

Napa County Sheriff's Department Report, Case Number 105907. 18 pages.

Napa County Sheriff's Department Supplementary Report, Case Number 105907, David Slaight. 1 page.

San Francisco Crime Report, Case Number 696314. 2 pages.

Record of Death. Paul Stine. 2 pages.

City and County of San Francisco, Coroner's Office - Necropsy Department. Case number 1976. Paul Stine. 5 pages.

Patterson Police Department, Case Number 7425. 2 pages.

Sheriff's Department, County of Stanislaus, File Number C62677. 1 page.

Sheriff's Department, County of Stanislaus, Follow-up Report, File Number C62677. 1 page.

Office of Sheriff – Coroner, County of San Joaquin, Standard Crime Report, Case Number 70-7475. 6 pages.

Department of Justice. "ANALYSIS OF ZODIAC HOMICIDES," 1971. 1 page.

Kinkead, Thomas. Letter to Earl Randoll. October 20 1969. 3 pages.

Coroner's Office. Autopsy report of Cheri Jo Bates. 31 October 1966. 8 pages.

Inside Detective. January 1969. "THROUGH HELL ON A BLUE PILL."

Record of Death for Richard Radetich.

Federal Bureau of Investigation. Report of Examination. DNA analysis. Case Number 95A-HQ-1282679. 11 pages.

Johnny Smith and Howard Davis. Interview with Kathleen Johns. January 1, 1998.

FOIA, Subject: Zodiac Killer, File Number: 9-HQ-49911, Section 1, Federal Bureau of Investigation. 89 pages.

FOIA, Subject: Zodiac Killer, File Number: 9-HQ-49911, Section 2, Federal Bureau of Investigation. 109 pages.

FOIA, Subject: Zodiac Killer, File Number: 9-HQ-49911, Section 3, Federal Bureau of Investigation. 258 pages.

FOIA, Subject: Zodiac Killer, File Number: 9-HQ-49911, Section 4, Federal Bureau of Investigation. 208 pages.

FOIA, Subject: Zodiac Killer, File Number: 9-HQ-49911, Section 5, Federal Bureau of Investigation. 373 pages.

FOIA, FBI Release, Case Number 9-HQ-49911. Section 1 (1078663) part 1. 151 pages.

FOIA, FBI Release, Case Number 9-HQ-49911. Section 1 (1078663) part 2. 75 pages.

FOIA, FBI Release, Case Number 9-HQ-49911. Section 1 (1078663) part 2. 76 pages.

FOIA, FBI Release, Case Number 9-HQ-49911. Section 1 (1078667). 172 pages.

FOIA, FBI Release, Case Number 9-HQ-49911. Section 1 (1078667) Part 1. 186 pages.

FOIA, FBI Release, Case Number 9-HQ-49911. Section 1 (1078667) Part 2. 186 pages.

FOIA, FBI Release, Case Number 9-HQ-49911. Lake Berryessa. 50 pages.

Major Verified and Suspected Zodiac Events

1962

Monday, April 9
Phone call (suspected)

Wednesday, April 11
Murder of Raymond Davis (suspected)

Sunday, April 15
Phone call (suspected)

Tuesday, April 17
Phone call (suspected)

1963

Saturday, June 1
Gaviota Beach sniper incident (suspected)

Sunday, June 2
Tajiguas Beach sniper incident (suspected)
Sniper shooting south of Gaviota Beach (suspected)

Tuesday, June 4
Killing of Robert Domingos and Linda Edwards (suspected)

1964

Wednesday, February 5
Killing of Johnny Ray and Joyce Swindle (suspected)

1966

Sunday, October 30
Murder of Cheri Jo Bates (suspected)

Letters mailed on Tuesday, November 29
Addressed to:
The Riverside Police Department
The Riverside-Daily Enterprise

Message on desk
Discovered in December
The Riverside City College library

1967

Letters mailed on Sunday, April 30
Addressed to:
Joseph Bates
The Riverside Police Department
The Riverside-Press Enterprise

1968

Friday, December 20
Incident involving Bill Crow and his girlfriend (suspected)
Killing of David Faraday and Betty Jensen (confirmed)

1969

Friday-Saturday, July 4-5
Shooting of Michael Mageau and Darlene Ferrin (confirmed)
Phone call to the Vallejo Police Department (confirmed)

Letters mailed on Thursday, July 31
Addressed to:
The San Francisco Chronicle
The San Francisco Examiner
The Vallejo Times-Herald

Letter received on Monday, August 4
Addressed to the San Francisco Examiner

Saturday, September 27
Sighting by three women (suspected)

Stabbing of Bryan Hartnell and Cecelia Shepard (confirmed)
Phone call to the Napa Police Department (confirmed)

Saturday, October 11
Killing of Paul Stine (confirmed)

Letter received on Tuesday, October 14
Addressed to the San Francisco Chronicle

Letter and card received on Monday, November 10
Addressed to the San Francisco Chronicle

Letter mailed on Saturday, December 20
Addressed to Melvin Belli

1970

Sunday, March 22
Kidnapping of Kathleen Johns (suspected)

Letter mailed on Monday, April 20
Addressed to the San Francisco Chronicle

Card mailed on Tuesday, April 28
Addressed to the San Francisco Chronicle

Letter mailed on Friday, June 26
Addressed to the San Francisco Chronicle

Letter mailed on Friday, July 24
Addressed to the San Francisco Chronicle

Letter mailed on Sunday, July 26
Addressed to the San Francisco Chronicle

Sunday, September 6
The Donna Lass incident

Card mailed on Monday, October 5
Addressed to the San Francisco Chronicle

Card mailed on Tuesday, October 27
Addressed to Paul Avery

1971

Letter mailed on Saturday, March 13
Addressed to the Los Angeles Times

Card mailed on Monday, March 22
Received by the San Francisco Chronicle

1972

Friday, April 7
Stabbing of Isobel Watson (suspected)

1974

Letter mailed on Tuesday, January 29
Addressed to the San Francisco Chronicle

Letter mailed on Sunday, February 3
Addressed to the San Francisco Chronicle

Card mailed on Wednesday, May 8
Addressed to the San Francisco Chronicle

Letter mailed on Monday, July 8
Addressed to the San Francisco Chronicle

1990

Card mailed in December
Addressed to the San Francisco Chronicle

Søren Roest Korsgaard (b. 1986) is a social critic, humanitarian, and author. He serves as the editor-in-chief of ww.CrimeAndPower.com and is the CEO of www.KorsgaardPublishing.com. Having wide interests and expertise in various fields, Søren is an accomplished statement analyst, graphologist, and currency trader. Furthermore, he is the webmaster of several prominent sites, including the website of Dr. Paul Craig Roberts, the Assistant Secretary of the US Treasury in the Reagan administration. He may be contacted via editor@crimeandpower.com.

www.ingramcontent.com/pod-product-compliance
Ingram Content Group UK Ltd.
Pitfield, Milton Keynes, MK11 3LW, UK
UKHW041831200726
13854UKWH00002BA/983